THE PORTFOLIO STANDARD

THE PORTFOLIO STANDARD

STANDARD

How Students Can Show *Us* What
They Know and Are Able to Do

Edited by
Bonnie S. Sunstein
and
Jonathan H. Lovell

Foreword by Donald Graves

HEINEMANN
Portsmouth, NH

Heinemann
A division of Reed Elsevier Inc.
361 Hanover Street
Portsmouth, NH 03801–3912
www.heinemann.com

Offices and agents throughout the world

© 2000 by Heinemann

Library of Congress Cataloging-in-Publication Data
The portfolio standard : how students can show <u>us</u> what they know and are able to do / edited by Bonnie Sunstein and Jonathan H. Lovell ; foreword by Donald Graves.
    p.   cm.
    Includes bibliographical references and index.
    ISBN 0-325-00234-7
    1. Portfolios in education—Standards—United States.   I. Sunstein, Bonnie S.
II. Lovell, Jonathan H.

LB1029.P67 P69   2000
371.39+   99-058143

Editor: William Varner
Production coordinator: Elizabeth Valway
Production: Colophon
Cover design: Jenny Jensen Greenleaf
Cover illustration: Peter H. Reynolds
Frontispiece and illustrations by Peter H. Reynolds
Manufacturing: Louise Richardson

Printed in the United States of America on acid-free paper
04 03 02 01 00 DA 1 2 3 4 5

CONTENTS

FOREWORD

We've never needed portfolios more than we do now. In a high-speed culture with more and more quick and easy assessments that govern instruction, this book comes as a refreshing reminder of what constitutes real literacy based on a partnership with the student. Most assessments do not engage the student in significant, self-evaluative, long-term thinking. Worse, when we speed up our curriculum and outstrip the possibility of the student as co-learner/evaluator we bypass the consumer for whom the education exists.

The Portfolio Standard expands current notions about how to help students be better learners. In the first chapter, Bonnie Sunstein shows how students have become forgers by replicating knowledge instead of acquiring the deep structure of significant learning. "Looks good on the surface," says Sunstein, "but what have you got?" Replication takes little time; authentic creation entails long, slow deliberative evolution.

The book asks more questions than it provides answers. The questions, however, cut to the heart of what constitutes a genuine education for all students in a democracy. Two chapters by teachers in Alaska and Puerto Rico show how portfolios authenticate a broad range of cultural engagement allowing for participation in democratic society as well as reversing the forgery trend raised by Sunstein. Danling Fu raises the most basic questions regarding our approaches to assessment when she questions the antithetical relationship between democracy and capitalism.

When portfolio use began fifteen years ago we reasoned that we and our students needed to see work collected over time. Students took on a different role in the evaluation process. They were asked to choose what went into their collection and then to give reasons for their choices. Portfolios worked quite well at the local level. Once portfolios left the local system and needed further review at the state or national level, their function was distorted. At state and national levels we needed assurance that it was possible to compare one portfolio with another. This required more standardization. The individual touch understood and prized at the local level produced problems for out-of-town evaluators. The authors in *The Portfolio Standard* have shown that the more personally relevant the artifacts in the portfolio, the more invested the student becomes in the learning process. For this reason many of the authors recommend the portfolio for local use only.

It takes time for teachers to help students become personally invested in the work in their portfolios. It takes even longer for them to learn to evaluate and recognize their own progress as writers and thinkers. But we are in a hurry for results. We want to know if our children are succeeding and competing with the best in the country. Indeed, adolescents know when the process of education does not include them, especially when teaching is in a hurry to cover a curriculum that does not engage them. They feel continually outside their subjects instead of inside them discovering, collecting, and exploring with intellectually stimulating teachers who use portfolios. Linda Rief shows this process eloquently with her student Molly Finnegan. Once again, long, slow learning with back-and-forth responses between student, teacher, and parent carry thinking beyond the classroom into long-term thinking about life itself.

The authors in *The Portfolio Standard* remind us that the portfolio is for our time—when we need the contributions of all our citizens. Too many assessments are culturally biased. Portfolios, with their inclusion of artifacts that represent the rich background of the student, have the potential to give new life to democratic ideals. Portfolios used at the local level can develop a kind of thinking quite antithetical to the quick-and-easy assessment mind-set.

The Portfolio Standard takes a long step back to look at our students in school and society. We need to step back still farther to examine the breakneck speed at which we travel in order to see the effects on the thinking and learning of our students and the serious implications it has for the future of our democracy.

The most serious consequence is the effect on long thinking. Quick thinking is prized and is needed but as James Gleick (1999) observes: "we have heard of unhurried qualities like wisdom and sagacity, but we think nonetheless that the students who plod through laborious calculations cannot be quite as smart as their comrades who snap their fingers and know the answer." Long thinkers like Darwin and Einstein, who called themselves slow thinkers, just might be lost in our schools. Long thinkers are able to sustain thought on a single problem for days, weeks, or years. Indeed, most of the problems of society require long thinkers who can persevere, create their own questions, and assess the validity of their answers. For this reason, I submit that it is the long thinker, who is used to sustaining thought, who will contribute to the survival of our democracy. Many of them are young adolescents sitting in classrooms today and irritating teachers who are sprinting through the curriculum.

The writers in *The Portfolio Standard* have slowed down the process of learning through collections, response, self-evaluation, and especially the inclusion of personal artifacts representative of a broad range of culture. Clearly, we see long thinkers in the making. Long thinking so obviously represented in the savvy professional, like many of the writers in *The Portfolio Standard*, will provide a wisdom transcendent of themselves and desperately needed by the complete learner today.

Donald H. Graves

REFERENCES

Gleick, James. 1999. *Faster—The Acceleration of Just About Everything.* New York: Pantheon.

ACKNOWLEDGMENTS

Making a book out of a conference is not an easy task. In fact, it's a bit like putting together a portfolio for the first time. You want to display the colors and conversations and literate digressions of real life. Yet you need to remember that you're shaping your display for someone who didn't live that experience. You need to transform three dimensions into two dimensions, and your tool kit is mostly black words and white pages. But then, in the course of writing the book, you sharpen your thinking—and even change it—so that the book is no longer an extension of the conference. In fact, it becomes a wholly new and unique entity. And so in writing these acknowledgments, we wish to thank those who contributed to both process and product for both conference and book.

Charleen Silva Delfino organized the 1998 conference with us and introduced three hundred people to her hometown, San Jose, California. She gave intellectual and practical shape to three panel discussions which raised the fundamental questions you will read about in this book. Linda Oldham, director of NCTE's Professional Development Workshops, envisioned the conference as part of her series and spent two years making sure it happened. Associate Dean Paul Bradley and the 1998 credential candidates in English Education at San Jose State University allowed us their spaces, offered us their equipment, and organized two days on their campus while they were on semester break. The California Writing Project, the National Writing Project, and NCTE's Assembly on Media Arts offered support and valuable leadership.

After the conference, as the book began to take shape, the locus of our process moved east. The Obermann Center for Advanced Studies at the University of Iowa, in particular Jay Semel and Lorna Olson, supported much of our communication with twenty-two authors in different parts of the country as well as time and space to form and articulate the ideas we share. Sandie Hughes, Beth McCabe, and Erma Statler of Iowa's Department of Curriculum and Instruction are a continual source of support and intelligent problem solving. We especially thank those colleagues all over the country whose words and names appear as little references on many of our pages but whose big ideas about portfolios, reflective thinking, and technology have been foundational to ours: Mary Chase, Bill Costanzo, Don Graves, Jim Marshall, Don Murray, Miles Myers, Donna Qualley, Tom Romano, Mary Ann Smith, Dave Stone, and Kathleen Yancey. In a fortuitous midnight phone conversation, Eunice Greer offered us our title and the focus of our book.

Finally but perhaps most important of all, this project moved further eastward to Heinemann in Portsmouth, New Hampshire, Elizabeth Valway and Maura Sullivan created the book as you see it, as did Denise Botelho of Colophon. We thank them for recognizing the art of book production. Bill Varner's continuous enthusiasm, ability to think broadly and edit deeply, and respond with the eye of an informed reader has inspired and taught us. In short, Bill has helped all of us show ourselves and others "what we know and are able to do."

INTRODUCTION

What is "the portfolio standard?" How do these terms connect? The term *standards* has recently come to mean "benchmarks" that students must "meet." That's a far cry from the display of individuality and growth we see in a student's portfolio. How might we understand what we observe of students' work in their portfolios in relation to the externally imposed standards that increasingly define our "success" as educators? Standards are necessary, we'd all agree, but not sufficient.

In the last ten years, many teachers have been caught between these two competing ideas: standards pulling at students from the outside (local, state, and national mandates) and, from the inside, learning processes, which cannot be "measured" or "standardized," pushing students from within to grow and to reflect on their growth. We hear phrases connected with "standards" projects: standards are "what students know and are able to do." But what about a single student? How does this "standard" phrase fit *one person*—the learner—who's engaged in meeting outside standards and also examining the inside particulars of his/her learning? In this book, teachers, students, administrators, and assessors all show us that a carefully rendered portfolio becomes an increasingly internalized standard against which learners can assess their own growth.

Portfolios give the responsibility of assessment to the assessed. The portfolio is a place where a student can set her own standard as she looks at the standards her institution sets for her and demonstrates how she meets them. Portfolios showcase one person's learning history, her individuality; the special "spin" he puts on an assignment or a personal creation. Portfolios can empower the powerless; they invite voices to speak in places which usually value obedient silence. Portfolios help us reclaim our identity in a world that uses standards to keep order and control. They're not a replacement for tests, nor an "alternative" to standards or assessment. Rather, portfolios can place value on literate activities that are undervalued in our schools. They can mark behaviors that go unnoticed simply because they are difficult to measure.

If someone's going to judge my portfolio, I need to learn to describe what's in it and why I put it there. I want to show my evaluator not only how I meet a standard (framework, benchmark), but how I define it in my own way. Often, how I exceed it. In order to do that, I must show not only that I understand the standard ("what I know"), but how I have met it in my own particular way ("what I'm able to do").

Keepers of a portfolio standard become conscious of audience, purpose, and voice—just like writers and speakers do. We must all learn to show our own work as it fits the expectations others have of us. Some people call this process reflection; others call it critical analysis. Whatever we choose to call it, we need to pay attention to the unique skills involved in collecting examples or "artifacts" of our growing knowledge and reflecting on what these artifacts tell us about ourselves.

The past decade bombarded us with portfolio experiments—portfolios as instruments for large-scale assessment, portfolios as formative devices for self-evaluation, portfolios as instructional tools for learning. Large cities and small towns, regional school systems and single buildings adapted and created their own versions of portfolios and of portfolio assessment. Some states mandated portfolio keeping. A few states came to offer portfolios as an option, allowing students to choose between using a portfolio or taking a set of standardized tests. Many colleges and graduate schools have come to recommend or even require portfolios for admission and graduation. Portfolios, in many varieties, are now a part of our academic landscape.

At the same time, federally funded projects like the National Board of Professional Teaching Standards and the New Standards Project spent much time and money using portfolios to expand our ideas of assessment. NCTE's Professional Development Conference series offered six national conferences over two years devoted to portfolios, reflection, and assessment. Textbooks developed their commercialized versions of portfolios. Teachers' organizations, educational businesses, and testing companies experimented with ways to market the portfolio idea. Indeed, in less than a decade, portfolio keeping has grown from a small local activity to one that is widespread, various, complex, and confusing.

Those of us who have advocated for portfolio keeping have wiped our brows and held our own in discussions about assessment. We've argued about who ought to be doing the assessing. We've created and rejected rubrics and holistic scoring scales. We've become frustrated as our students refuse when we offer them a chance to assess themselves. "It's too hard," they say. "It's too new." "It's YOUR job to tell us what we know and are able to do." Most exciting and complex of all, we've just begun to apply our portfolio knowledge to new technologies that our students often know much better than we do. Computers promise far more efficient ways to keep portfolios. Website designers are masterful portfolio keepers; they constantly monitor their work in progress and share it with a judging public.

SETTING A PORTFOLIO STANDARD

We're still not sure where portfolios fit in all of this confusion, but we've learned a lot during the last decade. We know the most effective portfolios are those that are owned by those who put them together. We know that if teachers keep portfolios, they are better able to help their students keep them. Most of us agree that it's unproductive to "standardize" or "grade" a portfolio, or to judge it without the portfolio keeper's help. Longtime portfolio keepers in the arts and in business have taught us that the best portfolio is one that never stops changing. A portfolio is one person's reflection of a moment in a process—captured in time like a snapshot—of a portfolio-keeper's identity, knowledge, accomplishments, and goals. We've come to see that a portfolio is not an alternative to assessment. It is, rather, a necessary complement.

With portfolios, students can put their own spin on standards, exceed expectations, adjust a curriculum to fit their interests, and then show us how they accomplish these goals. As they collect and then reflect on what they choose to put in their portfolios, students think like they've never thought before about how their own sense of themselves corresponds to what their world expects of them. Certainly it's hard, and certainly it's new, but when students become engaged in creating and articulating their own emerging identities in their portfolios, we remember why we became teachers in the first place. And we see that setting a portfolio standard applies to teachers, too.

Instead of a single classroom, strategy, or large-scale assessment report, we want to look around the country at what we've learned over the past ten years. We want to answer the questions: "So what's in portfolios these days, anyway? What can we learn about portfolio keeping from what's in them?" "How do portfolios work in a climate that is currently insisting on large-scale standards and assessment measures that are keyed to these standards?" And, as one high school student asked, "What do we do with the unflat stuff?" How do we and our students learn to document our knowledge in a contemporary world that enables effective and artful technological documentation? In short, how do we help students set portfolio standards, all in their own different ways—and still meet the standards our institutions set *for* them?

Our twenty-five authors were all presenters at a January 1998 conference.[1] They share diverse projects (single classrooms and individual students, elementary through graduate school, statewide and university-wide efforts, and both "hard" and "soft" multimedia portfolios) from Alaska to Kentucky, Puerto Rico to Minnesota, California to Maine. We hope this book will reflect the spirit and enthusiasm we shared as we asked questions that arose from what we learned by looking inside today's portfolios, and how our outsider roles as assessors influenced our understanding of what portfolios were and what purposes they served.

OUTSIDE IN AND INSIDE OUT

As we venture inside portfolios, we ask questions about how we learn. But looking outside portfolios, we're hit with questions about what we're supposed to learn, how we teach and evaluate. The politics are provocative. The ironies and the rewards are rich. And so we ask:

- What "stuff" should a porfolio include?
- Who ought to be evaluating portfolios?
- What is the teacher's (or school's) role in a student's portfolio?
- How do the artifacts in a portfolio help students define their emerging and changing ideas about their "literate identity?"

These questions provoke tension. Inside our classrooms, we want to encourage students to select the items to place in their portfolios. We understand our students through their choices of what to include, and we are struck by their differences. We wonder how to help students learn to "reflect upon" and "critically analyze" their self-chosen artifacts. But we feel pressure, too, from outside our classrooms. States mandate specific lists of standards, asking for "outcomes-based assessment" while teachers and students want to experiment, to leave portfolios open to change. These questions and practices—ours, our students,' and our institutions'—challenge our traditional definitions of terms we thought we understood: "literate behavior," "evaluation," "assessment," "reflection," "analysis," "school reform," "standard," and even "portfolio." And so we ask:

---

[1] Our chapters are revised from presentations at an NCTE Professional Development Conference, *Inside Portfolios: Interpreting the Cultural Artifacts of Literacy*, held at San Jose State University, San Jose, CA, January 15–17, 1998. The conference was co-sponsored by San Jose State University, the San Jose Area Writing Project, the California Writing Project, NCTE's Assembly on Media Arts, and the NCTE Commission on Media, and co-chaired by Charleen Silva Delfino, Jonathan H. Lovell, and Bonnie S. Sunstein.

- What implications do these new understandings have for our roles as evaluators, as classroom observers, and as individuals helping to set policy at the school, district, regional, and national levels?
- How should we define the balance of roles we play—as both interested observers and sometimes collaborators, working alongside our students with the body of data they've collected and displayed—but also as judges of our students' work?
- If we allow our students choices, how do we make sense of our students' self-chosen artifacts as we move from the role of supporters to the role of assessors?
- How do we broaden our definition of "cultural artifacts" and "literacy" in portfolios to include media beyond print?

We can't offer answers to these questions because everyone answers them differently. But we believe we can't find a better way than a portfolio for our students to show us what they know—and how they've come to know it. That's why we think portfolios are worth our continuing attention. That's why we believe each of us has, in fact, a "portfolio standard."

This book features mixed age groups and a variety of types of school programs. We include lots of perspectives to illustrate the complex context in which we find portfolios these days: students, parents, teachers, preservice teachers, administrators, test makers and assessors, researchers, and historians. We begin with Don Graves' foreword, a retrospective of the last decade's worth of portfolio activity since the publication of *Portfolio Portraits* (co-edited with Bonnie Sunstein) and a prospective view toward the future of portfolios. Don reminds us that sometimes we need ideas more than new materials, and energizing principles more than careful designs to give new life to students' identities.

Our cover and in-text line drawings throughout are by Peter Reynolds, CD-ROM artist and illustrator, FableVision Animation Studios, who impressed participants at the conference with his demonstrations of classroom portfolio Website possibilities. As an artist, Peter has been a portfolio keeper for years and describes his portfolio as a place where he "rethinks thinking." In our effort to bring some clarity to the complex set of questions we've had about portfolio keeping and assessing in the last decade, we've organized our collection of essays and examples into three sections.

SECTION I: A STANDARD SET FROM THE INSIDE

Our collection of chapters looks first at what's inside portfolios. Here are the questions we ask about what our portfolios actually contain:

1. How does a portfolio's contents define the culture to which its keeper belongs?
2. What artifacts are we encouraging students to gather?
3. What ways are we finding to offer students time and skills to analyze these artifacts?
4. What role should a student's interest in popular culture assume in a portfolio?
5. What's the role of media/Internet projects in student portfolios?
6. Do our students, or we, know what we mean when we use the term *reflection*?

In Bonnie Sunstein's opening chapter, she thinks more about reflection as she compares "inauthentic" portfolio keeping to art forgery and suggests that analytical self-reflection is the "technology" students can learn to document their learning. Next, in a chapter based on his opening keynote speech, Jeff Wilhelm discusses what he calls the "design portfolio" and shows how eighth-grade students in Maine use the contents of their portfolios while they work on projects across the curriculum. From Pennsylvania, Tom Stewart helps us visualize a portfolio-centered student conference as he talks with elementary preservice teachers about the portfolios they keep, and how these portfolios have helped them set standards for themselves as new teachers. Mary McGann describes two Indiana students and the portfolios they keep as reluctant writers. By adding artifacts from their outside lives, eighth grader Jerimy and second grader David (her own son) discover the connections between school and home as well as find value in what they write. Now teaching in New York City, Susan Stires discusses the evolution of her own assessment practices, focusing on using primary students' portfolios as a basis for their end-of-the year parent conferences at the Center for Teaching and Learning in Maine.

In a braided portrait of parenthood, teacherhood, and studenthood, Linda Rief, Cinthia Gannett, and Molly Finnegan give us a close-up of a New Hampshire middle schooler (Molly), her mother (Cinthia), and her teacher (Linda), as Molly develops her portfolio with Linda's and Cinthia's responses. From Puerto Rico, Miriam Dempsey Page describes her class of college freshmen as they respond to her writing "invitations" in order to develop portfolios that reflect their culture, language, and emerging identity. And at a college in Alaska, two instructors (Marilyn Barry and Yaso Thiru) use portfolios to assist and assess students' views of how they meet their university's general education requirements. Finally, Elizabeth Chiseri-Strater's college students in North Carolina discover that the "artifacts" they collect for their research portfolios, including journals, family letters, heirlooms, diaries, photo albums, yearbooks, video and audiotapes, and Websites, lead them to a whole new notion of what constitutes historical "facts."

SECTION II: A STANDARD SET FROM THE OUTSIDE

Our next section examines the pressures and expectations "outside portfolios" as we ask the following questions:

1. How are schools, districts, and regions evaluating the products of student portfolios?
2. Are our means of evaluating what we find in portfolios offering new understandings for us and for our curricula?
3. For us, how does interpreting portfolios reflect our understanding of teaching, our assumptions about our students, and our definitions of literacy?
4. Whose "reflections" do we value? Do our institutions value?
5. Whose responsibility is it to decide whether a student's work is work of consequence?

In this section, Danling Fu's provocative opening chapter connects portfolios with her bicultural view of American values. As our conference's final keynote speaker, Danling silenced the audience with her descriptions of two minority students—from their parents' and teacher's perspectives as well as from theirs and hers. Florida third grader Martin and New Hampshire high schooler Tran have what she calls "invisible portfolios." Their involvement with "skillbuilding" leaves no time or opportunity for portfolios. Danling's conclusions are both disquieting and riveting as she reminds us how portfolios might help students whom traditional assessments have served to marginalize and even silence.

From Kentucky, Liz Spalding describes teachers in a statewide educational reform program focusing on portfolio keeping. She captures their discussion of one high school's senior class in which every student was a portfolio keeper. Also related to the questions of state demographics, James Williams describes a research report from Illinois, a quantitative study that frankly asks what issues influence the "outside judges" who assess students' portfolios: socioeconomic status, ethnicity, gender, and even handwriting. From Iowa we offer perspectives from portfolio "assessors" themselves: Julie Cheville, Sandra Murphy, Barbara Price, and Terry Underwood. In this statewide, foundation-funded experimental project, responses from the "judges" came as interpretive descriptions and responses to the portfolio keepers. In Joe Potts, Ron Strahl, and Don Hohl's report on a five-year program for preservice teachers at the California State University at Long Beach, students, mentor teachers, and professors discuss the surprising new roles and relationships that the preservice students' keeping of portfolios engendered.

The two chapters that end our book ask particularly uncomfortable questions from the "outside"; concerning the dangers we encounter when we establish fixed external standards against which we evaluate a portfolio's content. In the first, John Schmit and Deborah Appleman, from their vantage point in urban Minneapolis, raise a question—one that James Williams' study hinted at earlier—a question we tend to whisper: Is it fair to use portfolios as assessments of reading and writing in urban schools? They ask "would the use of portfolios for assessment turn a powerful pedagogical tool into a dull knife or even a blunt instrument?" We conclude our collection with Judy Fueyo's half-satirical, intentionally critical, and thoroughly authentic look at the current state of portfolio keeping. Judy asks why portfolios "are being perverted across the land," questions her own complicity, and envisions ways to marry form and function with more satisfactory results for students and teachers alike.

SECTION III: A PORTFOLIO OF PORTFOLIOS

We've expanded our questions as we've tried to manage portfolios in the last ten years. At first, we wondered what the difference was between a scrapbook and a portfolio. A scrapbook, as some of us like to say, is a "pasted down" moment in time. But a portfolio is its opposite: it is a shifting document of the multiple processes of learning, constantly changing as a student continues to learn. We asked for a long time about where we ought to keep portfolios—at school or at home. Well, lots of us have answered, it depends on the conditions of the classroom, the materials at hand, the students and their home conditions and commitments. We wondered about how to share portfolios with parents and administrators—and we developed ideas about portfolios for parents' nights, portfolio panels or performances, demonstration sessions with peers and community people. We speculated about where to put the stuff we remove from portfolios as we insert new stuff; we put it back where it came from in the first place!

But as we've worked with student portfolios, we've observed deeper dilemmas: "Okay, okay, I love portfolios, but I can't afford a utility vehicle to haul them home in. And, truth to tell, even if I did, I do have a LIFE outside school." "Yeah, I tried them for a while. My students did such complete jobs that I didn't have time to do them justice." "Well, the more attached my kids get to their portfolios, the less they want to turn them in. And I don't want to force them." "I'd never,

never want to pass judgment on my kids' portfolios; they're all so different. I refuse to put a grade on a portfolio." "I don't want them to take MY portfolio home; why should I take THEIRS?"

We want to see students' portfolios, every page of every portfolio, each time they change. But as teachers we also know that's an unrealistic expectation for ourselves—and for our students. And so we've developed a few shortcuts, none of which gives the full impact of a real portfolio, but all of which make it more realistic to include portfolios as part of a working classroom inside an institution that is run by curriculum, standards, and expectations. When we're required to record grades at the end of a course, we can ask students to choose a few items from their portfolios that are relevant to the course and submit them for grading.

But the most important strategy we've used is a double strategy. It includes two pieces of paper (well, sometimes more than two):

1. an annotated table of contents
2. a "one-pager" about the portfolio's contents

Several times each semester, students submit two pieces of paper. The first is a table of contents made from a list of the artifacts in the portfolio at that time along with annotations or explanations in short sentences or phrases ("reflective windows," Post-it Notes, "captions," "thought balloons") that accompany each one. The second piece of paper is a one-page analysis of the current contents (a "portfolio letter," "one-pager," "reflective commentary"). This one-page analysis offers a portfolio keeper an opportunity to explore the portfolio's overall themes: connections between items, between school and home, between past and present, between one subject and another, between performance and goals. With these two documents, we can get a clear picture of a student's portfolio and progress. Like much else in life, there's no substitute for the real thing, but during our regular classroom portfolio-sharing sessions, this process of collecting snapshots of our students' portfolios offers a chance to view each student's emerging body of work several times and record notes about it.

And so in this section, we offer samples of this strategy—two-dimensional word portraits, in a way, of six sample portfolios: elementary, middle, and secondary students, a college student, a teacher education student, and a college professor. The keepers are all teacher-authors or students we've mentioned in this book. Each person's two-part sample contains an annotated table of contents and a reflective analysis of those contents. Of course, it's not the real thing. It's missing the colors, the textures, and the "unflat" surprises. But it's a good way for teachers to see the essence of one portfolio, peruse many portfolios, and develop more questions. And so we invite you to reflect on the ways that port-folios might fit into your own teaching lives, your students' learning lives. And we all invite you to consider how to assist all of your students, one at a time, to develop a portfolio standard as they tell us what they know and are able to do.

Bonnie S. Sunstein and Jonathan H. Lovell

I

A STANDARD SET
FROM THE INSIDE

1

BE REFLECTIVE, BE REFLEXIVE, AND BEWARE
Innocent Forgery for Inauthentic Assessment[1]

BONNIE S. SUNSTEIN

A forger only works on the surface; his work falls apart with the layers below. . . . Great artists change their minds a lot as they try to get it just right. . . .

Eugene Farrell

If you're a teacher, you probably have one or two forgery stories. My favorite comes from my years teaching junior high school English, and is about an eighth-grade girl who'd mastered the genre of the absentee note. One Tuesday morning, she handed me this note: "Please excuse Marie from school yesterday," written on embossed blue-note paper with rounded flourishes astride long elegant script, "as she was sick with a cold and low-grade fever." Her use of the phrase "as she was sick with" was a perfect rendition, I thought, of American suburban maternal discourse patterns. But as she closed the note, Marie gave herself away: "Luv ya, Mrs. Smith."

Marie's adolescent voice was her fingerprint. She'd absorbed her mother's note-writing style from years of careful observation: the handwriting, the stationery, the word choices, the appropriate language register for an absentee note. Marie was an artful forger. Expert forgers, we know, especially in the world of the arts, are disciplined students. As pretty good artists themselves, they must choose their specialties of style and period, mastering the techniques of the masters they imitate. But, like Marie in my eighth-grade class, forgers in the art world leave

[1]A version of this chapter previously appeared in *The Clearing House* 72:1, September/October 1998. Thanks to Sandra Murphy, editor of that journal, for encouraging me to think out these thoughts. Thanks, too, to my colleagues Deborah Appleman, Julie Cheville, Mike Evces, Mary McGann, and Joe Potts for reading and responding to drafts and offering information and insight as this article developed. My "Approaches to Teaching Writing" class (Spring '98) assisted me as I tried to bring a crazy analogy into focus—from smoking guns to fingerprints, from expectations to standards.

tell-tale fingerprints which keep buyers, dealers, patrons, chemists, scholars, lawyers, and historians very busy. And they've been doing it for centuries.

THE ARTFUL FORGER

There have always been innocent forgers, imitators who pay homage to a master artist by copying style, subjects, and techniques as intricately as possible. Art schools encourage students to echo traditional techniques for mixing paint and stretching canvas. Their assignments regularly include copying the master paintings and drawings in museums, trying old techniques, but always understanding that the art student's copy will not be exact—either in size or completeness of subject, and of course that it will not attempt to present itself as the original work of the master.

Some art forgers are not so innocent; they imitate for profit and they imitate well. Sometimes, like Marie's "Luv ya," no matter how well rendered the painting is, the forger leaves a fingerprint. There is an often told anecdote among collectors and curators that the French impressionist painter Corot made "two thousand drawings in his lifetime, ten thousand of which are in the United States." In another forgery story, a Victorian sculptor created a "Renaissance" Adam and Eve with Eve carefully clothed in a turn-of-the century bathing suit. As the famously generous "father" of the French impressionists," Pissarro discovered a forgery of one of his own works, where the forger had omitted an s from his last name (Waterman 1994, 76). Stories of Van Gogh fakes, rendered innocently and in homage by his colleagues, subversively by others, have circulated since his death in 1890 (Norman 1998, 4).

More often than not, forgers leave a well-rendered but superficial imitation of a master's product, difficult for all but the most experienced viewer to detect. As they work, forgers force themselves to slip into the mind-set of the master artist: "the same personality produced them, so a forger must, for a time, imitate the artist's soul" (Cebik 1989, 148), and as a consequence they force the loss of their own uniqueness. The artistic forger, then, sells his soul for another artist's soul, hoping to collect a fortune in a high-stakes game.

THE STUDENT AS INNOCENT FORGER

As I read about art forgers, I find myself thinking embarrassing thoughts about school assessment practices and students' ideas about meeting school standards. Forgers work like many of our most academically successful students: "What do I have to do to get an A?" "What am I supposed to prove?" "What do you want me to say?" "How many pages do you want this paper to be?" And then they "slip into the mind-set" of the assignments we create in order to render a product according to our requirements: size, style, voice, genre, period, signature. With clear stakes, drawn lines, and lots of practice with convention and technique, our students learn not only how to value their own work according to the standards we set for them, but also how to sell their work successfully "back" to us. We do not encourage them to set their own standards or goals within a set of curricular options. Their job is to meet, not adjust to, standards set by an outside curriculum or a set of outside assessors. So students, like forgers, are denied "the subconscious conviction of a truthful purpose," as art forgery expert Alan Burroughs writes, "[and] the forger can [therefore] imitate only superficial qualities" ([1938] 1965, 70). We must question the standards that we require students to meet as well as question our own role as evaluators seeking ways to judge the authenticity and value of their work.

Many students judge their work by the grades they get, filling their portfolios with "A" papers, chosen to represent "best work." We are happy to offer our students choices in the artifacts they collect in their portfolios, but then we watch as they choose an item simply because a teacher has deemed it "A work," or because a panel of judges has given it an award.

Where's the place to show the instructive failures? The unfinished magnum opus that will take longer than a semester or a report period to complete? Why are the risky attempts at modes or styles of expression that don't fit into easy categorization so infrequently on display in a student portfolio? Our students learn to value the preset, post-judged work rather than the "subconscious conviction of a truthful purpose," as Burroughs puts it, or the "artist's soul," as art critic L. B. Cebik (1980) writes. Grades, standards, or rubrics can't measure authenticity, experimentation, development, or soul in student work any more than styles, signatures, colors, or techniques can in paintings.

And so I wonder about the way we use the word "authentic" when we speak of assessment; the word "standards" when we speak of diversity. Are we in the business of encouraging the production of fakes when we specify that student work must meet standards we've set? Are we encouraging imitation with the rubrics we design, even as we aim to encourage and promote authenticity? I wonder how we might allow our students to craft their work more like masters than like forgers.

SEARCHING UNDER SURFACES: ART SLEUTHS AND AUTHENTICITY

As writers practice thoughts with their drafts, painters practice poses, angles, details, and overall composition. And as they work, they leave an invisible trail of their processes, covering and recovering drafts and sketches with new layers. Rembrandt, for example, experimented with lots of alternative hand poses, sketched and painted directly on his canvas before deciding which position would best create the overall composition of a portrait. Van Gogh, often too hurried and financially pressed to prepare enough new canvases, layered entirely new paintings over older ones. The artist renders and rerenders, sketches and oversketches, until he's satisfied with the soul of the work—his unique "signature," his fingerprint, which shows through in his finished product and identifies his art.

But when forgers work to reproduce a master's paintings, they work only on the visible surface. Those whose business is to uncover forgeries—the sleuths of the art world—design ways to look beneath the paint in order to determine whether a painting is authentic. "With Xrays, spectroscopes, ultraviolet light, gamma rays, luminescent photography, scientists can look under the surface of a painting, inside of a sculpture, and into an artist's mind" (Waterman 1994, 80). Art sleuths determine the chemical recipes for pigment in paint and match it to what they know about a painter's history. The color Prussian blue, for example, was rendered from blood residue in the eighteenth century, later from ammonia and charcoal, then from sugar-beet molasses and natural gas. Determining the chemical composition of a color can offer clues about when that paint was made.

Forgery experts, then, identify inauthentic art by looking carefully under the surface of a finished painting. "You can't slap together a Rembrandt and sell it to the Louvre," comments composition teacher Mike Evces, "but you can slap together a student paper and torture a teacher with it. The teacher can't send the paper to the lab to be X-rayed, even when she knows it's a forgery and stares holes in it trying to figure out why."

So how do we help ourselves look beneath the surfaces of our students' work? And more important, how do we help our students determine and define their own authentic "fingerprints?" Portfolios, I believe, with their emphasis on critical self-analysis—the acts we've come to call "reflection" and "reflexivity" (Sunstein 1996)—offer us and our students a way to determine, define, and display our work with windows into the processes we've used to produce it. Like the art sleuths' gradual development of spectrograph X rays and chemical analyses of paint for authenticating art, reflection is our own developing technology for searching beneath the surfaces of a piece of work, for helping students to find—and learn to value—what's authentically theirs. With this "technology" of reflection in mind, I'd like to explore a few of my most recent questions—as both teacher and portfolio researcher—and offer some ways to begin developing answers:

1. Be Reflective: How can we help students authenticate their work?
2. Be Reflexive: What techniques can students use to recognize and display authenticity?
3. Beware: How do we know how to ask? And how do we avoid getting only what we ask for?

Be Reflective: How Can We Help Students "Authenticate" Their Work?

Stephanie, a high school sophomore, made this observation about her work to researcher Joe Potts during an interview (Potts 1996):

Joe: If a person were to pick up your portfolio, and she toured it like we just did, what would she see?

Stephanie: She would see part of me. She would see me in my introduction and in my work, because that is really me in my work, but then, if she looked at my reflective analysis, she would see somebody who is fake, because I am writing fake in my reflective analysis.

Joe: You are writing fake?

Stephanie: Yes, I am not writing what I really mean because if I put in what I really mean, I wouldn't get a good grade.

Stephanie knows that an observer of her work would see the "fake" as well as the part of her that "is really me." To her, writing is real but reflective analysis is "fake." Her teacher has required that she "reflect" on what she has included in her portfolio, but has not offered strategies for reflection. Stephanie offers, rather, her own strategies for meeting her teacher's standards, her own version of artful forgery:

> I wrote this paper because he said write about a person, and I wrote this reflection because I wanted to make it look good. [She reads:] "The most important thing that I learned is how I actually learned about the friend I wrote about." I mean, give me a break. I already knew how I felt about her. This is all bullshit. I mean, this stuff is just bunk. I knew that he [the teacher] would want to hear this. This is what he wants to hear, so I wrote it.

As she reflects authentically to Joe in this interview, Stephanie doesn't realize she's reflecting at all—or even that her reflection was also in her writing. In fact it is the reflection, she claims, that's fake. Stephanie has studied her teacher's standards carefully; she knows how she will be assessed and she is aware of the "two parts" of her that function in her collected works: the real and the fake. But in order to understand her own process, accomplishments, and her real learning, she must learn to reflect as authentically and specifically as she does in this interview.

Like spectrographic light technology or the chemical analysis of paint, our technology for determining authenticity, I believe, is teaching our students and ourselves strategies for reflection. Reflection, the act of seeing one's own work and its relationship to the self and explaining it, is not an automatic skill. In fact, reflection rubs against our learned behaviors for "success" in school. Too much "self" is inappropriate, we are taught to believe. We learn quietly over years of schooling that it's the "other" who can assess us best. We don't trust ourselves to engage in thorough analysis of our own work for the purpose of individual display, and our assessment traditions discourage it.

With good reason, teachers and students fear superficial reflective comments like these:

- "My portfolio shows who I am as a literate person."
- "Welcome to my portfolio. As you look through its contents, you'll see that I am a reader, writer, and thinker."
- "A door leading to my thoughts and memories is left open for others to enter if they choose."
- "The writings contained in this portfolio reflect many thoughts, feelings, memories, and ideas that I have had through the course of my life and in my writing class."

These are the "just bunk" statements that make Stephanie feel as if she's "writing fake." Vapid reflection seems, at best, an exercise in self-indulgence, and we rightly resist self-indulgence without a purpose. But careful, detailed reflection is not among the "basic skills" that our assignments, assessments, or our school calendars allow for. Yet reflection is a strategy for searching through our processes and probing beneath the surfaces of our work. With it, we and our students can take stock of learning represented in a given collection of work at a given moment in time.

In a 1996 survey (Sunstein and Cheville), forty-two teachers around the country, all of whom were dedicated to the practice of having their students keep portfolios, discussed how they help students achieve a "reflective stance." What kinds of questions, we asked, do you ask students in order to encourage reflection? Some ask a series of related questions, aimed at generalizing about learning over time:

1. What do you know that you didn't know before?
2. What can you do that you couldn't do before?
3. What do you do that you couldn't do before?

Alan Purves, SUNY Albany

1. How are your writing and your composing processes different now than they were when you began compiling this portfolio?

2. Which class activities (journal writing, peer response groups, revision, etc.) have affected your writing and your composing process this semester, and what effects have they had?

> Jeff Sommers, Miami University of Ohio

Some sets of reflective questions ask for careful analysis of the actual pieces they've chosen for display and analysis in the portfolio:

1. If you were to choose one piece of work that represents your best effort, what would you choose?
2. Why is it a significant effort?
3. When you revise your work, what lenses do you use to determine what to change?

> Sally Hampton, New Standards Managing Director,
> 1992–1995 ELA Portfolio Project

1. Why have you chosen these specific pieces for your portfolio?
2. What makes these pieces interesting to you?
3. What surprises you about your work?
4. What would you do differently?

> Brian Huot, University of Louisville

1. What do you want people to learn about you from reading your portfolio?
2. Show me where or how they would learn those things from looking at your work.
3. What's something that you've been working to improve? Trace your growth in that area through the collection of your work.

> Eunice Greer, Harvard PACE

Still others emphasize specifics, asking students to make personal connections between themselves, their understanding of curriculum standards, and the artifacts they've collected:

1. How many pieces of writing did you finish this semester? What genres are represented among these pieces?
2. What's the most important or useful information about conventions of written English you've learned this semester?
3. What will you try to do in your writing in the future?

> Nancie Atwell, Center for Teaching and Learning,
> Edgecomb, Maine

1. After looking over all your artifacts, what is missing?
2. What connections exist between your artifacts in your portfolio? Explain the connections.

> Lora Wolff, Keokuk High School, Iowa

And finally, two teachers choose one single critical question to elicit reflective analysis, a question they ask repeatedly, each time students review and re-analyze their portfolios:

- What is different in your portfolio now than six months ago?
  Jane Hansen, University of New Hampshire
- If you think of your work according to "level of difficulty' what would you choose as hardest and why? Please describe what you were trying to do, even if you did not achieve it.
  Judy Fueyo, Pennsylvania State University

"The work has a history—or more correctly—a biography. . . ." writes L. B. Cebik (1989, 147) as he describes the process of looking for authenticity in paintings. Students' reflections about a piece of work can highlight that work's "biography." Commentaries drawn from reflective questions such as the ones above offer students a chance to describe the learning processes they use to craft their work:

- "As I look through this portfolio I notice slight improvements . . . the way the paper flows came from learning about transitions . . . I made fewer errors in grammar and usage because I started to look them up when I revised . . . maybe writing is something that there is no right or wrong way to do it." (a high school senior)
- "I feel like I have a lot of strong points in my writing. I can pick a topic and expand on it without swaying off the subject. I am very orderly in my writing, and I can create stories off the top of my head. Following the writing process is another one of my strengths. But tagging along are also some weaknesses. I sometimes have weak openings and my endings don't conclude my thoughts. I also need to improve my vocabulary and spelling." (an eighth grader)
- "I am taken aback by the realization that I've categorized my portfolio much like I categorize my life . . . Is it education, or writing, or reflection, or family?? . . . I have learned that I am a novelist dying to get out. Perhaps a stand-up comedienne, as well. The stories from family shout to be released on paper. My personal writing shows this over and over again." (a veteran teacher)

Be Reflexive: What Techniques Can Students Use to Display Authenticity?

And so the reflective stance, like spectrography, searches under the surfaces of students' work, uncovering its biography of lessons learned, risks taken, strategies tried, intentions explored. But reflection by itself is not enough; students must learn to take a reflexive turn when they evaluate their work: a turn back from the self to the other. Students must look at their learning in relationship to what the "outside" expects: standards, curriculum guidelines, admission or graduation requirements. A well-honed portfolio not only says, "look at me, here I am and here are my fingerprints"; it also says "this is how I meet (exceed, adjust) your expectations for me."

Neither expectations, standards, nor curricular goals should be mysteries for students, nor should assessment be inaccessible. Curricular mystery encourages confusion, and that encourages innocent forgery: "What do I do to get an A?" "What is the paper supposed to say?" "What am I supposed to think?" And under such conditions, students are clueless about standards or any evaluative criteria we or our schools have for them. "Here are my collected papers," such a student says as he hands his portfolio to a teacher or an outside assessor. "Now you assess them."

But that's not the point. The technology of portfolios—reflection and reflexivity—is not the technology of grading. As teachers, it should not be our job to assess the piles of artifacts students collect and display in their portfolios; it should be our job to assist students to do it themselves, according to the particular expectations of our class, school, district, or region, with reflection and reflexivity as tools. With reflective portfolios and a reflexive stance, we can instead observe: "Here are your collected papers, and with your reflective comments they explain who you are and what you've learned. Now show me how they meet this set of requirements—the ones we have for all students in this (class, school, grade level, district)."

Here are some examples of reflexive questions—ones that take a turn toward the institutional "other," to encourage students to view and articulate their work in relationship to a set of standards:

- What should I know as a reader about this piece that will help me understand your thinking and work? What would you do next to this piece to have it "tell your story" even more clearly?

  Linda Carstens, San Diego Unified School Dist.

- If you are reflecting for personal reasons about your work, do you have a life or a school career pattern into which these reflections fit? If you are trying to show someone else something about your reflections, how will you make these reflections visible and meaningful for the other person?

  Miles Myers, executive director, NCTE

- What do you want your work to say (to others) about you? What does your work say about you? What are the differences?

  Sara Jordan, SUNY Albany

- What things can you show me about your learning that I would otherwise not know about?

Tom Romano, Miami University of Ohio

- Look over the curriculum guidelines for all students at your "level." Find places in your portfolio that illustrate that you've accomplished each guideline. Mark them with Post-it Notes, and then explain how they all work together.
- How do the contents of your portfolio meet the six objectives for this course?

Bonnie Sunstein, University of Iowa

For the teacher, the student portfolio functions like a spectrograph. With X-ray vision, we can watch as a student tours us through her process and explains each critical moment of the drafting of a piece, the making of an artifact. For the student, the portfolio is not only the frame and the canvas for a finished piece; it holds the early sketches, the experiments in composing, the erasures, stops and starts, rearrangements, coverings. Only the student knows how those processes unfolded, and she ought to have the authority to explain and document her work as it stands in relationship to required standards:

- "I've learned that I think by making up stories. When we studied evaporation in science, I wrote 'The Raindrop Who was Afraid to Fall.' I made a main character, Chip, who was a raindrop who lived inside his mother, a cloud. It helped me learn about how evaporation works." (a third grader)
- "I think I've been looking a lot for metaphors in my reading. This is a result of my change in writing—or vice versa. I think now I look for things that aren't so obvious . . . the words that are unwritten teach much stronger than words on paper." (an eighth grader)
- "I think I am a pretty diverse writer. I can argue different opinions, stand up for how I feel, and compose things using things that other people say. I can analyze my feelings and I can revise a poor essay in order to make it a good one." (a tenth grader)
- "My literacy is the part of myself about which I feel the coolest. . . . I think of my portfolio as a living being . . . I control my literacy but my literacy controls my portfolio. . . . School does not have a particularly large representation in my portfolio. I think that this is because I was 'idiot-tracked' first through eighth grades . . . I had awful handwriting and handwriting comments were all I got. I am quite surprised I became a writer at all." (a college junior)

- "What I learned about writing: 1. Revise, don't edit; 2. Slash adverbs, crush passive voice, and mutilate dull verbs; 3. Respect words; 4. Look for the extraordinary line. It is simply the ordinary brought into focus. . . . " (a middle-aged preservice teacher)

Beware: How Do We Know How To Ask? And How Do We Avoid Getting Only What We Ask For?

It is chilling to think of the expression "Beware of what you ask for because you just might get it" in relationship to our traditional assessment practices in schools. We create the market for forgery in writing when we encourage superficial adherence to style and form. By privileging the surface features in students' writing, we create a demand for a superficial kind of product, a forgery of sorts, using curriculum guidelines to shape student texts and ideas. But the practice of keeping portfolios by both students and teachers, along with the additional practice of analyzing their contents with rigorous questions that demand reflection and reflexivity, lets everyone know we welcome the search beneath the surfaces. No one can fake that.

Alan Burroughs writes, "In some cases the intimate view, obtained by studying alterations and the development of a design, compels the critic to revise his estimate of the artist's personality" ([1938] 1965, 89). And that's the challenge to us as teachers. Perhaps those "school smart" students whose successes lie in curricular imitation will not be the same students as those whose close analysis will document breadth and depth of cognitive growth. Perhaps the bulk of the learning of curricular standards will emerge from a product a student submits late or incomplete. Or perhaps a major epiphany will occur out of an instructive failure. Students will be able to document that kind of learning, like master painters under the surfaces, with rigorous habits of reflection and reflexivity. We must be prepared to meet all students' authentic self-portraits with the same scrutiny we use to detect the inadvertent fingerprints on their forgeries. And we must be ready for disappointment, confusion, and lack of confidence as we do it. Cebik writes:

> We lack confidence in the work, in its being what we have taken it to be. More significantly, we lack confidence in ourselves. We no longer know how to respond to the work, either cognitively or emotively. . . . No longer does form and color challenge or delight us. Instead we focus upon dirt on the surface. (1989, 148)

Cebik's words to art scholars are equally important to us. Teachers, too, must learn to be connoisseurs of our students' work. It doesn't take blatant forgery like Marie's absentee note to shake our confidence. Our confidence is often shaken when we read student writing under the pressure of grades, when we try to distinguish between form and content, between adherence to convention and pushing beyond boundaries of style or genre, between risk and safety. We need to serve as buyers, dealers, docents, chemists, scholars, lawyers, and historians. And, more important than that, we must be curators and patrons at the same time. We need to find ways to support our students to authenticate their collected body of works even as they are in the process of collecting it. We cannot wander around the museum as casual onlookers, asking students to "reflect" without offering them the tools and the stances to help them do so. Nor can we spend all our time in the workshop studio, tinkering and creating without stopping to document what we've done. And certainly we don't want to spend all our time (after the papers are turned in) in the lab with our spectrographs scrutinizing every misplaced modifier and unfocused verb and hounding ourselves about what's authentic. Instead, we need to teach ourselves and our students to function more like the masters—to know how to work with passion and a discernable soul, but also to understand both how and when to hang their work on the walls for others to see.

REFERENCES

Burroughs, Alan. [1938] 1965. Art Criticism from a Laboratory. Westport, CT: Greenwood.

———. 1926. "Art and the X-Ray." *Atlantic Monthly*. April; 137.

Cebik, L. B. 1989. "On the Suspicion of an Art Forgery." *The Journal of Aesthetics and Art Criticism* 47:2. (Spring): 147–56.

Drobot, Eve. 1989. "The Real Fake." *Saturday Night*. (March): 31–39.

Graves, Donald H., and Bonnie S. Sunstein, eds. 1992. *Portfolio Portraits*. Portsmouth, NH: Heinemannn.

Mundy, Alicia. 1992. "The Artful Forger." GQ. 62.(6).

Norman, Geraldine. 1998. "The Van Gogh Fakes." *New York Review of Books*. (February): 4–7.

Potts, Joseph P. 1996. "Assessing Portfolios: A Study of the New Standards Project 1994–95 Field Trial Portfolios in Three Tenth Grade Classrooms." Unpublished doctoral dissertation, University of Iowa.

Sunstein, Bonnie S. 1996. "Assessing Portfolio Assessment: Three Encounters of a Close Kind." *Voices from the Middle* 3:4 (November): 13–22.

Sunstein, Bonnie, and Julie B. Cheville, eds. 1996. *Assessing Portfolios: A Portfolio*. Urbana, IL: National Council of Teachers of English.

Sunstein, Bonnie, and Joseph P. Potts. 1998. "Literacy Stories Extended: Of Reflection and Teachers' Portfolios." *Teacher Education Quarterly*. (Winter): 61–72.

Waterman, Frederick W. 1994. "Those Fabulous Fakes." *Hemispheres*. (July): 74–80.

2

CURATORIAL COLLECTIONS
Cross-Curricular Design Portfolios
JEFFREY D. WILHELM

A teacher, ideally conceived, is a designer who helps learners to design themselves.
David Perkins, Knowledge as Design

A seventh-grade student of mine, named Walter, once told me that "in school all you do is a bunch of crap for other people." This stood me up a bit because, though Plato doesn't use the word "crap," this is pretty close to his definition of slavery; namely, that anyone who does someone else's work is a slave.

You don't create, define, or find meaning for yourself by doing someone else's work; you do it by creating and constructing meanings in actual situations that are of great personal relevance and social significance. You achieve it by doing work of importance to you and to the communities with which you are engaged. You construct knowledge and identity as you engage in such work.

When our students create portfolios, they are telling the story of their learning, and in a very real way they should also be telling the story of who they are, who they want to become, and who constitutes the various communities they might want to work and live in. More than that, portfolios can become arguments about the world, how it is, and what it should perhaps become, and how we can all participate in this act of becoming. This kind of "critical literacy" and "social action" is often lacking in current versions of portfolios.

But as we provide students with the time, opportunity, and choice to construct their own meanings and to live and document their own learning story, we must not forget to assist them to more competent learning performances (Tharp and Gallimore 1988). If we do not lend them our own and others' expertise, and support them in developing a wider repertoire of more powerful strategies and expert understandings than they currently possess, then we can certainly not be said to have taught them. And if we have taught them, the best portfolio should both contextualize and demonstrate this learning in actual performance.

A "WORKING" PORTFOLIO

To be most useful, portfolios should do work for students, teachers, and a larger community of learners. The best portfolios, I think, do "work" by making cases, providing documentation, and making arguments—by participating in larger conversations about meaningful topics.

I'm saying that first, a portfolio should demonstrate student learning, accountability for what is learned, and understanding of how and why this learning should be enacted. Student portfolios should not just demonstrate procedural learning, but should argue for what is at stake around issues, or "contact zones" (Pratt 1991; Bizzell 1994) of significant, highly contended and debatable issues that the student has come to understand and make judgments about. A contact zone can be conceived as an actual geographical space in which different parties with differing perspectives vie against one another. Or, as I use it here, such a zone can be simply an issue around which various points of view exist.

Personally, I agree that all facts are social constructions (see Hillocks 1995) and that therefore even the sciences and maths are full of contact zones—important issues that can be viewed from a variety of perspectives. Student portfolios can be records of how and where various "facts" were collected and how they speak to each other. Students can then learn about the various ways knowledge is constructed, and can personally participate in current debates about what different "facts" culled from different sources and through different lenses might mean.

Second, student portfolios should demonstrate teaching and learning that is visible, justifiable, and answerable. When learning is made visible through language or an artifact, it can be held steady and used as a tool to think with. In effect, our thought has been placeholded. When learning is made visible, it can eventually be built into a coherent knowledge artifact. The stuff of the portfolio can stand behind such artifacts to provide evidence and support.

Third, student portfolios should demonstrate how knowledge can be used to make a difference to a community of practice.

CURRICULUM AS "DESIGNING KNOWLEDGE"

To do all of this, I suggest that we conceive of curriculum as "designing knowledge" (Perkins 1986), and of portfolios as

1. the procedural record of questions pursued, alternatives considered, decisions made, and justifications required in the process of designing knowledge artifacts; and
2. the products that are the knowledge artifacts themselves.

If we make such an instructional move toward a design curriculum, I believe we will immeasurably enliven classroom work and encourage substantive learning. A design curriculum will also help educators conceive of literacy and composing in a broader sense to include the various ways of making meaning through electronic, visual, and symbolic means. We'll accrue other benefits, too, such as the development of more sophisticated, student-centered, integrated, and inquiry-driven curricula.

I further believe, given the current politics of schooling and standardized testing, that reductive notions of learning can be fought only with real performances and design artifacts that demonstrate knowledge in actual, situated accomplishment. "Design work" can demonstrate both procedural and conceptual knowledge in powerful and irrefutable ways.

GETTING AN EDGE ON IT

Many of the portfolios I've seen in my own and other classrooms have me concerned. At worst, portfolios can be inert collections of the same old work that kids have always done, as Walter puts it, for "somebody else." The work may be considered acceptable even though it is of no use beyond the classroom, and even though the conceptual and procedural understandings that are expressed are not really accountable to what is understood in expert communities of practice.

For example, in a sixth-grade science class I've worked with, students were assisted through a guided set of activities with electricity. As they did so, they built a portfolio of observations and operational definitions about electrical phenomena. The observations were shoddy and the definitions and conclusions totally wrong. Kids wrote things, such as, "the lightbulbs drink the charges and use them to be bright," and "the battery keeps making electricity until it's all out."

Our teaching team introduced a project—designing a security system (or another electrical system of their choice)—that would require students' accurate knowledge of electrical circuitry. We then devised activities that would confront their current misconceptions. Only when their portfolios demonstrated their competence could they move on to actually designing their system. This provided great motivation, particularly to the more reluctant boys, and their portfolios became important documents and repositories of something that might be called knowledge and that could inform them as they designed their projects.

Because I value the move toward more authentic learning and assessment, I've been led to ask: what literacy and learning performances do we enact as adults and experts in the world outside of school?

My answer is that we use literacy to design things—to design knowledge and knowledge artifacts that address human needs and solve human and environmental problems. And whenever we design, we create shared community standards of what counts as success. In this chapter, I argue that instead of loose collections of work, portfolios should be curatorial collections of the processes and products of design, and of the work that supports and justifies the validity and usefulness of these objects.

SCIENTIFIC DESIGN: A PROJECT WITH MOTION

One of the great challenges of teaching is to tease out, teach, and assess cognitive processes that are fairly opaque, if not invisible. Neil Mercer (1995) states that students must demonstrate their achievement by "making their learning visible and their reasoning accountable" (x). This is exactly what I think a portfolio should help them to do.

While team teaching a sixth-grade science unit on kinematics, or the study of motion, we began our work by helping students to ask questions about motion. Questions were asked about the speed and direction of thrown and hit baseballs, about the design of roads and the acceleration of automobiles. There were lots of questions about bodies falling from space. We differentiated between those questions that were really about motion and those that were about something else, then proceeded to create a series of activities to help students explore some of their questions. The questions were theirs, but the path to expertise surrounding these questions was laid out by the teachers. The students, in turn, were to document their emerging understandings in ways that were visible and accountable.

Early in the unit, students busied themselves with ramps, steel balls, stopwatches, measuring tapes, and a variety of other resources as they pursued a number of guided activities. Throughout, they were asked to predict the outcome of certain circumstances—for example, when the pitch of a ramp is increased—to elicit prior knowledge and misconceptions; to engage in experimental activity around their prediction; to record results; to articulate their own operational definitions of concepts such as *acceleration* and *uniform motion*; and to construct "laws" or "rules" of the natural world based on their observations. They were continually asked to justify their definitions and emerging understandings.

This is the same process that real scientists use, and is unlike the "backward science" of typical school learning where we provide students with information, and then have them do experiments to prove that the information was correct—a situation which often leads to the "drylabbing" or faking of results instead of the careful construction of meaning through scientific thinking. Backward science encourages drylabbing and does not help students learn the real scientific processes.

The students were asked to build and write out understandings that they could justify and make visible. Their observations, their data, their definitions, and their articulation of conceptual understandings were all part of their "portfolio." Even so, some of the students' data was faulty, and many of the students' initial misconceptions continued to persist. In a science class, this was not good enough.

Teaching science showed me in a new way that I need a constant window into students' interests, ability, and current thinking so that I can adjust and redesign instruction to assist them in addressing difficulties and in developing more competent ways of knowing. The portfolio allowed for "instructive failure" because kids demonstrated what they knew (and didn't know) and why they were thinking that way. An important element in this process was the reflective writing that the kids completed about each activity—what they learned from it, what knowledge they used from past activities, and so on.

We continually asked students to "make public" what they knew and how they knew it. In one case we did this at a simulated physics conference. One group of boys insisted on philosophical grounds that uniform motion could not exist. They cited the concept of inertia and argued that "everything is either speeding up or slowing down." A group of girls presented their study next, and they argued that uniform motion did exist. They used graphs to prove it: "When we measured how long it took the ball to travel one meter at the top of our ramp, and how long it took the same ball to travel one meter at the bottom of the ramp, it took the exact same time. So we have proven that uniform motion exists!"

The discussion that followed explored what counts as evidence in a scientific community, how evidence must be collected and explained, how reservations must be responded to. The boys quickly set up their own ramp to replicate the girls' experiment, and found the same results. They revised their argument to coincide with the view that uniform motion does indeed exist. Sharing portfolio results allowed for students to learn from each other, and for failure to be instructive and forward looking.

Throughout our unit, we continually pitted various student methods and interpretations against each other, and confronted student misconceptions or impoverished conceptions with experiences and experiments that would help them to see evidence they had missed. We did this in the service of "assisting students to more competent and expert performances" (Tharp and Gallimore 1988).

At the end of the unit, small groups of students decided to create 3–5-minute video documentaries exploring a question involving motion in the context of their lives. Groups presented their research issues to the class in the form of a roundtable discussion. One group wanted to explore whether a hockey puck could achieve uniform motion. Another group proposed to gauge the speed at which cars went by their homes. They proposed ingenious methods for ascertaining their answers. When another group proposed to see how many free throws a student could shoot in one minute, the class immediately critiqued their question as not being about motion. Critiques and shared understanding continued to be a source of dialogue through the completion of the final videos, and a review board was set up to approve viewing of the videos by third grade-reading buddies.

Anna
Video Documentary on Speed of Cars Going by Tammy's House
Portfolio Contents

1. Question Brainstorming Sheet
2. Question Justification
3. Roundtable Presentation Sheet
4. Peer Comments—Roundtable
5. Revised Question and Justification—Teacher Sign-off
6. Data Collection Proposal
7. Peer and Teacher Approval of Data Collection Methods
8. Data
   a. Day One—4 p.m—15 cars
   b. Day One—5:30 p.m—23 cars
   c. Day Two—8:30 a.m—7 cars
9. Data Representation—Graph
10. Outline of Proposed Script
11. First Draft—Script and Visual Displays
12. Peer Editing and Teacher Approval Sheets
13. Review Board Approval Sheet
(also see our videotape in Tammy's portfolio)

GROWING COMPETENCE

In a science classroom it seems pretty clear that we want students to pursue and construct justifiable understandings about the natural world. We wouldn't want students to walk around with misconceptions about electricity, for instance. We wouldn't say, "Well, it's all right, at least he constructed his own misconception!" Yet I'm afraid that all too often insufficient student work in the language arts is celebrated. It is celebrated even though substantive conceptual understandings are not made evident. It is celebrated even when procedural understandings (or ways of knowing) are impoverished. It is accepted when conventions of language use (or ways of representing knowledge) are totally off the mark when compared to the work of experts.

This is not to say that we should insist on "correct" answers. There are certainly a range of possible answers and solutions to rich design problems. However, we should insist on growth toward fuller understanding and more answerability for our work. If students had left my science class with no new procedural understandings of how to pursue scientific inquiry, apply scientific knowledge, or represent scientific data and did not possess a more justifiable conceptual understanding of "uniform motion," then I would have had to regard my teaching as unsuccessful.

Why, then, would some language arts educators and students themselves be satisfied with a student story that did not convincingly demonstrate growth in ways of shaping narrative, and of conceptual understanding of the issues or themes the story explored? Is it because it is not clear what is at stake? Because the reading, writing, and learning we do in the language arts is not contextualized in purposeful situations? Because the work we pursue with students has no real audience or purpose? Because there is no real answerability? I think all of these issues are part of the problem, and the antidote I propose is the model of student-design learning (Lehrer 1993).

CONDITIONS FOR KNOWLEDGE

The conditions of knowledge are accountability, applicability, organization, and extensibility (see Wilhelm and Friedemann [1998] for a full discussion). When a community of practice creates knowledge, that knowledge is justified in terms the community values; the knowledge can be put to use and inform action; it is coherent and patterned; and it can be adapted, built upon, revised, and extended by other members of the community.

In the world outside of school, people produce knowledge for specific purposes. When this knowledge is collected, say, in a professional portfolio, it exhibits actual accomplishment, is used to fulfill real purposes, and serves as an incubator for further inquiry, learning, and adaptation. We move constantly between learning, knowing, doing, and learning more.

Portfolios are also a perfect way to track and document the process of design, and to make that process accountable to the community and the conditions of knowledge.

Perkins (1986) argues that design is the appropriate metaphor for knowledge. When students design "knowledge artifacts" such as prosthetic joints, a water purification system, a plan for improved cafeteria service, video documentaries, museum exhibits, Websites, hypermedia documents, dramas, and the like, they make their learning public and their reasoning accountable. The process and product of design provide multiple ways to demonstrate and assess what students know and are able to do, and multiple opportunities to assist them to more competent performances in the context of meaningful work.

What's more, design projects are problem-driven, personally relevant, socially significant, situated in real-world use, and are created by a community of learners connected to wider communities of learners.

WHAT IS STUDENT DESIGN?

Lehrer (1993) proposes that student-design learning with hypermedia requires students to identify topics and or problems, formulate questions, find information, organize data, analyze data, represent and justify what has been learned (e.g., through a knowledge artifact), revise the representation (or artifact) based on testruns and feedback, and present the artifact to an audience in a context where it may be useful. His model, as I have found, can be useful with many different kinds of knowledge artifacts such as video and drama, art and models, hypermedia and Websites (Wilhelm and Edmiston 1998; Wilhelm and Friedemann 1998).

HISTORICAL DESIGN:
A CULTURAL JOURNALISM PROJECT

I recently worked with several groups of seventh-grade students engaged in designing historical journalism projects. The purpose of the unit was to help students understand the workings of particular cultures and historical periods, and to explore how history is represented, how cultural information is passed on through time, and other issues around creating and understanding the past. We made sure to include both conceptual goals (a deep understanding of both general and particular historical-cultural concepts, e.g., knowledge of cultural institutions such as education, and of how this institution was enacted and how it shaped culture in the particular society) and procedural design goals (ways of asking historical research questions, of finding and validating historical information, or of representing this information to others, etc.).

One group at Mattanawacook Academy in Lincoln, Maine decided to design a classroom museum of ancient Egyptian culture, under the direction of their teacher, Julie Housum. Another group of five boys, under my direction, decided to create an interactive multimedia document that explored how French culture was brought to this country and continued to shape community life in their town.

We began the unit with a process drama in which we discovered, as archaeologists, a lost culture. The purpose of the drama was to introduce the students to the notions of history, culture, and cultural conflict. We then attempted to define culture and some questions we had about particular cultures. After some shared readings, groups formed and began to refine their own research questions.

In both Julie's class and my own, students chose to design projects that would be museum pieces, created to answer the questions that visitors to a museum would actually have. We planned to actually create the museums and invite visitors. The resulting video and multimedia document would subsequently be shared as museum exhibits with various groups. They would also be permanently "published" and made available in the school library.

In both classes, the work of creating the museum was framed as a "mantle of the expert" drama (Heathcote and Bolton 1995). (See Wilhelm and Edmiston [1998] for a full treatment of how drama can be used to front-load, motivate, and guide sophisticated sequences of instruction.)

In this kind of work, students are asked to take on the roles of "experts" in a community of practice. In our case, students became curators and exhibit designers. Oftentimes, the work is only dramatic and no concrete products or artifacts are created. In our work, however, students actually designed museum displays and exhibits.

First, we had to understand the problem and the context we were addressing. We brainstormed who would be likely to visit our museum. What would they already know—or think they knew—about our topic? What questions would they have? What kinds of exhibits would interest and excite them? Since there would probably be adults, peers, and smaller children visiting, how could we accommodate the needs and interests of various audiences, while still accurately representing what we had come to know?

Julie's class generated questions about pyramid power, how the pyramids were built, curses related to mummies, the class structure of ancient Egyptian life, Egyptian religion, fashion, food, and art. As they progressed, they also came to ask whose stories were missing from history, and how these voices, e.g., of the slaves, could be included in the museum. My group asked more immediate questions, such as why the local church no longer held services in French, why speaking French in school had been outlawed during previous generations, how the French they spoke was different from that spoken in France, and why and how French culture was still expressed through holidays, cuisine, fashion, folklore, and the like.

For two months students collected information by reading: picture books, myths, poetry, stories, songs, articles, and reference books; by visiting and cross-referencing a variety of Websites; by interviewing informants (Julie's class worked with anthropology students from the university; my group interviewed local folklorists and historians). As they processed the gathered information, students began to organize it, notice gaps, and pursue further research.

All their notes and plans were kept in a kind of process portfolio that would be used to develop and justify their resulting exhibit. Some students "made up" information and stories that they wanted to put into the museum. This led to a dramatic meeting of our "Museum Board" to discuss what could be put in a museum, what kind of inferences we could justifiably make, what steps we had to take to verify the information related in our displays.

Throughout both projects, Julie and I attempted to make students answerable for their thinking and for their work. A few days before the Egyptian museum was to open, I visited the displays. Upon entering, I followed a winding paper version of the Nile River back in time. It had been decided that most of the students would be in role as ancient Egyptians in a kind of "living history" museum, so that they could answer questions and provide the perspectives of ancient Egyptians. At each exhibit, I quizzed the student curators/actors about their display, and asked how they knew their information was accurate.

At the fashion display, I was able to apply *kohl*—eyeliner—and other kinds of authentic makeup from that period to a papier-maché face. While dressing paper dolls with period robes and headdresses, I asked why makeup and dress had changed during the three periods of ancient Egyptian civilization that were displayed. I asked about the symbolism of color, about how Greek and Mesopotamian culture had influenced notions of style. I asked if all Egyptians, or only the rich, were influenced by fashion. I asked about the sources of the girls' information—how did they know what they said they knew? How were they sure they'd gotten it right? My two hosts answered my questions confidently and discursively, and we ended up engaging in a long discussion about "defamiliarization" and how popular culture is always changing and differentiating itself from what is currently in vogue.

As I moved on to the next exhibit, one of the girls told Julie, "He really pushed me. I liked it. It proved that I really know my stuff."

There were other exhibits where there were problems. Prior knowledge was assumed in the Sphinx exhibit; I had some reasonable questions about the pyramids that could not be answered. These boys once again hit the books and improved their exhibits before the grand opening.

The same kind of justification was pursued with the boys creating the multi-media display of Franco-American culture. As we discussed their hypermedia presentation, they theorized about notions of assimilation and resistance, of cultural and personal identity; they argued for preserving diversity because it ensured various kinds of choice, dialogue, and vitality; and they made comparisons from the condition of their culture to the cultural situation of many Native Americans. They also made predictions about the future, and devised plans for preserving their culture. These ruminations later became part of their multimedia document's argument.

Throughout this process students had created and made use of various ways of collecting and representing information, all of which could be thought of as pieces in a "portfolio" of learning. For instance, their logs and notes were a kind of process portfolio and data bank that provided answerability for their progress and for their learning. Their emerging design plans provided a placeholding function, something to reflect upon, critique, and grow from. The actual museum exhibits were representations of what had been learned. Further, these exhibits were set to work to teach real audiences, which included other students. As a kind of "jigsaw classroom" was created with the design artifacts (or portfolios, if you will), a body of knowledge was pieced together that taught other students what one group had learned and how they had learned it.

Authentic performances of the kind expected of expert adults were modeled and enacted. Skills, strategies, and knowledge were developed that transcended individual assignments, assortments of facts, and specific content areas. A marriage of learning, thinking, knowing, sharing, and doing was achieved. (For detailed descriptions of how students can be assisted to find information, ask questions, organize and analyze information, etc., during the process of a design project, see Wilhelm and Friedemann [1998].)

BUILDING CRITICAL STANDARDS

A portfolio, like any display of knowledge, must involve the articulating and meeting of critical standards. Early in the projects described here, we began to generate criteria for the successful solution of our problems. As Tharp and Gallimore (1988) point out, critical standards don't just emerge. Students must be assisted to articulate and apply them. Having a real audience and purpose was an immeasurable help. As Tharp and Gallimore argue, "all designers need an audience . . . idle talk palls."

Critical standards are best negotiated, implemented, and revised in a community of use. In such a context, there can certainly be a range of excellent performances, but there are just as certainly appropriate and inappropriate solutions, valid and invalid conclusions, higher and lower qualities of design. When students are helped to develop their own critical standards, we can nurture their desire for learning, for social action, and for quality, and provide them a means to achieving a personal sense of excellence.

When students are guided to determine their own goals and standards and then to enact them, this self-determination becomes self-definition. School should be a place where they engage in significant work together in ways that help them to know and to become more than they already are. A portfolio, in my opinion, should be a record of this kind of work, and a visible demonstration of what has been achieved through it.

At a pizza party to celebrate our museum exhibits, students were excitedly sharing what had flopped, what people had questioned, what had gone well, what had been great fun, and what they would do differently next time. My group discussed donating their multimedia document to the local history museum, or perhaps even putting together a bigger and better display for them. Julie's group wondered if they should have resequenced the exhibits to give visitors a better sense of travelling through time, or of moving from the experiences of slaves up through the social classes to that of the Pharaoh.

When this kind of thinking happens, the portfolio has become a platform from which to reflect on learning over time, and from which to continue knowing about and creating the self, and from which to venture out into that vastly wonderful and mysterious place called the world—maybe even to make a difference in the lives of others while we are there.

REFERENCES

Bizzel, P. 1994. "'Contact Zones' and English Studies". *College English* (56) 2: 163–169.

Heathcote, D., and G. Bolton. 1995. *Drama for Learning: Dorothy Heathcote's Mantle of the Expert Approach for Teaching Drama.* Portsmouth, NH: Heinemann.

Hillocks, G. 1995. *Teaching Writing as Reflective Practice.* New York: Teachers College Press.

Lehrer, R. 1993. "Authors of Knowledge: Patterns of Hypermedia Design." In S. Lajoie and S. Derry, eds., *Computers as Cognitive Tools,* 197–227. Hillsdale, NJ: Lawrence Erlbaum.

Mercer, N. 1995. *The Guided Construction of Knowledge.* Adelaide, Australia: Multilingual Matters.

Perkins, D. 1986. *Knowledge as Design.* Hillsdale, NJ: Lawrence Erlbaum.

Pratt, M. L. 1991. "Arts of the Contact Zone." *Profession 91*: 33–41. New York: Modern Language Association.

Tharp, R., and R. Gallimore. 1988. *Rousing Minds to Life.* Cambridge: Cambridge University Press.

Wilhelm, J., and B. Edmiston. 1998. *Imagining to Learn: Inquiry, Ethics and Integration through Drama.* Portsmouth, NH: Heinemann.

Wilhelm, J., and P. Friedemann. 1998. *Hyperlearning: Technology, Literacy and Integrated Project Learning.* York, ME: Stenhouse.

3

GETTING REAL
Talking to Students About Portfolios
THOMAS STEWART

GETTING STARTED

"Enjoy your holiday!"

With an ironic wave of a mitten, the last of my office-mates for the semester disappeared down the hall. I looked wistfully at the snowflakes settling on the single tree outside my window. In the window's reflection, I could see the pile of colorful portfolios that awaited me, resolutely staring me down in the glass.

I was exhausted and relieved as I finished examining student portfolios that semester. I was also a bit disappointed with what I was seeing. The course I had taught, a writing methods class for elementary education majors, was one of a series of classes the students took which focused on critical theory and pedagogy. As I looked at the portfolios, the critical part seemed to be missing.

When the portfolio was initially assigned, students were given a sheet listing what was required in the portfolio—a few of their best pieces, a photo or artifact from one of the projects they had done. Meant as a general guideline, the students picked the assignment sheet apart like a team of lawyers examining a contract. "How many pieces do I need?" "What exactly counts as an artifact?" "What can I use for a theme?" As an answer, I usually reversed the question: "How many pieces do you want to include?" and so on. In a final crescendo to the semester, I interviewed fifteen students for a half-hour each about their portfolios—how they had come up with themes, why they had chosen the pieces they did. It was a chance for the students to talk about the portfolio-making process.

When I had finished the interviews, though, I couldn't help but feel that they were superficial and unsatisfactory. Was I alone in my disappointment with the portfolios? I shared my thoughts with a colleague. She, too, was disappointed. As superficial as the portfolios had been, the interviews were even more so. What we were hearing in the interviews was students telling us what they thought we wanted to hear. Both of us had come to the field of education from a writing background. Authenticity was critical. The first step was a more authentic interview, where students felt empowered to say what they were really thinking: to get real. I wanted to know: Were students making any connections when they created portfolios that were meant to connect the three classes? Did students reveal any sense of critical awareness during interviews about the portfolios held at the completion of the courses? In the following, I share the manner in which two undergraduates, Janine and Olivia, completed and discussed their portfolio assignments during my second semester as an instructor for the course.

A NEW APPROACH

It was something of an ambush: The portfolio interviews during the spring semester were marked most significantly by the absence of innocuous questions like, "Which of these are your favorite pieces?" The second time around, the questions were more critical: "How was this process of assessment different from some other ways we could have done this?" and "What does being a critical teacher mean to you?" With the voluntary cooperation and permission of the participants, I recorded the interviews. After the interviews were completed, I listened to each one. I was primarily interested in interviews in which participants

- made connections between the work in their portfolios and critical issues
- were able to articulate some concept—rather than a particular concept—of what critical meant to them
- articulated how the portfolios became a visual representation of the cognitive activities they had done in the courses.

While listening to the interviews, I examined the participants' comments about their work and analyzed them in conjunction with the products themselves: the portfolios.

STUDENT PORTFOLIOS

Interviews with two of the students, Janine and Olivia, stood out in terms of meeting the above criteria. Janine's and Olivia's portfolios, like those of many of the students, are more visually than critically oriented. Both portfolios are elaborate visual "productions"; each features a brightly decorated cover and is cleverly designed on the inside.

Janine's Portfolio

Janine's portfolio cover and title theme are borrowed from Dr. Seuss's (1990) book *Oh, the Places You'll Go!*, to which Janine has added, "With reading and writing we learn and grow." In her introduction, Janine notes that she has included pieces that will "show me the real reasons I have chosen to become a teacher." She continues, "Each piece shows that I have come one step closer to my ultimate goal [of becoming a teacher]." Janine carries the book's motif throughout the portfolio, as cut-out sections of Dr. Seuss rhymes appear with each artifact she has put in the portfolio. Among the works, Janine includes a critique of a piece of children's writing. In her summary of the piece, she notes that the assignment "helped me to learn and grow as a writer and as a teacher of future writers." In writing about her group presentation, another item she represented in the portfolio, Janine notes that the presentation "has shown me that the reading and writing process extends much further than a pencil and paper or the pages of a book."

Another artifact Janine includes is her read-aloud, an assignment in which students were required to read a book to an elementary student and then evaluate the student's reading. On the original assignment, Janine and her partner received an unacceptable mark. After redoing the assignment, they received an acceptable mark. Janine writes in her reflection, "Our unacceptable mark allowed us to realize what we did and did not know and grow in our new knowledge. . . . All of these pieces illustrate that I really have learned from my mistakes." When asked about the inclusion of this assignment, Janine said, "If [the instructor] wouldn't have given me the chance to redo it for an acceptable mark, then I would still have no clue what I had done."

Olivia's Portfolio

Olivia chooses as her theme, "Elementary educators are lifelong learners." She notes in her introduction, "The pieces that I have chosen demonstrate my understanding of how important learning is to a teacher." Among the items she includes are some from a group presentation on multiculturalism: visuals from the presentation and a sheet filled with feedback from her instructor. She writes that she includes this piece because her group was forced "to take our topic and present it in a way that would be interesting and informative to others in the class." During her group's presentation, Olivia and the group made most of the class feel the effects of discrimination by responding only to students who exhibited certain physical characteristics. She continues in her written reflection on the piece, "We intended to shock our [classmates] into understanding what it feels like to lack the perception of the dominating culture. We knew that there was a possibility that our presentation would fail, but it was successful and we were able to get our point across." During her interview, she noted that she also chose to represent the presentation because "this is the first [group presentation] that actually went well. . . . Everyone put an idea into it, and we were able to build something together." In her reflective summary statement for the portfolio, Olivia writes, "Each of these projects [in the portfolio] has shown me what an important role learning is [sic] for a teacher."

PORTFOLIO INTERVIEWS

Rather than simply "turning in" their portfolios, students were asked to talk about them in individual half-hour interviews scheduled with one of their instructors. I transcribed the interviews of Janine and Olivia after carefully listening to all of the interviews. My examination of their interviews revealed that, rather than following my lead and talking about critical issues of race, class, and gender, what both students stressed was the practical value of the portfolio. Attempts to bring up critical issues were met with resistance. When asked what being a critical teacher meant to her, Olivia responded with uncertainty: "I guess really being critical I would think that you would really . . . you know what I mean . . . you would take a real specific interest in each student maybe and then go through their work."

I attempted to get at notions of *critical* through the work Olivia and Janine had included in their portfolios. Janine had included several pieces representing a group presentation on discrimination during which the group did a survey. I challenged Janine: "On your survey, the one answer that surprised me came in response to the question, 'Do you think affirmative action programs discriminate against the majority?' And almost everybody said yes that they do discriminate against the majority." She responded, "Yeah I think a lot of times people will give what they think we want to hear." This has clear connotations for a person like Janine, who is becoming a teacher: After all, what does it mean when students say what they think the teacher wants to hear rather than what they really think? What does it mean when a teacher encourages that kind of response?

Olivia also made responses to critical issues when talking about her group's presentation, for which they chose the topic of multicultural-ism. "We sat down," she began when explaining how the group grap-pled with the issue, "and tried to figure out what multicultural really is because you can take it from so many different angles. I mean we would talk, and it seemed like everyday we were changing what we thought it was. . . . In some cases we were focusing on discrimination, and then sometimes we went a totally different route. So what we tried to do was we tried to keep it basically about culture—not so much about gender or race or anything like that." I challenged her by noting, "You're not going to get very much resistance [on a college campus]. . . . How would you handle it if you were trying to present the same ideas to a more hostile audience, maybe, just for example, in a school district [in which] some of the teachers don't agree with multiculturalism?" Olivia responded by saying, "I think you can do it without saying [you're do-ing it]." Curiously, in the reflections about the group presentations that Olivia and Janine wrote for the portfolio, they reflected exclusively on their process in doing the presentations—Olivia, for example, noted, "This is a great assignment for collaborative learning"—rather than on the critical issues that came up through the content of their presenta-tions. The students were more intent on the experience itself than on the meaning of the experience.

Both students seemed more comfortable when talking about the portfolios as metacognitive tools. The chance to see their work as a whole was, as Janine noted, "a lot more fun I think than just sitting there studying, because I got to see what I had done . . . and it was worth it." As Janine noted later in the interview, putting together a portfolio "really made the whole class come together and made me un-derstand why I was doing this. And as far as assessing myself [with the portfolio], I now know that [teaching] is what I want to do." Further-more, Janine articulated a professional value to doing a portfolio in a methods class: "I may forget [the assignments] by the time school starts next year, but then I can bring [the portfolio] out when I finally am a teacher. I may have added 500 new things to that, and I can have that with me so that my students can look through it, or if I need an idea . . . I have it all right there." Janine made note of the excitement generated by the visual aspect of her portfolio: "I was really excited about it. . . . My roommates were all studying for accounting tests, and I was finish-ing my semester!"

The portfolio also helped Janine in a broader way: "During the se-mester, I fell into a kind of slump where I thought, 'Well, what am I doing?' I had no idea where [the block of classes] was going, because I felt like I didn't have anything concrete that I could take anywhere . . . until the end of the semester when I did this, and it was like, 'Oh!' For some people, it may have clicked all semester, and for others it didn't. . . . Doing this made it all worthwhile." Seeing the work come together in a visual way through the portfolio helped Janine make the connections among the courses.

Olivia found that the portfolio required a higher order of thinking. "I think," she began in her interview, "it makes you think more about what you do than if you have a question, and it just asks you to give the answer." Olivia stressed the importance of the visual aspect of portfolios in relation to integrating knowledge: "When you try to integrate them all together, you can kind of see what you learned. If you can integrate everything together, I think it shows you learned something." Once again, it was the process of graphically organizing the work through the use of the portfolio which allowed the student to make connections between the work. Rather than having a student "chuck it and forget everything . . . and have nothing to show for it," as Janine noted, the portfolio brings everything together. As Olivia concluded, the portfolio "kind of gave me a way to end what we learned . . . to actually go back and reflect on everything that I learned."

USING PORTFOLIOS TO "SHOW" LEARNING

Both Olivia and Janine use the word "show" to describe what the portfolio does. The portfolio shows these students something (e.g., the importance of lifelong learning) that was merely an abstract idea; it articulates something (e.g., the goal of becoming a teacher) that was only a vague sense to the students. It also becomes a physical piece of evidence that shows that they have accomplished something. As Janine notes, the process of creating the portfolio helped her overcome a slump because it revealed to her that she had done many things of which she was proud. Both students talked openly about the risk of failure. Janine mentioned her failure to get an acceptable mark on her read-aloud assignment the first time she turned it in. Olivia talked about the possibility of failing when her group did an innovative presentation. Yet both students' portfolios reveal how they took risks and ultimately succeeded. Not all students' portfolios were as refined as Janine's and Olivia's. Some wrote reflections that were little more than descriptions of what they had done. In those cases, the interviews were a good place to probe further, to demand a deeper explanation, and, in a few instances, to ask students to redo parts of their portfolios.

GETTING REAL

The metacognitive processes that Janine and Olivia went through in creating their portfolios expanded their understanding of the content they learned in the three classes. Neither, however, clearly expressed any notion of how doing a portfolio clarified any of the critical issues which were discussed during the semester. Further research is necessary to examine this issue.

Janine and Olivia focused instead on the organizational advantages of doing the portfolio and on the fact that it helped them to remember what they had accomplished in the classes. The two students, for the first time looking at their work in the three courses as a whole, essentially had to make sense of it all, whether they chose a theme first and then pieces to fit in with that theme or vice versa. Evoking what Wolf and Siu-Runyan (1996) theorized about the effects of portfolios, Janine and Olivia became reflective about their own work. During the process of writing reflections for each piece they chose, the students again had to think about what role each piece played in their learning. Through examining the body of work as a whole, students could "see" what they had done and "show" it to others. And by organizing the work into a coherent whole, they have developed reference books which they can use in the future, rather than, as Janine noted would happen without a portfolio, "throw[ing] all the papers in the back of the closet and wonder[ing] why the heck I did it." The portfolios and interviews are authentic methods of examining things that students have already "learned," and, in the process, they "relearn" them, making the material real to them.

REFERENCES

Seuss, Dr. 1990. *Oh, the Places You'll Go!* New York: Random House.
Wolf, K., and Y. Siu-Runyan. 1996. "Portfolio Purposes and Possibilities." *Journal of Adolescent and Adult Literacy* 40: 30–37.

4

WHEN A PORTFOLIO KEEPER
IS A RELUCTANT WRITER

MARY E. MCGANN

*In my classroom, portfolios have become the students' stories of
who they are as writers, readers, thinkers, and human beings.*
Linda Rief, Seeking Diversity

This is a story of two reluctant writers, David (aged 8) and Jerimy (aged 14). They did not know each other and they found themselves in two very different learning situations. What they have in common, however, is the growth in writing that portfolios encouraged for them. I had been fascinated with the development my own college writing students had demonstrated in their portfolios for as long as I had been structuring my classes around portfolios. As a teacher educator and writing teacher, I found myself doing research in Verna DeLuce's eighth-grade class where Jerimy was a student. David's literacy development took on a special resonance for me as his mother, especially as I began to realize that all the books, reading aloud, and writing—in short, the literate environment my husband and I thought we had created in our home—did not seem to help David avoid struggling with writing. David kept his portfolios out of school with a private reading/writing tutor and Jerimy's writing portfolio was compiled in an eighth-grade language arts class. As I looked at Jerimy's portfolio in the course of my research in that eighth-grade class, I experienced a shock of future recognition: this could be my son David in five years. Given David's struggles, he could become a writing avoider. I decided to look at these two different portfolios to see what could be learned about the ways portfolios help students who do not see themselves as writers. How do the portfolios of such reluctant writers help those writers define themselves? How do their portfolios help them develop as writers?

In looking at these portfolios, I tried to discern the ways in which these two writers' portfolios constitute a self-definition. David defines himself as first an artist; he is a child who takes great joy in what he chooses to draw, especially when it's a joke or bizarre kind of satire. Jerimy defines himself as someone who put a great deal of effort into his portfolio. Neither writer would have been a self-initiating portfolio keeper like Linda Rief's student Molly Finnegan. In fact, both writers would hardly have called themselves writers. David found himself in a third-grade class taught by a teacher who created a language-rich environment for her students, but who, nonetheless, felt constrained by the grade-dominated system of her building and school district. David's portfolio grew from his work with his tutor, Camelia Ibrahim, at that time a junior elementary education major at Indiana University. Concurrently, David was keeping a school writing folder. A look at David's two portfolios—his tutorial portfolio and his school collection—suggests that he did his best writing when he could chose the subject and format and when he could illustrate the writing. After much reflection, I believe that the tutoring portfolio was so successful because it was "underinvented" by his tutor; that is, she made few requirements, few interventions beyond serving as a highly interested and supportive audience. At the beginning of his third-grade year David's teacher was rightly concerned about his reluctance to read and write, and as committed and knowledgeable as his teacher was, with twenty-seven children and no aide, she was not going to be able to give him individualized attention. The only option of extra school help was an aide who used workbook exercises with a small group of children in a pull-out program. So I hired a private tutor.

Both portfolios—David's tutoring work and Jerimy's writing skills workshop portfolio—were created by a tutor and a teacher who understood the nature of underinvention, yet also knew how to create a low-risk atmosphere for writing and reflecting on that writing. Such underinvention, as Mary Ann Smith (1997) suggests, is part of the most viable of portfolio cultures, classroom cultures in which students have predictable structures that help them write and revise (148).

The evidence of Jerimy's early writing in Verna DeLuce's Writing Skills Workshop (eighth grade, August through December) suggests that he had not had much success with writing or reading, and thus tended to avoid both. During the eighteen weeks Jerimy wrote more, he told his teacher, than he had ever written. His teacher, Verna DeLuce, sees herself as a coach; at the midpoint and the end of the grading period, she views herself as a co-evaluator with her students. She also believes that by giving learners the responsibility for fulfilling a contract of what they will do in writing and reading, she is able to encourage more writing and better writing than most students have done before they have to come to her class.

Both of these writers wrote more than they had ever written when they found themselves in a portfolio situation. Both Verna DeLuce and Camelia Ibrahim see themselves as coaches, and acted accordingly. Papers were not marked up or graded. In Jerimy's eighth-grade writing workshop, DeLuce has multiple short conferences with all students and a formal evaluation conference with each student at the sixth week, the tenth week, and at the end; grades are based on the teacher's evaluation and the writer's self-evaluation of the fulfillment of a contract made at the beginning of the term. Looking at the quantity and quality of improvement in both writers, I was reminded of Paul Diederich's (1974) oft quoted statement about evaluation in language arts: "My predominate impression is that [language arts classes] are fantastically over evaluated. . . . Common sense suggests that grades ought to be reduced to the smallest number necessary to find out how students are doing toward four or five main objectives . . . but teachers keep piling them up like squirrels gathering nuts . . . I believe very strongly that noticing and praising whatever a student does well improves writing more than any kind or amount of correction of what he does badly, and that it is especially important for the less able writers who need all the encouragement they can get" (2). Diederich, a former Professor of English at the University of Chicago, went to work for the Educational Testing Service (ETS) where he developed Holistic Scoring as a process for assessing large numbers of student essays. His influence on the profession of English teaching and the field of assessment has been immeasurable.

JERIMY

Jerimy found himself in a writing skills workshop class at Tri North Middle School taught by Verna DeLuce; DeLuce and her colleague Lisa Riggins designed this course after reading Nancie Atwell's *In the Middle* and Linda Rief's *Seeking Diversity*. In the beginning of the course they had talked their principal into using faculty development funds to send them to Durham, New Hampshire, to visit Rief's classroom for three days. After five years, they are still tinkering with the course; changing it, refining it, and reflecting on how the students work within the portfolio culture they have created. DeLuce views herself within that classroom culture as a reader, coach, a prodder, an editor, and finally as an evaluator. However, she gives students a great deal of responsibility for their own writing and learning and even for evaluation. She structures the grading by a contract consisting of the student's promise to write and revise so many projects, select a certain amount of projects and to read and verify (with reading log entries) a certain amount of pages read during eighteen weeks.

Looking at Jerimy's portfolio with me, DeLuce expressed wonder that a student who came into her class with the skill level which Jerimy had demonstrated had even bought into her process: "So many students are afraid to attempt writing," she sighed. While Jerimy did actually accept the premises of the class, he showed his reluctance in other ways. Six out of eight writing projects came to DeLuce later than deadlines she had set. His final portfolio was missing a few pieces, although the bare bones of the contract—three projects selected and revised (out of eight), 250 pages read and verified and a reflective letter—were present. At the beginning of writing his first projects, Jerimy expressed the complaint that many reluctant writers express: "I don't know what to write about," so DeLuce had him make a time line and from this a few ideas came. One of these ideas, from the time line, was to write about a family trip to California. Here is how he began:

FIRST DRAFT

I went with my mom, brother, and grandmother To see my grandmother's sister and uncle Ron. We flow their. It was my first time to fly. It was neat. We missed our first plane and we had to wait for another plane to get their. It was neat to visit their cause it was hot their and cold here. California has lots of buildings and a lot of cars. We went to the ocean on a boat. We touched the ocean and it was cool.

**THIRD DRAFT (AFTER MAKING A
WEB TO GENERATE MORE DETAILS)**

I went to California with my mom, brother and my grandmother and we went to see my grandmother's sister and my uncle Ron. We flew there. It was my first time on a airplane and it was awesome. We missed our first plane, so we had to wait for another. California is a big state with many buildings and cars. It was neat to visit there because it was hot there and cold here. We saw the ocean sparkling from the golden sun and it was as blue as the sky.

In his reflection questionnaire (which DeLuce requires when students finish a project) Jerimy wrote about this paper: "The hardest part was the revision, to think back to when I was there and what it was like." In response to the question, What suggestions from your editors did you use and why? Jerimy wrote: "Most of it because it sounded better and went with my sentences."

In working with students and early drafts, DeLuce teaches various pre-writing and invention strategies—cognitive mapping, freewriting, listing,—and asks students to use several of them at least once and to demonstrate how they used them. Jerimy may have had a strong spatial sense, for the web seemed to work well for him and he employed it several times after DeLuce walked him through its use in an early conference on his first paper. An observer in her class, as I was, can see how much teaching she does in these short conferences. DeLuce has been teaching for a number of years, and she handles a class with grace and good humor; she moves quickly and energetically around the room, holding short miniconferences, demonstrating the use of strategies, leaning over a computer screen, or having students read aloud to her.

As an athlete, Jerimy seemed to have defined himself early on as a member of the "Sports Club" as Frank Smith (1988) might call it, but he seems to have defined himself outside the literacy club (1–5). Smith points out that members of the literacy club are "people who read and write, even the beginners. . ." (11). However, for the eighteen weeks Jerimy participated in DeLuce's writing workshop, Jerimy may have joined the club that probably had seemed quite elusive to him throughout his early school years. A comparison between his six weeks' reflective letter—a short paragraph—and the letter he wrote as he was submitting his final portfolio, suggests that he had come to an awareness about writing:

END OF FIRST 6 WEEKS REFLECTION:

Dear Mrs. De

I deserve a C because I haven't put all my effort in it but I put a lot of my effort. I thick [think] I did do good on my friend and I paper. I am all ways at my disk [desk] on time. I turned my parent letter in. I've turned my bumper sticker in and I've turned my book report in.

FINAL REFLECTION:

I used most of the editing strategies you gave us. I didn't use all of them because I thought it was fine. I had a good start with my Michael Jordan childhood paper. I also had a good middle in that paper by listing his accomplishment and awards, but I did not have a good ending or conclusion.

I have done good on pre-writing and drafting. I think the editing [having three editors] helped in many ways. I had more details in my final drafts. I need to improve in many ways. I need to write in different way and use more different words. But I put a lot of effort into these papers.

He still defines achievement in terms of effort, but for a reluctant writer like Jerimy, who has had little success in writing or reading, the expending of such effort is remarkable: He completed six projects and revised three of those projects considerably, although a look at the final draft of his early project on Michael Jordan suggests a great reliance on

Internet sources, which he summarizes. The projects on football and his family story, "Windmills, Wings and Water," (about the California trip) show considerable progression through the drafts. Unlike the Jordan project, these pieces, more closely connected with him and his family life, reflect his own voice and ideas. I asked DeLuce how she handles such a situation and she replied that in conferencing she prods the student with "Why don't you use your own voice? I want to see and hear you in this project." That response did little to induce Jerimy to change much. The piece about Michael Jordan came early in the workshop and it might be argued that someone like Jerimy thinks that printed or Internet sources are more authoritative than his own words, which he may deem inadequate.

DeLuce believes that the source of greatest success in her workshop is the peer review. DeLuce requires two peer editors (who read and edit the paper away from the writer) and an adult editor (in Jerimy's case, his mother read and signed two of his drafts) to read and sign off on drafts near completion. DeLuce points out that she gets a broad mix of abilities and backgrounds in her class so that a highly accomplished writer may be sitting in the same class with someone like Jerimy—and the two work together in peer reviews. Rather than view this broad range as a problem, DeLuce cheerfully refers to as "Failed Tracking," and uses it to help all her students work with each other.

In reflecting on Jerimy's writing during the twelve weeks, DeLuce believes that the fact that he learned about prewriting strategies, revising, editing verbs, and adding more details represented considerable change in his writing habits. Jerimy defines his success in the amount he wrote and in the fact that he went through several revising stages. Both are probably accurate.

While it is true that some teachers might look at Jerimy's final drafts and see deficits (and there are some), looking at how much he wrote and how his revisions changed qualitatively, and thinking about him as a silent, reluctant reader and writer who achieves athletically but does not place much value in school literacy, we may recognize a number of students who have sat before us, sometimes daring us to teach them to write. For such a reluctant writer, writing and rewriting as much as the portfolio system in DeLuce's class encouraged is quite an accomplishment.

The value of the DeLuce's portfolio system is that it creates an atmosphere where reluctant writers have the space and time to reflect and revise more than they might in other class settings. Such a classroom culture demands that students think reflectively (Smith 1997, 147). And DeLuce insists on students taking their writing and revisions seriously.

DAVID

Early in his third-grade year (September 1996) I began to worry about my son David's reluctance to write. While David had been read to since infancy, and possessed many markers, crayons, and pencils, using them on paper to create all kinds of signs, he seemed to avoid writing as much as he could in second grade when he kept a writing journal and a math log. As his mother, I was startled by this, because David had started school in a preschool and kindergarten where he had done a considerable amount of reading, drawing, and writing from age two until he had moved, at age six, to first-grade. In the fourth week of his third-grade year, he took a state-mandated test with a holistically scored writing sample, and I was pretty certain his scores would come back low. (This is a "high stakes" test designed for Indiana by CTB-McGraw Hill and administered to the children in grades 3, 6, 8, and 10). Knowing that the school and the teacher would be mandated by Indiana law to "remediate" David's skill levels, I wanted a tutor who would read and write with him in a low-risk setting. The only instruction I gave her was that I wanted David to write as much as possible and I hoped that she would have David keep a folder of what he wrote. Camelia Ibrahim began tutoring David in January 1997. As I had predicted, when the state scores came back in February, David's teacher scheduled a conference with me. The fact that David was working with a tutor saved him from state-mandated school remediation. More important, David seemed to enjoy reading and writing with Ibrahim.

David's teacher had twenty-seven students in her classroom. Such circumstances limit the ways such a teacher can create a culture which will encourage young writers. David seemed to have little investment in the writing he did in school. The exceptions seemed to be two inquiry projects, one on reptiles and one on volcanoes—two of his favorite subjects at the time. David's third-grade teacher had many good and productive ideas about how to teach literacy, but the circumstances of her classroom kept her from reaching David as a writer. David's teacher also asked her children to keep a cumulative writing folder. During the last two weeks of class, the children selected some pieces, supposedly to show their fourth-grade teacher. David took this instruction literally and the reflective sheet on every piece he chose but one, read "I want my fourth grade teacher to like me [or like my writing]". Interestingly enough one piece, a drawing showing a child's room with a locator key, was not even his but another little girl's. Obliviously, David had stapled a reflective sheet on Sarah's drawing on which he wrote "I chose this piece from my folder because I want my fourth grade teacher to like me."

On the other hand, the portfolio David kept with his tutor shows how David defined himself in relation to his artifacts. Since Camelia let him write about what he chose or to respond to readings he chose, the pieces he generated for her tended to be longer and written in a more exuberant voice than his school writings. These pieces show his love of sports, his interest in his biracial identity (he had chosen a library book about slavery above his level; instead of telling him that, Ibrahim and he did a paired reading and then he wrote "If I were a slave."), and his sense of humor ("This Thing Is Well Like Funny," a joke book in which a creature talks back to his creator, and "Mummy Medicine," a parody of an advertisement found in an Egyptian tomb).

With David's reading, we had a breakthrough in April when his teacher asked him to choose a book and read it independently and then do a book project. Ibrahim offered him several high-interest middle elementary paperbacks and ask him to choose one. He chose (as Camelia predicted he would) Jerry Spinelli's book, *Fourth Grade Rats*, about a group of fourth graders who terrorize a school playground with practical jokes only to be reformed by a third grader. David loved this book so much that he finished it in one evening and slipped a note under my door that read "Mom, I loved it. Finished it!" Reading *Fourth Grade Rats* led him to write about it (his teacher had asked for a book response) when Ibrahim asked him about the book. This was late March 1997, and he laboriously typed the piece on the computer and worked with Camelia on editing.

To her credit, David's teacher asked to see his tutoring portfolio and suggested he could use some of the pieces for his school portfolio. He chose "This Thing Is Well Like Funny" and "If I were M. J." to include. On those he wrote the only different reflective statement (i.e., different from "I want my fourth-grade teacher to like me or like it."). On "This Thing Is Well Like Funny" he wrote "I chose this piece because I have a tutor and her and I made it and I like it." In the text of the book, David's dragons appear to change shape, from one shamanistic demon to another. With words in cartoon bubbles, the monsters, some of them undrawn or unfinished, speak directly to David, and the writer speaks directly to the reader. David, who started calling himself an artist when he was four years old, loves to draw and especially likes to draw fantastic, even monstrous figures. He would much rather draw than write. In fact, one of his teacher's comments on his report card had been "If I let him, he would draw all day!" (I resisted the urge to ask "What's wrong with that?") David's teacher felt restricted by the curriculum, which mandates that student's write conventionally by the time they are in third grade. This curricular mandate is reinforced by the statewide test administered to third graders in the fourth week of the school year.

While David's teacher allowed choice and did not grade individual pieces of writing, she seemed to limit her students' literacy because of her perceptions of the curriculum.

Camelia Ibrahim, David's tutor, was not constrained by the state-mandated curriculum or the school district's emphasis on standardized tests. Ibrahim seems to understand Graves' contention that in teaching writing, we should first encourage fluency and wait to instill correctness. She also seems to understand the ways in which David was struggling with the conventions of writing. Although Ibrahim sometimes asked David to read a piece out loud and even to revise a piece, she did not correct his writing or ask him to do much editing. Later, at the end of the summer when she saw David for the first time after our vacation, Ibrahim asked him what he had done during the summer and he wrote about his trip to Rhode Island and then to Montreal, Canada. After he wrote, she asked him to read over the piece and see if he would like to change any words. He circled quite a few misspelled words without any prompting and she helped him find the words in the dictionary. He circled the words (his spelling: Momantreeal, speick [speak] frnich [French]), and then corrected them, and he added some details and words he had left out. What is most apparent in this is David's willingness to write more than a few sentences—especially since he really enjoyed his trip. He includes the most significant details to him—going to Old Montreal and its souvenir shops, and taking a 3-D movie ride (a twenty-minute attraction). He even added a marginal detail that might go into a revision—those on the ride could not unfasten their seatbelt:

> When I went to Canada I got so lucky. When I went to old Montreal I must have gone to 15 stores in one day and got stuff in each store. I went with my mom and dad. In this part of Canada They speak french. But most people speak English. There was this ride called the O-zone and you are in a car thing and you go slowly at first and then you go very fast. When you get to the end you will not feel like you are there.

While David demonstrates, with this piece, that his view of revision has grown to include adding words, the most significant element is still his willingness to write and the development of his voice. The second most significant element visible in this short piece is his willingness to edit—something he resisted at school and in parental homework sessions during the year. While David's skills may have been less sophisticated than those of some of the other children entering fourth grade with him in the fall of 1997, I knew that the key to learning these skills was a willingness to write. As I was working on an early version of this article, a year later, I asked David to look over his tutoring portfolio with me. He still loves "This Thing Is Well Like

Funny." When he reread the piece about wishing he were Michael Jordan, he said, "Mom, this is terrible." When I asked why, he replied with this evaluation, "Bad spelling and it does not make sense." Interestingly enough, in fourth grade he became an avid note writer and seemed very concerned about editing the notes (some of which could classify as letters) especially when they were written to certain girls in the class. His comment about the Michael Jordan piece may indicate that he is learning critical responses to writing and that he is becoming more aware of correctness.

Both of these writers, Jerimy and David, came to their portfolios as reluctant writers. I would suggest that they are not all that atypical, especially of the male school population. While not every reluctant writer is fortunate enough to have a tutor like Camelia Ibrahim, teachers like Verna DeLuce cast themselves in the roles of coach and collaborator. As teachers and teacher educators, we need to think about how to coach, to encourage, and to prod, we need to think less about correctness and more about fluency at least until students have begun to see writing as a means of self-definition. We cannot assume that such a realization will happen at the same time for every child. We can believe that the cultures we create at every grade level should accommodate writers at several different stages of fluency and competence, and we need to shape our classrooms to accommodate those differences. We should coach correctness through fluency; and wait patiently while students write before we zoom in with a correcting pencil. Mary Ann Smith (1988) points out that "Rather than manage, teachers in portfolio classrooms design in the best sense of the word. They set the tone, the openness to learning through modeling, through immersing their students in reading and writing" (148). Smith would probably agree that Camelia Ibrahim and Verna DeLuce are effective because in the portfolio cultures they design, the portfolios were "underinvented." The writing teacher who sees herself as a coach guides her students through the invention of their portfolios and their invention of themselves as writers.

REFERENCES

Atwell, Nancie. 1987. *In the Middle.* Portsmouth, NH: Heinemann.

DeLuce, Verna. 1997. Personal Communication. Tri North Middle School, Bloomington, IN, March 20.

———. 1998. Personal Communication. Tri North Middle School, Bloomington, IN, January 7.

Diederich, Paul. 1974. *Measuring Growth in English.* Urbana IL: National Council of Teachers of English.

Rief, Linda. 1997. *Seeking Diversity: Language Arts with Adolescents*. Portsmouth, NH: Heinemann.

Smith, Frank. 1988. *Joining the Literacy Club: Further Essays into Education*. Portsmouth, NH: Heinemann.

Smith, Mary Ann. 1997. "Behind the Scenes: Portfolios in a Classroom Learning Community." In *Situating Portfolios: Four Perspectives*, ed. Kathleen Blake Yancey and Irwin Weiser, Logan, UT: Utah State University Press.

Wiles, David. 1997. Personal Conversation, August 26.

———. 1998. Personal Conversation, January 6.

5

TO SIT BESIDE
Learning to Evaluate Reading and Writing
SUSAN STIRES

When I began teaching thirty years ago, I evaluated the way I had been evaluated: errors marked on papers and grades at the end of the quarter on report cards. I accepted it as a tradition, a necessary evil of schooling. I was too busy working with my fifth graders at the James Otis School in East Boston to think much about evaluation. I loved my kids and my school, and I was excited about teaching. I was also concerned about some other issues at the time, such as the placement of recently immigrated seventh graders in my fifth grade because they did not yet speak English.

When I moved to Maine and began teaching third grade, I started to question marking errors on papers and giving grades. I wondered about grading coming at the end of the quarter, especially after I had given Erin Frank a B in English, and Mrs. Frank stormed into school and told me that "Franks don't get B's; they get A's!" I don't recall what I told Mrs. Frank, but it had something to do with use of skills learned, and I showed her some of Erin's writing as my evidence, thereby justifying the grade I had given her daughter. She calmed right down. Certainly, I could have gone on in such a manner, but I came to realize the different values that people place on grades—for the Franks it was a certain status in the community—as well as their arbitrariness and their subjectivity.

In 1980, when I began teaching writing through a process approach, I began to evaluate differently. I kept notes of my conferences, and I had my students collect their writing and all of their drafts in cumulative folders. I also conducted a two-year case study of a writing student with a learning disability, which accelerated my development as an evaluator. This case study, which I conducted during a school writing project under the direction of Nancie Atwell, influenced my teaching so dramatically that I was launched into qualitative assessment, particularly through the use of interviews and field notes.

Donald Graves' and Jane Hansen's work on self-evaluation further influenced my development (Graves 1991; Hansen 1998). As a result of studying their work, as well as Linda Rief's classroom research (1992; Rief and Barbieri 1995), I conducted my own classroom research in self-evaluation in writing. I learned to set goals with my students and to have them set their own goals. I had heard my students' voices in their writing, and as I developed questions, forms, and formats for my students to use in evaluating their reading and writing, I began to hear their voices in these self-evaluations as well.

Throughout my teaching since 1980, I have focused on both formative (on-going) and summative (end-point) evaluations that I learned about from Thomas Hilgers from the University of Hawaii (1986a, 1986b). Both have come to be reflected in my students' portfolios, as conceptualized by many researchers, including Robert Tierney (1991) and Bonnie Sunstein (Graves and Sunstein 1992). My students displayed what they knew and were able to do through samples of their work and photos of their projects and performances. I helped as they learned the process of pulling together their samples of evidence. My experience with collecting samples of evidence goes back to my nine years as a resource room teacher, when I wrote goals and objectives for my students and was required to provide evidence of these goals being met. Since I did not wish to waste my resource room students' time with tests, most of my evidence was drawn from work samples and my notes. At the time, I kept folders from which I could draw samples that showed what the students could or could not do. It was natural for me, therefore, to take the next step when I became a primary teacher and have my students display this evidence in a portfolio.

SAMPLES OF EVIDENCE

Closely monitoring one's students is not easy, and the more students that one teaches, the more one needs to set up systems in which the students assist in the process. Interviews and self-evaluation forms are joint ventures between the student and the teacher. They require both parties to take responsibility for the material. In interviews and self-evaluation formats, the teacher is responsible for conducting the interview and recording the responses, while the student is responsible for thinking hard about the questions and answering accordingly, sometimes orally and sometimes in written form. Further, the student needs to reflect on his or her responses and reactions.

Other areas of data collection also require both student and teacher input. For some, the student takes most of the responsibility while the teacher helps out; for others, the teacher takes most of the responsibility while the student helps out. For convenience' sake, I will call these areas *student generated* and *teacher generated* data. Student generated data includes record keeping in the forms of reading and writing topic lists, peer conference forms, group conference forms, and editing checklists. Teacher generated data includes conference record forms, teaching journals, and notes. Interviews and self-evaluations involve data that is generated equally by both student and teacher.

In the past, recording data for the purpose of evaluating a student's learning has been primarily a teacher's responsibility. However, my own experience led me to involve not only myself as the teacher, but also my students and even their parents in these activities of recording and evaluating. But while I found that many parents were keenly interested in their children's work and self-evaluations, and even helped set goals for their children, I believe more work needs to be done in involving parents in more active roles in this area.

INTERVIEWS AND SELF-EVALUATIONS

When I began teaching at the Center for Teaching and Learning in 1990, I decided not to use any of the interviews or self-evaluation forms that I had used in the past: the Burke Interview (Weaver 1988), the Writing Survey (Atwell 1987), or other adapted forms (Stires unpublished ms.). I made up a self-evaluation form that my primary students could fill out by themselves with some help from me. Instead of conducting interviews with my students at the beginning and end of the year, I used these self-evaluation forms at the end of each term. In the beginning of our work at the Center, we had parent conferences and wrote narratives three times a year. The next year we revised our schedule to hold parent conferences twice a year and to write a substantive narrative report at the end of the year. All of the students in the school used portfolios as a way of collecting, selecting, reflecting on, and presenting their work in all areas of the curriculum.

During the third year the faculty adapted a student self-evaluation interview from the questions Linda Rief includes at the end of *Seeking Diversity* (1992). The one I developed was appropriate for primary students and included the following questions from the

Burke Interview: "When you are reading and you come to something you don't know, what do you do about it?" and "If you knew someone who was having difficulty reading, how would you help that person?" (Weaver 1988, 10).

Since the self-evaluation interviews I conducted in the first (fall) term were extensive, I used them as a basis for my fall parent conferences. As a faculty, we also read and discussed Robert Anthony's (1991) work on student-led conferences, deciding to have students conduct their own conferences during the second (winter) term. In these winter-term conferences, students' voices absolutely boomed. After his conference, Eben commented to his mother, "Now I know what education is all about. It is about knowing stuff and telling people about it and what you are going to learn." For this winter term, I continued to use the original self-evaluation form I had developed in 1990.

The more comprehensive interview, based on Linda Rief's work, was good for the fall-term conference because it brought the student's voice into the conference. Although the students were not present at the fall conference between the parents and the teacher, their "echoes" could be heard in the richness and extensiveness of their self-evaluation interviews. While these interviews were time-consuming to conduct students elaborated on their responses because they were oral. Since I had a relatively small class, I was able to conduct these interviews as formal conferences during my reading or writing workshop while either the teaching assistant or a parent volunteer worked with the rest of the class. I was able to complete four interviews during the hour of each workshop, finishing them in one week's time.

These fall self-evaluation interviews yielded some important data. In addition to stating the number of books read and pieces of writing completed, the students also answered what genres they had tried in writing and how they rated their reading books: holidays (easy for the reader), just rights, and challenges (hard for the reader). The next question on each interview had to do with what the student had learned in terms of process and content as a reader and writer. In her writing interview, Christine, who finished eighteen pieces of memoir, poetry, nonfiction, and letters, said, "I see if it sounds right and looks right. I put in shapes (in poetry) sometimes. If I want to leave white space in a chapter book, I do." She added that her writing focused on things she did and places she went. In spelling words, she said she wrote the sounds she heard or she just knew the words from practice. She wasn't sure what to say about punctuation, but concerning capitalization, she knew to use a capital when she began a sentence.

The next two questions were about goals: hers were to become better at spelling words and to try her hand at making up a story (fiction).

Christine identified "conferences—to see if I should add anything—and Have-A-Go sheets" (Routman 1994) as the most valuable things she had done in writing workshop. I particularly liked Linda Rief's question, "What do you do at home as a writer that I don't know about?" because I was often surprised by the responses I received. In her writing self-evaluation interview Christine said, "When I am in my room, I write letters and send them to my mom and dad as paper airplanes asking, When can I come down?"

The parallel question about reading background satisfied my need for background that I had not yet gleaned from daily references to reading and writing at home or conversations with parents. Christine answered the question by telling me that "I collect and read books. When mad or sad I read a book—or at nighttime. I did read *Island of the Blue Dolphins*. I got up to the tenth chapter, but I didn't finish it." I did know that Christine's father had read the O'Dell book aloud to her, but I didn't know about her own attempt to read it. Nor did I realize that Christine read at home in part to cope with her anger or unhappiness.

At the beginning of the reading interview, Christine told me that she had finished twelve books and all of them were "just rights." She explained her reading process in this manner: "I choose a book I haven't read yet that I think might be interesting like one you read and I want to read myself. I start reading it. I read it to myself." She added that what she found in books were "white space—mostly in poetry books, shapes, periods, chapters, characters—maybe funny or strange things." In answer to the questions "What do you do when you're reading and you come to a word that you don't know?" and "Do you ever do anything else?" Christine responded, "I try to sound it out, I see if I remember the word. I had to do that in *The Wednesday Witch*, or I guess or skip the word. Sometimes I look at the picture." To the question "If you knew someone was having difficulty reading, how would you help that person?" Christine replied, "I [would] help them sound it out, skip it, or look at the picture. With Becky [her younger sister], I read a word and she copies it."

Christine was unable to respond to what she would like to do better as a reader, but she knew that she wanted to try "more chapter books and long books with pictures and lots of words in the books [illustrated storybooks]." She identified learning about endings (er, ed, est, ing, ly, and y) and r-controlled vowels as information that was helpful to her. The winter-semester form—my 1990 form—that she completed herself was much briefer, but it did ask Christine about something that she learned that helped her and what she planned to do next in both writing and reading (Figures 5–1 and 5–2).

For my students' self-evaluation in their final (spring) semester, I asked how many pieces they had written and books they had read, but I

WRITING SELF-EVALUATION (1-2)

NAME _Christine_   DATE _3/23/9-_

How many pieces did you write? _8_

Pieces of writing
from this term:

1. _PoeTTY folder_
2. _SKiing_ ✗
3. _EmiLY_
4. _EmiLY_
5. _SanTa_
6. _Maya_
7. _anne_
8. _EverY RabiT was once a Bunny_ ✓

Put a star next
to your favorite
or best piece.

10. _____

Why did you choose this piece as your favorite or the best one?

I choose IT Becase IT Was MY first Time SKiing.

What is something you learned to do in writing this term that helped you?

The ✳

What do you plan to write next?

a STory.

FIGURE 5–1

then used the broad self-evaluation questions from Donald Graves and Jane Hansen that I had used in my former first-grade classroom. My reasons were mainly practical: they allowed for general goal setting at the end of the year. For example, Christine said that what she wanted to learn next in writing was "cersof" (cursive writing). Also, the self-evaluation did not take a lot of time because most of my students could complete the forms themselves without my interviewing them. However, it tended to produce general responses like the one above by Christine. Interviewing at the end of the year, while more time-consuming, provided more specific and elaborate responses.

READING SELF-EVALUATION (1-2)

NAME _Christine_____ DATE _3/23/9__

How many books did you read? _2 ½_   Challenges _1_
Just Rights _19_
Holidays _6_

Please write down
the titles of five
books that you
read this term and
liked a lot.

1. _The enchanTed Book_
2. _The Magic twrWing st_ ★
3. _The HundIed DresseS_
4. _HecKedy Peg_

Put a star next to
your favorite book.

5. _ThumBelina_

Why did you choose this book as your favorite?

I LiKeIT Becase ~~IT~~ IT Has
magic and I Like all sorTs of
magic.

What is something you learned to do in reading this term that helped you?

MarCin 6 PaGes in BooKs,
IT HaIPes me To RemambeI

What do you plan to read next?

aLoTe of
CapTeI BooKs

FIGURE 5-2

There was nothing absolute about any of the forms or any of the
questions that I used in interviews or self-evaluations. They simply
helped the students and me hold a formal conversation about how they
thought they were doing in reading and writing, based upon what they
learned and what I taught them, as well as their own insights. As a
teacher, it was useful for me to reflect upon which questions enriched
my conversations with my students and helped us to set goals and make
plans and which did not.

TEACHER RECORD KEEPING

Besides the formal conversations about evaluation, there are many informal conversations and actions to keep track of. To me, this was like collecting sap from a maple tree to be boiled down later into the maple syrup of an overall assessment. It is in the act of discussing and recording, in the collecting, that both students and teachers find the value in what they do every day. My use of field notes in qualitative teacher research studies and three years of keeping a teaching journal in the 1980s, as well as my knowledge and occasional use of anecdotal records, all contributed to my ability to keep track of my students' learning.

During my last years of classroom teaching, I still made journal entries if I was trying to make sense of a particular student's learning, or if I was interested in recording particular commentary about reading and writing. However, what I used on a regular basis was a kind of shorthand method of collecting daily information about the reading and writing activities of my students. It was a conference form, with everyone's name printed on the front and back side of a grid—front for week-by-week writing activities; back for week-by-week reading activities. As a form for evaluation collection, these grids were far more useful than my teaching journals because at any point during or after the semester I could lay the pages out and read across the week-by-week grids. In the process, I would find information, discover patterns, and pose questions.

Other teachers might use a clipboard with individual mailing labels that they could then attach to pages with the students' names, individual student notebooks, a single teaching notebook with sections for each student, or other formats. The ways are as individual as the teachers who use them, but the objective is the same: to collect the conversations and behaviors of the students as they read, write, and speak about their reading and writing.

STUDENT RECORD KEEPING

From the time I began teaching process writing in my resource room, my students kept track of their pieces of writing by recording the number, the topic (which was often the title), and the date they completed the piece. They were very successful at this task and enjoyed seeing the growing record of their work. It was only natural, when I aligned my teaching of reading with my teaching of writing, that I had my students record the books that they chose and read. They numbered the books and recorded the date when they completed them. When I returned to classroom teaching in 1988–89, I extended these requirements and forms, having students write to me in a journal, and writing back to them about what they had read. These journal entries constituted written conferences about their reading and were part of the accumulated data they recorded about their reading in my class.

In my primary classes at the Center for Teaching and Learning, I continued to use reading journals according to their original design. However, I expanded the recording form for reading to include more information. Since my students were aware of authors through author studies and information that I provided them in class, it was important to record authors by their last names on their reading list. The faculty had discussed Ohlhausen and Jepson's article (1992) on the "Goldilocks' principle" of levels of difficulty in reading as perceived by readers rather than externally imposed formula. As a result, we had our students rate their books as H for "holiday" (easy to read), JR for "just right," and C for "challenging" (difficult or a stretch for the individual). It became part of the data for which the students were responsible, recorded by them on the list that they kept in their reading folders. At the end of the term, the students counted up the different ratings to determine how many of each they had read, as well as the total number of books read (Figure 5–3).

Similarly, in writing I added "Audience" and "Genre" to the recording sheet because it reflected my classroom emphasis on the kind of writing my students were doing and who might read their writing. Young children typically write for themselves, but I was interested in expanding first and second graders' notion of audience (Figure 5–4). Letters my students wrote also expanded their notions of audience, but since these letters did not conform to the format I'd developed, students kept them in a separate "Letter List" that was included in their writing folders along with their Writing Lists. When the students counted up the pieces of writing that they completed during a term, they added the letters to their other writing to determine the total. Most of the students had more difficulty remembering to record their writing than to record their reading, probably because they finished books more frequently than they finished pieces of writing. Although most students had recorded information about their reading and writing in kindergarten at the Center, it took some first graders all year to become proficient at it. With a few exceptions, second graders had no problem keeping track of their writing or their reading.

In writing, the students also kept track of the conferences that they had with each other. I used the peer conference form that was used in the school and that outlined the steps for a peer conference. My young students were just beginning to develop their skills as peer responders and recorders of their conferences. Some of their comments and ques-

_____'s **Reading List**

No.	Title	Author	Rating H/JR/C	Date
1X	Duncan and Dolores	Samuels	1 JR	3/23/9
2	The Terrible Fight	Zemke	9 JR	3/27
3	The Tale of the two bad mice	Potter	3 JR	3/28/9
4	The Tale of Peter Rabbit	Potter	4 JR	3/28
5	Birthday Present	Rylant	8 JR	4/7/9
6	Those Bottles!	Miller	6 JR	4/11/9
7	Amazing Monkeys	Hyner	2 JR	4/26/9
8	Musical Instruments	Jeunesse	JR 8	4/27/9
9	Lights! Camer! Action!	Gail/Gibbons	JR 9	5/8/9
10	Fire! Fire!	Gail Gibbons	JR 10	5/13/9

FIGURE 5–3

tions were fairly standard, but some of them were extremely meaningful and insightful. For example, after Eileen responded to Anna's poem orally, she wrote: "You sownd (sound) like a real purfesahal (professional) poite (poet) when you say there is a wale (whale) in the distence (distance)." When Sam responded to Eileen, he left her with these more typical written questions: "Why do you have two books in one? Why does it say 'the end' two times?" Sometimes, however, the students wrote evaluative comments to one another not on the forms but in "letter-notes" such as Sam's to Becky (Figure 5–5).

When students shared a piece of their writing-in-progress with a whole group, they needed a record of this conference. In these instances I recorded the responses because the student writers were busy either sharing, listening, or responding, and because I could write the fastest. However, I considered this part of the student's record keeping responsibilities. After the conference, the student took the notes and used them to revise his or her writing. Eventually, the conference record was added to the collected drafts that were filed in the cumulative writing folder.

When I first started teaching process writing in 1980, I used forms developed from the Boothbay Writing Project, including a student

_____ 's Writing List

No.	Topic	Audience	Genre	Date
1	My House Is In...	Class	essay	10/13/9_
2	It was Halloween	me	poem	11/2/9_
3	Halloween Night	Class	poem	10/15/9_
*4	The trick	me	memoir	11/4/9_
5	The Puppy	?	fiction	11/18/9_
7	My Shell, 3rd trem	Mom and Dad	poem	1/11/9_
6	THE ELEPHANT₂	CLASS	poem	Dec/9_
8	The Snow₃	CLASS	poem	1/4_
9	The Valentines ⁴	Mom and Dad	poem	2/11/9_
10	Hot Warm Could Cool ⁵	CLass	poem	2/15/9_

FIGURE 5–4

_____

editing checklist. These forms required students to fill in their name, the title of the piece, the date, the audience, and the skills they identified. They edited for those skills or had a peer edit for them. The form was stapled on top of the writing when the piece was submitted to the teacher for editing, and the teacher in turn edited and made comments and notes. Although I used this form with my intermediate-level resource room students, I did not find it as useful with my primary special education or primary general education students. It required more recording time than I thought was worthwhile, and I also found that keeping a skills list was burdensome for primary students.

As I taught my first- and second-grade students at the Center about editing, however, I knew that they needed a guide. For their self-editing of their writing, therefore, I devised an editing checklist. My first graders experimented with it, while my second graders became proficient at using it. The checklist format allowed them to concentrate on their developing skills rather than on the recording of the skills. It required the students to focus on four areas in their writing—their spelling, capitalization, punctuation, and handwriting. It asked them to make a check beside the appropriate box if they had done such things as "looked at every word" and "corrected the words I know," "capital-

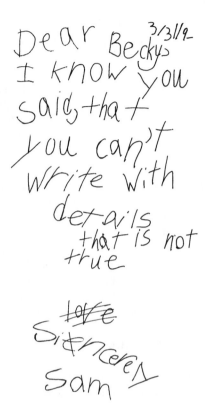

Dear Becky 3/31/9_
I know you
said, that
you can't
write with
details
that is not
true

love
Sincerely
Sam

FIGURE 5–5

ized the beginning letter of every sentence" and "capitalized proper nouns," and so forth for ten simple statements. It is difficult to get young writers to take full responsibility for editing and proofreading their work, but it is important to get them started. Also, it is important for them to be the keepers of this information.

As students mature, it is possible to have them take greater responsibilities for their writing and reading records. Other primary teachers have undoubtedly had students take responsibility for other parts of the process. I began with the writing folder and the reading list because I believed these were the most effective starting points for students.

SUMMATIVE EVALUATION AND REPORTING

During the 1989–90 school year, when I was consulting in school districts in various parts of the country, I began to read more about the many efforts to find evaluation formats that matched with process reading and writing. One of those formats included samples of evidence displayed in portfolios. My understanding of portfolio keeping was very new during my first year at the Center, but I collected some pieces which I put into an academic portfolio for each child at the end of the year. In these portfolios, my students engaged in formal and informal self-evaluations, selected pieces of writing to be displayed, and kept reading and writing lists. Also I included notes and some photographs I had taken.

My colleague Donna Maxim and I wrote narrative reports three times a year for our first classes and I used the information that the students and I collected for their portfolios to write my reports in anticipation of holding conferences with their parents. The following year, we decided to consolidate our efforts and meet with the parents during the first and second terms and write an end-of-the-year report. We had notes for our conferences and made those available to the parents. It was during that second year, when I taught first and second grade, Donna taught third and fourth, and Nancy Tindal came to teach kindergarten, that we all adopted portfolios. The following year, when Susan Benedict joined us as the fifth- and sixth-grade teacher, we initiated the student-led conference during the second trimester.

I added a list of minilessons and activities to my end-of-the-year report, similar to what I had done in my public school first-grade class, but in an expanded form. Donna had already begun to do this, and it was an important addition to the report. My students continued to work on their portfolios, and I taught them the principles of portfolio making that I learned from Jane Hansen: collect, select, reflect, and project. Since I highly valued the selection process, I asked the kids to make hard decisions about what papers and projects represented them as readers, writers, and learners, and I asked them to reflect on their selections orally and in their self-evaluations. I did not have them write their reflections because I had difficulty justifying the amount of time it would have taken for the students to do this writing.

The student portfolio pages for a single term began with a copy of my report or conference notes which served to identify the term, and a miscellaneous page where photos of oral share or playtime were displayed. This was followed by the reading section. At the very least, it contained the reading self-evaluation, the reading journal selection, the list of books read, and an example of a page from a selected "just right" book—a practice I borrowed from Susan Benedict. The students also included other artifacts they considered important, including photos of their reading activities.

The writing section consisted at the least of a spelling example, the writing self-evaluation, the list of pieces written, and a writing selection. The math section included the math self-evaluation, a selection from the math journal, and one or two math work samples, while the science and social studies sections held two or three science examples and a selection or two from the social studies journal. The final section held places for art, music, physical education, and Spanish. Since the art and physical education teachers were also part time assistant teachers in the school, they also developed self-evaluation forms appropriate to their areas. Each of these sections also held photographs of the activities that could not be represented by pieces of paper. Photographs were particularly numerous for science and social studies, which consisted of many hands-on activities. As with reading, students included other artifacts that represented them in their different academic areas.

Since the students constructed their portfolios by making the selections and putting them into plastic sleeves (something many of the first graders needed help with), they were keenly aware of what the portfolios showed about them as learners. Although many of them needed much help with selection in the beginning of first grade, they became quite skillful as they went along in making their choices of materials. Because they started the process in kindergarten, most students could assemble their portfolios independently by the end of the first grade. While some continued to need help in second grade, all the students could talk about the contents of their portfolios, which they did formally in the student-led conferences.

One year, I asked my students how they felt about leading these conferences, and they gave a variety of responses. The majority of their responses showed their positive feelings:

> "Staying still was hard, but it was good because both my mom and dad were there."
>
> "It was hard to stay cool, but it was fun."
>
> "My dad came for the first time—that was good. It was hard not to try to get candy from his pockets."
>
> "It was hard because I couldn't remember all of the things, but good because I could think about them and be there."
>
> "I didn't have to explain to two people at once. I could concentrate on my mom."
>
> "It was fun to read about the different things I did."
>
> "I didn't really like it because I was embarrassed."
>
> "It was hard to be still. It was good to show my mom and dad."
>
> "It was lots of fun. My mom and dad liked it."
>
> "I thought it was hard to sit still, but I had a good time."

"It was hard to remember all of the things, but I liked reading my self-evaluations."

"It was fun because I got to be part of the conference and lead it."

"I liked it, but it was hard to do it all."

Reporting to parents is a step in this continuum of development that we take as evaluators. Involving them in more direct and genuine ways seems a logical next research step for me. Other teachers will have other concerns because their understandings about evaluation may be different than mine. Throughout, I believe that we must remember that the purpose of evaluation is to inform teaching and learning.

CONCLUSION

There are some other issues and challenges concerning evaluation that I believe need to be addressed. There are many abuses of evaluation going on today, from wide scale, narrowly focused testing to "padded" portfolios. These abuses cause evaluation to serve itself rather than students and their education. I am especially concerned when I see portfolios used as scrapbooks or photo albums to re-create the curriculum or showcase the teacher's methods. Portfolios, with all their potential to correct the abuses of formal evaluation, are as vulnerable to abuse as other methods.

The student should be at the center of evaluation, because ultimately it is the student whom the evaluation serves. The more opportunities that a student is given to participate in the evaluation process, the more sophisticated he or she will become as a self-evaluator. Teachers and parents should work in partnership with the student in this ongoing process of evaluation. All parties should be aware of the fact that growth is not linear for most learners, despite the fact that linear systems have been set up to measure it. The practice that I found worked best for me in my own classrooms was to look at growth over time. I discovered that I could do that best by closely monitoring what my students did and said every day. Evaluation is part of the learning process, but it also serves the teaching process. It needs to reflect the curriculum and the instruction and be aimed at improving them. It is through curriculum and instruction that we make students aware of what is possible.

Evaluation is one part of the whole cycle of planning, teaching, and evaluating that comprises a teacher's work. It is also one part of the cycle of learning (becoming acquainted with concepts, trying them out, and evaluating one's involvement and gain) that is part of a student's work. Evaluation is a crucial step in both cycles; portfolios are the display cases of evaluation. Evaluation played this major role in my teaching and my students' learning. It did not get shortchanged or reduced to some cryptic number or external letter grade. It was a dynamic, ever-developing part of the teaching and learning cycle. The student portfolios that grew day by day, week by week, month by month, and year by year documented the cycles of teaching and learning in which my students and I engaged.

REFERENCES

Anthony, Robert, Terry D. Johnson, Norma L. Mickelson, and Alison Preece. 1991. *Evaluating Literacy*. Portsmouth, NH: Heinemann.

Atwell, Nancie. 1987. *In the Middle: Writing, Reading, and Learning with Adolescents*. Portsmouth, NH: Boynton/Cook.

Chew, Ruth. 1972. *The Wednesday Witch*. New York: Holiday House.

Graves, Donald. 1981. *Build a Literate Classroom*. Portsmouth, NH: Heinemann.

Graves, Donald H., and Bonnie S. Sunstein, eds. 1992. *Portfolio Portraits*. Portsmouth, NH: Heinemann.

Hansen, Jane. 1998. *When Learners Evaluate*. Portsmouth, NH: Heinemann.

Hilgers, Thomas. 1986a. "How Children Change as Critical Evaluators of Writing: Four Three-year Case Studies." *Research in the Teaching of English* (20).

———. 1986b. "Writer's Evaluations of Writing: A Comparison of Criteria Used by Primary-school and College Students." Paper presented at the New Directions in Composition Scholarship, Durham, NH.

O'Dell, Scott. 1960. *Island of the Blue Dolphins*. Boston: Houghton Mifflin.

Ohlhausen, Marilyn M., and Mary Jepsen. 1992. "Lessons from Goldilocks: 'Somebody's Been Choosing My Books But I Can Make My Own Choices Now!'" *The New Advocate* (1), 32–46.

Rief, Linda. 1992. *Seeking Diversity: Language Arts with Adolescents*. Portsmouth, NH: Heinemann.

Rief, Linda, and Maureen Barbieri, eds. 1995. *All That Matters: What Is It We Value in School and Beyond?* Portsmouth, NH: Heinemann.

Routman, Regie. 1994. *Invitations: Changing as Teachers and Learners K–12*. Portsmouth, NH: Heinemann.

Stires, Susan. Unpublished ms. *Trying It Out: Learning to Teach in the Language Arts Through Research and Reflection*.

Tierney, Robert J., Mark Carter, and Laura E. Desai. 1991. *Portfolio Assessment in the Reading Writing Classroom*. Norwood, MA: Christopher Gordon.

Weaver, Constance. 1988. *Reading Process and Practice*. Portsmouth, NH: Heinemann.

6

WHO'S THE TEACHER?
LINDA RIEF, MOLLY FINNEGAN, AND
CINTHIA GANNETT

> . . . the heroine of E. B.White's Charlotte's Web responds to a
> question from her friend and protege, Wilbur the pig. He has
> noticed that she has painstakingly made, in a high corner of his
> pen, a round fuzzy object, and asks, "Is it a plaything?" She
> responds:
> "Plaything? I should say not. It is my egg sac, my magnum opus."
> "I don't know what a magnum opus is," said Wilbur.
> "That's Latin," explained Charlotte. "It means great work. This
> egg sac is my great work—the finest thing I have ever made."
> Her egg sac, in the fullness of time, releases five hundred and
> fourteen tiny spiders, all but three of whom float away on
> balloons of silk let loose from their spinnerets, to add to the
> world's arachnid population. . . .
>
> John Updike, "Magnum Opus"

WHAT STUDENTS CAN TEACH US ABOUT
LITERACY PORTFOLIOS,
LINDA RIEF, TEACHER

Molly Finnegan's portfolio in eighth grade was, and still is, a great
work, sending out the threads of ideas about all a portfolio can and
should be. As I paged through it I realized how much more I was learning about her, and from her, despite the fact that I had had her in class
for two years—both as a seventh and eighth grader. Molly's portfolio
was an in-depth conversation so full of choice and design that the work
she chose to represent "all she knew and was able to do" orchestrated
her own reflection and evaluation. She took the work of developing
her portfolio seriously. It was not a plaything.

Here was the first portfolio from an eighth grader I'd seen in which
the student had truly broken down the barriers of her learning environments—in and out of school—and constructed a full picture of just
how deeply literate and articulate she really was. This fourteen-year-
old was sending out "balloons of silk" that would change the way I constructed my portfolio and encouraged, guided, and taught subsequent
students to consider theirs.

What did I learn from Molly? Some very important insights:

- *A real portfolio is as unique as a thumbprint.*
- *Who we are today as literate human beings is intricately tied to our history as learners, especially with regard to reading and writing.* When we ask our students to construct a reading-writing autobiography we can begin to discover how the *then* and *now* are related, and what works for them as learners.
- *Real learning occurs when students are encouraged to pursue those things in which they are deeply interested.* A lot of Molly's writing and reading in eighth grade was tied to her interest in women's early literacies, tied in with journals she was transcribing, her interest in quilting, and her attempts to find her place as a writer and a person, with her peers and aside from her peers.
- *We need to extend our notions of literacy to include the visual and performing arts, as well as the literary arts.* Many times Molly found her way into words through art or drama. She drew numerous self-portraits and reflected on what each one told her. She was an active member of a local theater group, taking on roles of characters that let her think about her own personality and how she interacted as self with others. Once I learned how important art and oral language were to Molly, I began to pay more attention to how they were important to other students. Nick as a radio disc jockey. Ailis as an artist. Rob as a performer.
- *Convincing students to show us who they are as literate human beings outside of class takes constant encouragement and prodding.*
- *Portfolios are not something one constructs the last week of school.* They evolve over a long period of time, with students immersed in reading and writing, and in the process of collecting, selecting, and reflecting with evidence and artifacts.
- *Every item in a portfolio should be there for a reason.* Molly's selection process was simple: "If I don't know why something's in my portfolio, it shouldn't be there."
- *The social context in which a student lives at school often influences what they allow us as teachers and peers to know about them.* I was not surprised by Molly's decision to remove her section about diary transcriptions and the section about quilting. She told me both sections felt "too nineteenth century" and she wasn't sure how her peers would react to that aspect of her literacy. I wanted her to feel comfortable with the choices she made and gave her the option to remove those sections in relation to her audience. When she shared the portfolio in our "read-around," she'd removed those sections. I asked her to let me see her portfolio on my own and asked her to consider adding those sections back in. She did.

How did my portfolio change as a result of Molly's portfolio? What was it like before? After reading Molly's work, I thought about my roles as a literate person: teacher, learner, writer, reader, and editor. Who was I? Who am I? What do I want to become? What do I keep in? Take out? I searched for pictures of anyone reading to me when I was little. A book in my hands, perhaps? A crayon, drawing my first picture? A pencil, setting down my first notion of words? Unlike Molly, I have none. I am still composing my reading-writing history each year, digging for the layers of who I was by talking to aunts and uncles who might remember. I do not have a rich literary history.

Therefore, the focus of my portfolio at the moment is in who I am as a reader/writer, and who I have been evolving into a learner/teacher over the past twenty years. Currently I use pictures to introduce each subsection:

- students working in the classroom and pictures of resources around the room
- students with visual and performing art projects
- students working on community projects as extensions of the language arts
- teachers as students in university courses and workshops I conduct
- doctoral students and interns working with me in the classroom
- my office and library at home
- my letterwriting, from my first letter to Santa in 1952 to a letter to Naomi Shihab Nye, which I just recently wrote
- family pictures tied to stories I want to write out

The reading and writing I select to include is woven through each sub-section, and changes with each teaching year.

I am still rearranging where these items best fit based on the three major sections of the portfolio: Who was I? Who am I? What do I want to become? What I am realizing as I assemble and reassemble this portfolio is that students are at the heart of all I do, whether they are eighth graders or teachers-as-students. I learn from them and with them. They inform and extend my teaching, my reading, and my writing.

Not all students are as smart with, as intrigued by, and as passionate about words as Molly is. But all students have some interest they are deeply invested in that can be connected to who they are as literate human beings. We have to listen hard peripherally to find out what those interests are, because those areas are our entry points to either helping our students come to words, or encouraging them to teach us what they have already done with words, so we can build on their strengths and areas of expertise.

Nick writes a note on the board for us to listen to his radio broadcast from WUNH on Saturday night. In his portfolio he includes with my encouragement a tape of one broadcast, a schedule of a program and the songs he will play, and a description of what he had to do during a thirty-hour apprenticeship to pass FCC regulations and gain a spot as a DJ on this radio station.

Seth brings a sixty-pound pack to school he'll need for a hiking trip Friday afternoon. By the end of the year his portfolio is filled with descriptions of solo hikes, recommendations of books about hiking and backpacking, a videotape of his description of the appropriate equipment, and a query letter to AMC *Outdoors* with a sample of his writing for a possible article.

At lunch Tania mentions her grandparents' visit from Bulgaria, and how she prefers to go to Bulgaria to visit them because she can speak Bulgarian but they can't speak English. Her portfolio ends up filled with stories of visits to her grandparents: driving the wagon to gather hay, canning vegetables, and standing in line at the tiny shop to buy loaves of bread in town. It is a portfolio rich with her family history.

I notice a beautiful art book on the science teacher's desk that she is giving to Ailis as a thank-you for a project she did. When I ask Ailis to show me some of her art I am stunned to see the sophistication of her work and the connections she makes to her reading.

Trapper's parents ask me if he has shown me the articles he writes weekly for an on-line mountain biking magazine when I ask them to come in and talk to me about their son's failing grades in language arts. The articles are highly technical, practical with recommendations depending on the use of each part he has been sent to test out and write about, and sophisticated in the levels of design concepts for which he has clear understanding. Trapper knows his audience, his subject, and his purpose in the articles well. He simply never included them because he "didn't think they counted."

The portfolios of these students are now rich with the evidence of who they are inside and outside the language arts classroom. I learned to pay attention to them and encourage the inclusion of all they know and do, and care about, through Molly and other students like her and very different from her.

I am still struggling to define my role as a portfolio keeper myself, and as a teacher who requires portfolios in the classroom. How do I document and construct myself as a literate person? How do we create our own categories for selection and reflection? How do I get students to represent their school literacies and life literacies? How do I encourage students to extend their notions of literacy based on their strengths and interests?

We need to convince our students that the work we do on a daily basis is important work by giving them life work. All of our students may not produce a magnum opus, but it will be great work for the moment.

STUDENT, DAUGHTER, TEACHER?
MOLLY FINNEGAN

For those of us who live and create in a multigenre world, the portfolio seems a brilliantly made-to-order outlet; it is a format that allows our own words and images and artifacts to celebrate and assess all the ways we learn and teach ourselves and each other. I love watching my portfolio grow and squirm, watching it change, watching my perception of a year or a project change. But I was not fluent in this language of learning and evaluation immediately; I had to learn my own version of portfolio. I have worked with and against the ebb and flow of my own understanding and the rise and fall of my teachers' knowledge of portfolios.

Years One and Two: Mr. T. Tries Out Portfolios:
Focus on Learning and Choice

My first encounter with the word *portfolio* was in fourth and fifth grade primarily as an end-of-the-year "evaluation tool." The first year was a rough draft. Not understanding terms like *assessment*, I regarded this project as a sort of a scrapbook and joyfully collected my favorite pictures and school assignments and letters and baseball cards to represent who I was. I realize now I was taking the first steps in portfolio making by connecting my in-school and out-of school selves, but my "scrapbook" concept was pretty incomplete.

Other than that, we (the students) didn't put much conscious emphasis on selecting or explaining the types of work and artifacts we chose to put into the collection. I don't think our teacher knew exactly what he wanted the portfolio to be or do, so he didn't give us too much direction. We were a bit confused (and a little intimidated) by the freedom of choices we had, but since he seemed confident that our efforts were going well, we gave it a shot, searching for something we assumed was harmless and easy.

He seemed a little confused when we all shared our portfolios—we discussed our favorite animals, our favorite sport, what we wanted to be when we grew up. The discussion of writing and school work and evaluation got lost in the pile of photographs and pictures and baseball cards. This was an experiment that may have been introduced too little and too late in the year to go where he had wanted, but WE were happy with our first efforts.

Fifth grade brought a more refined understanding for both the teacher and the students. We were brought into the portfolio assignment earlier and given a sheet which had suggestions about how one might take on this project, including some general categories to help us organize our work. He occasionally worked with us in conference to challenge us, to articulate the importance of each tidbit by asking why. Why did you include this? How does this reflect you as a member of this classroom? As a learner? At first, I was startled by the suggestion that if I didn't have specific reason to include something, it shouldn't be there. But I began to write commentaries on some of the entries, adding Post-it Notes from time to time to describe an artifact, as I started to understand why it was important to understand and interpret the significance of the choices.

For both years, he asked us to produce a short assessment essay that asked us to reflect on different areas (reading, writing, specific units) across the year and through all of our work and to include it at the back of our portfolio. While it was IN the portfolio, the assessment essay was not produced from the portfolio process. That is, we didn't create our reflections as we constructed the portfolio, or even as we read over the finished product. While the evaluation of the year's work was not yet integrated into the portfolio itself, I was beginning to understand the flexibility of the portfolio to include both the process of learning as well as the products, and to see the portfolio as a space to examine all the ways I used writing and reading and language in school and at home.

Sixth Grade: Mr. P. Stakes Out the Showcase Portfolio: Focus on Display

My first year in middle school was very different from all of my years in elementary school. We wrote a very large number of book reports, which was a genre that I had only once been acquainted with—in third grade. This was a year of "important" reading and assigned supplemental responses. The main difference between elementary school and middle school was the lack of choice in the curriculum, and then, in our portfolios.

At first, I was relieved when my teacher asked us to bring in $2.50 for a binder he would purchase for each of us to keep our best works in. I was very glad to engage in a now familiar activity, which was actually undefined territory for our teacher, who had never used portfolios before. Then we got them, beautiful maroon binders, and they were all the same. Mine was no more unique than the other twenty-three people's in the class.

"You can put something on the front, if you want," our teacher offered us.

In this class, we were to choose a range of different works, but only the best ones, and only from the language arts class, and arrange them in order, preferably chronological. Then we were to write a letter to our parents, inviting them to see what we had accomplished in his class. I think that these portfolios were less about the student's experience of the curriculum and more about the teacher's presentation of his curriculum.

And then came the bomb.

"Are we supposed to write about our artifacts? Or how our year was?" I asked him.

"Nope. You don't need to."

No?!? What was wrong here? This response seemed totally and completely wrong; it seemed illegal in some way to be keeping a portfolio and not to have any real voice in its development, no real opportunity to reflect on or evaluate our own work. I abandoned much of my zest for the project, carefully placed my prettiest work in the plastic sleeves and dutifully gave it to my parents. In my mother's written response, she began cautiously, as she realized how we had been limited by this kind of portfolio, "This portfolio seems to center around your writing about reading, i.e., response/book report." This was true; everything was centered, strictly focused on product. Although I still have a difficult time accepting this as a valid form of portfolio, I can see how it was in some ways a useful project, teaching me about careful selection, about focused work, and about the presentation of one's best work. But my own developing idea of portfolio was already at odds with this narrowly focused, teacher-evaluation-based project.

I remember how I invited readers to look at it: "Gasp as you look deeply into her wonderful portfolio!"

Deeply?!? Sounds now like I was trying to convince myself.

Seventh Grade: I Make My Own Portfolio

Seventh grade is THE foundation year, a curriculum filled with introductions, where every single student *gets* taught about short stories, myths, how to research and write nonfiction and of course, THE applicable literary terms (*flashback, foreshadowing, inference* . . .) We did not keep portfolios that year. Maybe the sense was that the curriculum was so structured that the teaching team didn't think it would be of much use to keep a portfolio; after all, there isn't a lot of choice in seventh grade. And isn't that what a portfolio is? Choosing? And explaining your choices?

So at the end of the year, I was left with a lot of stuff I didn't quite know what to do with. Put it in another box? Like first through fourth grade? No, I decided I needed to put it away with some sort of conclusion, some final effort. I knew my mom was still keeping a portfolio, and I knew that kids my age got to go to her Teaching of English classes and show her students their collections. Besides, this portfolio thing already had some momentum behind it. The resulting big brown binder that I entitled "STUFF: The Good, the Bad and the Unrevised" was borne out of the desire to be organized, to keep my work for myself (and maybe someday to share with college students), and to be an intellectual, a serious writer.

In went all of the stuff I thought was important, good, or relatively substantial from my year: a Greek tragedy I wrote in social studies, several lab reports from science, a story about a girl and her abacus for math, a brochure about spotted turtles from language arts, etc. Except for things that were really ugly, really poorly written, or really poorly graded, I put in my whole year. It was to be my own personal testimony of seventh grade, and of how happy I was to be going into eighth.

Eighth Grade: The Portfolio Grows Out

Obviously, we all have lives outside of school. We all have interests and abilities that matter to us and should matter to our teachers. One of the most important things Linda Rief did in eighth grade was to allow me to bring in my other types of literacies back into the classroom, through the portfolio, as I had begun to do in elementary school. I was able to break down the boundaries of both my learning environments—the one I am in from seven to two, and the one I am in the rest of the time—and savour and celebrate myself and my discoveries during eighth grade. Her version made every way I used language a valid use, and I knew it was appreciated by a fellow user. So instead of being a collection of my finest works (like a showcase portfolio), or simply a measure of progress in school, I decided to create a full, round, multi-layered, multi-textured organic "thing," including most of my drafts for each important assignment and the origin and story of each piece or artifact. (It is this portfolio which is included with an annotated table of contents in another section of this collection.)

In Part I, I started with a series of images, lists of traits, and other artifacts that introduce me, then described in detail each member of my family and their influence on me. As a cornerstone to my "identity kit," I put in a drawing and letter from my mother and a drawing she had done of me to accompany several self-portraits I had done over fourteen years. This artifact was important because it was not just about me creating me, it was about how we co-create each other through words and images. My mother has always encouraged my learning and writing and it was necessary that her voice be included in this forum. In further sections, I considered my own meanings and content of the word *art*, drew connections between my own artwork and some of the "masters," and discussed other arts: drama, singing, storytelling.

The second section focused on reading and writing. It was important to me to show that my growth had been affected by my teachers of all kinds. Even though it was required that we include some full case studies of our writing, I wanted to make Linda's voice heard throughout, so I put in all of my case histories, several of my drafts, and our joint evaluations of each piece, so it was clear that I wasn't doing this on my own. I tried to make the teaching/learning process visible in other ways, too, including reading responses and letters back and forth about reading and writing from my classmates. I also included a few pages at the back, asking for comments and questions to keep the portfolio alive and responsive to its readers.

And though I tried to keep it open to all of my audiences, to every learning community I shared myself, I was also in eighth grade so I was—well—leery of sharing certain aspects of my literacy. As I became more aware of the multiple audiences for portfolios, I realized that I could insert or remove some sections. Part I, for example, included two other sections, sections that constituted a significant part of my literacy, and which I periodically took out if I knew I was going to share it with kids, then reinserted if I was to show it to an adult.

One section contained all sorts of poetry, quotes, feelings, and personal stories I had recorded about quilting, which had become my medium of choice, combining writing with textiles. I felt that, unlike my section titled "Art," this was not a kind of art that other eighth-grade kids would respect me for. I was feeling "way too nineteenth century."

The other section, which was clearly too nineteenth century, was the result of several years of work I had done with my mother transcribing a set of Civil War–era diaries written by a woman who had lived nearby. As a writer, I enjoyed the possibility of a universe so close to mine, yet gone for over a hundred years. I had transcribed a large portion of the diaries, done lots of historical research, written poetry about them, and taken many photos of the remaining sites she was connected to. Naturally this would be a part of my school portfolio. Or not? I had debated this several times. It found its way in there, but it didn't find a way into my portfolio conversations with classmates. I usually "neglected" to share it when I showed the portfolio to my friends.

Looking back, I know that most of my peers really liked my portfolio, and some even asked me if they could borrow ideas from it. It seems a bit silly to me now that we were presented with an open opportunity to show everyone exactly what we were and what we did, and I ended up censoring myself, making my portfolio somewhat like what I had been fighting in its earlier sixth-grade reincarnation. In sixth grade I had thought the teacher had sent me into a "portfolio regression," by working in a form that forced me to step in line with the twenty-four other red binders. What I had loved about this matured version was using the portfolio to differentiate myself from the rest of Linda's one-hundred-and-twenty students by forming my own individual voice. But by excluding this part of me, I realize that I, too, may have been guilty of restricting the portfolio and restricting myself. I cannot say, however, that it was a totally negative thing. It was definitely an effective lesson on audience, even if I was ahead of myself in realizing it. In subsequent portfolios, I have chosen to include opportunities for the reader to ask questions or contribute anything they feel is missing in the collection, so it is enlivened by the voices and visions of those who inhabit my learning communities.

High School: The Portfolio Grows Up

In the past two years, my understanding of the portfolio has changed again and again. After a few years of trial and error, I now jump into portfolios with great energy, attempting to find new ways and words to describe the benchmarks and watermarks of my education. Just recently I created a portfolio for a poetry class. I spent close to twenty-five hours taking pictures, drawing pictures, typing and retyping and reformatting poems, finding the right quotes, making collages, and introducing and evaluating my poetic identity. My idea and expectation of the portfolio changed again, from the comprehensive (nearly 4 lbs.) collection of nearly everything I had created in the year, to a focused and selective (yet very full) reflection of myself in terms of one identity. In this current portfolio I am a poet, exploring my communities, my challenges, my literary influences, my stories, and my histories.

I see this very powerful tool has engaged me in the education of my evolution, and the evolution of my education. While some use it as a tool to close a year or course, I have begun to understand that it is an opportunity to split open what I think I know about myself and my explorations. I must attempt to dissect my ideas, and taste them, and to keep adding a little here or there, so that my portfolio will continue to squirm and change. I do not believe that learning can be restricted to the hours of the school day; why do we limit our own precious testimonies as learners to being about a narrow range of activity or time?

Portfolio is unique to its owner. In trying to create a running account of myself as a literate being, I realize that my language of portfolio is my own. It has many forms and many purposes and many audiences, composed of nouns (teacher, student, process ..) and verbs (evaluate, cultivate, celebrate ..) constructing the language I will use to communicate with others about the ways we learn.

CONSTRUCTING THE PORTFOLIO AS PEDAGOGY: FROM PIDGIN TO CREOLE
CINTHIA GANNETT, MOTHER

The most transformative potential of "portfolio," as I have come to understand it, is its ability to connect instruction and assessment dialogically. That sentence is easy to write, but not at all easy to do. As with any innovative pedagogical practice, portfolios are developmental. That is, we teachers develop our portfolio pedagogies over time, by observing what kinds of instruction, guidance, formats, and requirements work best for particular purposes, for particular students, or types of classrooms, and by being in dialogue with other faculty who are using portfolios themselves.

Certainly, portfolios are also developmental in the sense that teachers need to keep portfolios themselves, to learn from their own experience of portfolio keeping over time, if they expect to harvest the rich potentialities that portfolios promise. Sheri Everts Rogers and Kathy Everts Danielson remind us in *Teacher Portfolios: Literacy Artifacts and Themes* (1996), "Just as we learn to read by reading and we learn to write by writing, we must learn about portfolios by keeping them ourselves. Teachers must also keep portfolios, not only to model the process for students, but to grow themselves as readers and writers" (4). While I have certainly grown as a reader, writer, and teacher from my portfolio keeping, my own developmental course suggests that teachers are not the sole, nor necessarily the best, sources for "modeling the process" of portfolio keeping.

Indeed, my own experiments with portfolio keeping and portfolio pedagogy over the last several years have shown me how very challenging it has been to fuse the very different, and seemingly incompatible, languages and practices of instruction and evaluation.

I worry. What happens when students enter texts or artifacts that I didn't assign? How does regular student reflection and self-evaluation throughout the process change what and how I teach? Or possibly more important, what they learn. How do I work with, value, or evaluate artifacts that aren't texts? How do they? Don't I have to set the categories for entries, even if I allow students to choose the specific sample of that category, so that they accord with my class design, or so that my evaluations will be standardized and fair? What happens when students set their own categories? Is it possible to collaborate on the selection of process and product artifacts? How do we represent both school literacies and life literacies? And how do I/we/my students balance the act of making a summative reflection on the portfolio? Who's the teacher? Who's in charge?

Having been trained, both as a student and as a teacher, to see in-struction (coaching/guiding) and evaluation (judging/ranking/gate-keeping) as very separate roles, with very distinct vocabulary and language attached to each, I would characterize my efforts to "con-struct" the portfolio, to work at joining these discrete, seemingly op-posing discourses, as rather like learning a pidgin. Historically, pidgins have been trade languages that develop when speakers of one language first come in contact with a group of speakers of a completely novel tongue. They merge the vocabulary and syntax of both, often drawing more vocabulary from one, while retaining some of the syntax of the other. These rather crude and simple hybrid forms of speech do work, but they are rough at the seams and full of holes.

While I continue to work at synthesizing the teaching/learning functions of the portfolio with assessment and evaluation, of learning to talk this new talk, my own uneven portfolio development and port-folio practice, is indicative, I think, of the narratives of many teachers who are working through this process. I also have discovered that—at some level—my most effective guides in the process of building this new language have been the next generation of portfoliokeepers. Lin-guist Derek Bickerton and others (1983) have found that the children of pidgin speakers, because of their built-in language capacities, natu-rally develop more fully elaborated "creole" language systems from the limited and sometimes confusing linguistic input of their parents and other adults. A similar phenomenon, I have come to believe, is occur-ring with portfolios. Given the opportunity to develop portfolios with-out the explicit or tacit injunction that learning and assessment are separate activities and separate languages that the teacher controls fully, I find that our children can often develop fuller, more textured portfolios than those I or even my graduate students are likely to pro-duce on the first few rounds. These portfolios are like creoles—lively languages that bring learning, teaching, reflection, and evaluation to-gether in new and unexpected ways. I learned this, in large part, by watching my daughter come to terms with the idea of a portfolio in el-ementary and middle school.

Cindy's Pidgin Portfolios and Molly's Creole Portfolios

In 1993, Molly and I both started keeping portfolios. I was 42; she was 10. We were, in a word, NOVICES. She was in the fifth grade; I was entering my twentieth year of college teaching. I started my portfolio when I assigned one for the first time in a course on the teaching of writing. I was terribly proud to share my work on it (mostly toward the end of semester); it was a big binder of material. It certainly showed a much broader range of my academic writing than other vehicles might have, and it even showed one piece of writing-in-progress. (I was daring enough to add a short section on teaching writing toward the end.) As proud as I was of my creation, as I look back on it now, it seems my focus was solely on demonstrating that I was a successful producer of academic prose. For all my practice with the vocabulary on portfolios, I had barely produced a proto-form of the "showcase portfolio." *No tickee, no washee.*

By the time I was ready to begin my second full portfolio (1994–1996), I had read more and thought more about the complex and combinatory nature of a portfolio. I had also witnessed my own graduate students' first efforts to develop their own portfolios based on my narrow understanding of the concepts, processes, and products of portfolio keeping. Most important, I had observed and participated in my daughter's early portfolio efforts. This second portfolio has a whole different feel. My notion of valued and valuable literacies started to stretch beyond the academy to letters of complaint written to an officious orthodontist, readings of my daughter's writing-in-progress, journal entries, behind-the-scenes pedagogical work, drafts of a developing memoir, and all kinds of journal work and invention activities. I began to incorporate visual imagery, and incorporate various artifacts. Most important, I began to create my OWN categories for selection and reflection. I invited my graduate students to perform their own experiments, find their own artifacts, create their own categories and assessments. Finally, the beginnings of a developed literacy portfolio. Rough in places, but more communicative. As they say in Belizean creole, "*Neva kal haligeta big mot sote you don kras the riba.*" (Never call an alligator Big Mouth until you have crossed the river.)

Since then I have created multiple portfolios for my own professional development, but have also continued to explore the potential of the portfolio to document and construct myself as a literate person. Molly and I share our portfolios-in-progress. Sometimes we even share artifacts, as our literacies evolve through shared family activity and experience, although we interpret them from our own unique and individual experience.

Molly's interest, for example, in sketching out extended family influences on her developing literacy has acted as one prompt for my current portfolio-in-progress. This portfolio is a focused project which reopens and "breaks up" the literacy memoir I recently completed, "The Grammar of Memory," to elaborate and situate the various family influences and my own lived ways with words. It includes early photographic images of reading and writing and visual literacies in our family: my mother reading, my father at the typewriter or taking photographs of the internal universe of a flower. It includes a grainy but powerful image of my father's birth mother, Hattie Bird Wilmoth, at seventeen, standing tall in the door of a one-room schoolhouse in West Virginia—one of the few young women in that time and place to finish grade school. There is a tiny typescript collection of careful love poetry, written by the man who would adopt my father at age four when Hattie, broken by poor health and poverty, was forced to give up her eight children. This man, Heroumian Kostenski, whom I knew as Herman Gannett, emigrated from White Russia at age ten, struggled to learn English, and married the Pennsylvania Dutch tutor, Gracie Soliday, to whom the poems are dedicated. They both became teachers. Artifacts like these enact the commitment to intergenerational literacy and learning that have been central to my own literate identity.

Watching my daughter develop her concept of portfolio, I observed the ways in which she negotiated the explicit instruction and tacit assumptions of her teachers, who were themselves often novice practitioners—users of "pidgins" much like my own. I began to notice how her portfolios shifted from year to year in form and function. During the first two years (fourth and fifth grades), she produced what I would call a primitive learning/literacy portfolio, somewhat uncertainly cast by her teacher as an "assessment tool," but loose enough in conception to invite students to construct and demonstrate their learning from across and beyond the curriculum. Molly's NEATO PORTFOLIO, as she titles it, includes photos of family and favorite places, with commentary woven across the page. She even includes her nature journal, a nonflat artifact under an interesting section called "Investigations."

In the sixth grade, her language arts teacher was also trying out the portfolio concept for the first time, but in a very different dialect. This showcase portfolio was restricted to the best samples of work. This portfolio is more elegant, coherent, polished, impressive; it functions primarily as a "performance" for parents. Yet it is missing a sense of agency, an attention to process, a place for student reflection. What is most important, however, is that these early pidgin portfolios gave her the ground to create her own language for portfolio practice. They also helped me reconsider the relationship between my portfolio assignments and my students' interpretations and responses to those assignments.

Although I did not fully appreciate it at the time, her new portfolio language took its first tentative form the next year, her seventh-grade year, when there was no formal portfolio assignment. Curiously, she created her own folder, called STUFF: *The Good, the Bad, and the Unrevised. My Portfolio (1995–1996)*. Even though it is a large, unwieldy collection of process and product, this self-sponsored project, collected, organized, and titled, demonstrates a powerful harnessing of instruction and self-assessment. The first entry acts as an interesting invitation. There is a square abstract block in the middle, and the large print text reads: "Alright, Harold. Now we will play some mental games. I will show you a picture and you can tell me what you see, OK?" Below the block, the response reads: "Ah . . rest & relaxation & freedom & doing things because you want to." When I asked her about it she pointed out that it was a place where she both could collect "stuff" (artifacts) that interested her about her learning across the year; she also wanted it as a permanent trace of her progress and accomplishment that she could use for future years. "I wanted to know what I had done in and out of school EACH year."

In the eighth grade, Molly and I both had the good fortune of her having Linda Rief as her teacher and portfolio guide. This portfolio can really carry on a conversation; it is full of choice AND design; it integrates and orchestrates reflection, self-evaluation and teacher evaluation; it is open to many of Molly's representations as a literate and knowing self. This portfolio begins to approximate Paula Salvio's (1994) description of the ideal literacy portfolio: "In ideal terms, the cultural portfolio invites children to collect the objects that represent their literacy practices and to interpret the significance of these artifacts by tying them to a larger social and political field. In this sense it is a habitat for students' literacy practices, for their 'habits of literacy' are interpreted in relationship to the social contexts they once, now, and one day do hope to inhabit" (420).

Now I always bring elementary school children into my graduate classes on the teaching of writing to discuss portfolio keeping and to share their portfolios in small groups. They are helping us, present and future teachers, learn to talk the talk.

REFERENCES

Bickerton, Derek. 1983. "Creole Languages." *Scientific American* 249: 116–122.

Gannett, Cinthia. 1999. "The Grammar of Memory." In *Ordinary Lessons: Girls Growing Up in the Fifties*, Ed. S. Franzosa. New York. Peter Lang.

Rogers, Sheri Everts, and Kathy Everts Danielson. 1996. *Teacher Portfolios: Literacy Artifacts and Themes*. Portsmouth, NH: Heinemann.

Salvio, Paula M. 1994. "Ninja Warriors and Vulcan Logic: Using the Cultural Literacy Portfolio as a Curriculum Script." *Language Arts* 71 (October): 419–424.

Updike, John. 1999. "Magnum Opus." *The New Yorker*, July 12.

7

FREEDOM AND IDENTITY
Portfolios in a Puerto Rican Writing Class
MIRIAM DEMPSEY PAGE

Portfolios invite freedom and creativity, and the place to start is student writing. Any final collaborative role in evaluation or assessment will mean more if students are free to choose their topics. In my writing course at the University of Puerto Rico at Mayaguez (on the west coast) I extend to my students four familiar writing invitations, which they use to develop portfolios and which organize the course: (1) a personal essay, (2) writing to inform/place or nature writing/a travel narrative, (3) a problem-possible solution or analytical essay, and (4) an argument/persuasive essay. There are only two stipulations: (1) students must choose their own topics; and (2) "new rhetoric" or literary (creative) nonfiction is allowable and necessary in many cases. Academic discourse, or thesis with support, is discussed as an option, but only as option, if the writer's purpose and audience call for it. I emphasize variations on the modern essay, deriving from Montaigne. In responding to the four writing invitations students can be as creative as they wish. They can write autobiographical essays, other personal essays, narrative essays, memoirs, descriptive essays, fictional essays, symbolic essays, analytical essays, and argumentative essays, often with genres blurred—and, always, in terms of life experiences, background, and culture. As a result, students develop portfolios that explore and reflect not only rhetorical variations and purposes but also the nuances of Puerto Rican culture.

With Spanish as their first language, the students in our classes explore their life experiences and culture through a second language,

English, which presents both opportunities and challenges: opportunities for expressing and translating for a non-Spanish-speaking audience things that matter to them, thereby developing creativity, critical thinking, and bilingual fluency; and challenges to present or render cultural experiences, traditions, beliefs, and language that are not easily translatable. The portfolios are truly the students' own, becoming even more so in a deeply reflective and reflexive writing workshop (Qualley 1997).

Students share up to three drafts of each piece in both large- and small-group workshops. In the large-group workshop, two students share copies of their writing with the entire class each week. In the small-group sessions, students bring five copies of their writing-in-process—four copies for their group and one copy for me. This way each student receives weekly responses on their writing-in-process.

In the personal essay, students are writing their life experiences. That speaks volumes on an island that is both modern and developing, an island that is predominately Catholic, with some Protestant sects, but an island where Santeria, Voodoo, and *Espiritismo* (especially *Espiritismo*) are also practiced.

In writing to inform or in the place/nature pieces, which most often turn into storytelling or travel narrative, students write their life experiences and memories. The travel narratives to date have taken them around the island to the United States or other countries, or to other islands in the Caribbean—all interesting cross-cultural journeys.

In the "problem" pieces, Puerto Rican students are concerned with the same issues that bother most college students. Parking on the UPR-Mayaguez campus, abortion, personal relationships, gender, sexual orientation, and religion, for example, deeply concern them. But these issues, of course, are viewed in terms of the perspective and culture of the Puerto Rican students. For example, "machismo" (traditional male dominance and patriarchal attitudes) appears frequently in their writing. Puerto Ricans are just now beginning to come to terms with a newly emerging sense of male-female relationships in a modern society.

The argumentative essays also pick up this gender issue as well as subjects that concern college students anywhere. But one special issue continues to re-emerge: the statehood question. This issue is highly volatile in Puerto Rico, with considerable debate occurring on the island and in the United States Congress around the question of independence, commonwealth, or statehood for Puerto Rico. The students write often and with much feeling on this subject.

The following selected student topic choices from the first semester of the academic year, 1997–98, show the wide range of individual interests. One student entitles his symbolic autobiographical essay, "*Gallo*

Pinto" (multi-colored rooster), and writes a poignant story of his being Puerto Rican and the history of his island. Another searches in "Identity" for ethnic and cultural heritage, finally celebrating his multiracial background and Puerto Rican identity. In "Flavio's World" and "A Man of Peace," two students face the bitter realities of racism both in their own lives and in others' and dream of a world where peace and mutual respect prevail. A young Catholic tells of his own spiritual odyssey and of his deepening faith as a college student, even of a growing tolerance for other faiths. A recovering substance abuser recounts his hellish journey through alcohol and drugs to a miraculous recovery. Two surfers describe the awesome force of the waves, the exhilarating yet frightening experience of being "lost in the tube," conquering the ride into shore, like young warriors returning to their lairs. A pre-vet student discovers the power of reflective and reflexive science as she spends a night discovering sea turtles off Culebra.

Their writing takes me all over Puerto Rico—to *El Yunque* ("On Top of the World"), the only rainforest in the United States National Parks System; to Isabela ("Jobos Beach") on the Atlantic coast; to the healing waters of *Banos de Coamo* ("A Place to Cure Illness"); and more. Occasional pieces describe Caribbean cruises to the other islands—"One Day in Barbados" (with stops at other islands), "Voyage" (a piece on returning to San Juan and Puerto Rico)—and reflect the deep love of home, family, and culture among these students.

A future cardiologist traces his family's roots back five generations to Spain. Another student passes family landmarks as he climbs 4,000 feet to his grandmother's house, nestled high in the *Cordillera Central* at Utuado. Puerto Rico for them is not only physically beautiful; it is a deeply symbolic and spiritual place. At the end of many pieces describing a trip to the United States or to other islands, are the words, "It was so good to get back to my beautiful little island."

From time to time I can see influences from the other islands. Bob Marley, a favorite Jamaican reggae artist, has been the subject of several essays. Even Voodoo has appeared, in a piece titled, "Obeah Night," a short story/essay on a Voodoo ceremony set during the time of slavery by a student from Antigua. For the most part, however, I read about the things unique to Puerto Rico—"Our Special Lullaby Singer" (ubiquitous green tree frog indigenous to Puerto Rico); "Living in a Paradise"; "Puerto Rico—*La isla del encanto*" (*el coqui*, Phosphorescent Bay, *fiestas*); "*Fiestas Patronales*" (festivals honoring the patron saints); Three Kings' Day; and many more celebrating special Puerto Rican customs. The students also take great pride in their athletes—those that represent Puerto Rico in the Olympics, the many that go to the major leagues, and those who play in the more local leagues on the island. They write of basketball, boxing, and baseball. I've also had one tennis champion in my classes, and one student described the long tradition of cockfighting in her family.

Puerto Rico, discovered in 1493 by Christopher Columbus, has a long history dating back to the Taino Indians. With the Spanish conquest and later the importation of the slaves from West Africa, the island has drawn its Indian, Spanish, and African heritage together to form a rich, diversified culture. Some of the foods, for example, *pasteles*, may be of African and Indian origin. The people value their traditions and heritage. To be here today is to be a part of an old culture that is becoming increasingly modern. The students are computer literate and blend their amazing knowledge of the Internet ironically with pieces telling about their sadness at the disappearance of *el jibaro* (peasant or folk hero) and the sugar cane fields, the coffee plantations, and the mango groves.

But a new Puerto Rico is emerging and with it new attitudes concerning the roles of men and women. Traditionally a patriarchal culture, Puerto Rico is just now beginning to feel the struggles of gender resistance. Recent student topic choices reflect this newly emerging awareness—"The Development of the Woman in Our Culture," "Women in Computer Engineering," "Looking for Equality," "Women vs. Men in the '90s," and "Waking Up." Sexual liberation and its consequences have followed suit: "The Turn Around," "The Loss of Innocence," "From Grandmother to Granddaughter," "You Want to Play, or Not?" and "Homosexuality."

Citizens are entering the twenty-first century talking about new roles and new responsibilities, with all eyes turned now as well to environmental issues. Deforestation, endangered species like the sea turtle and the manatee, and many other issues both on the island and along the coasts figure prominently in student writing with powerful titles, like "Massacre in Our Resources." Some students (and student divers) belong to environmental clean-up groups, many talk about recycling, and others are active in Greenpeace and other environmental groups.

When I give the writing invitation to argue or persuade on an issue that they care deeply about, the topic choice I see most, however, is the statehood question. One student wrote a prayer-essay on the eve of the birthday of the discovery of Puerto Rico (November 19, 1493), pleading for respect, dignity, and freedom. And others followed, with titles such as: "A Whole Century's Quest" (referring to the uneasy relationship between Puerto Rico and the United States for a hundred years, since the 1898 invasion in the Spanish-American War); "Puerto Rico: Wake Up!"—an argument for independence; "Our Struggle for Independence";

"A Republic in Puerto Rico"; "Boriken"–the Indian name for the island before the Spanish conquest; and a well-argued one for statehood written by the son of the Secretary of State. The recent debate over the sale of the Puerto Rico Telephone Company, also related to the political status issue and the island's freedom, produced passionate writing. Some of the titles: "Sell, the Best Decision"; "The Puerto Rican Telephone Company Sale"; "Privatization of Public Agencies"; and "More Professional" (a letter-essay to the governor).

The rich responses to the four writing invitations with their variations give me an opportunity to guide the students to diversity of rhetorical purpose, audience, content, and form. I also invite those so inclined to write poetry, fiction, or drama. So the portfolios become filled with writing the students really care about, portfolios resonant with the beauty, richness, complexity, and paradoxes of their culture— even with its many problems and challenges, still *"La isla del encanto"* (the island of enchantment). The portfolio writing matters because it matters to the students. They lose their stiffness, their resistance to writing, and their self-consciousness with language.

POST-PORTFOLIO: A FINAL EXAM

A final exam is required at UPR-Mayaguez, so I create a range of topics to reflect what the students have been writing about all semester. Without the department requirement, I would not follow the portfolio with a final exam. The exam in this case (December 1997) was more an extension or a deepening of earlier ideas written during the semester. I distributed the topic choices a week ahead. The students were free to use any form they wished. They came to the exam and wrote on one of the following topics:

1. Puerto Rico's Political Status
2. Male-female Relationships in Puerto Rico at the End of the Twentieth Century
3. Sexual Liberation and Its Consequences
4. Puerto Rico and Sports (team and individual)
5. One or More Things Unique to Puerto Rico or to Puerto Rican Culture
6. The Role of Science/Technology in Puerto Rico's Development
7. Free Choice (prompted by a student who told me he didn't like any of the topics, proving my point about freedom of topic choice; he wrote on the way women are depicted on television)
8. Response to the Long Work (novel or book-length nonfiction required in the course):

    a. Discuss the theme of the long work and one key way the au-
       thor develops the theme.

    b. Discuss the significance of one character to the long work
       you've read.

A student choosing to respond to the long work question wrote on
Rosario Ferré's *The House on the Lagoon*. Daughter of Luis Ferré, former
governor of Puerto Rico, Rosario Ferré is one of Puerto Rico's foremost
women writers. The student concluded that the novel did not have a
single theme, but rather intertwining themes emphasizing the mixing
of blood and intersecting life situations across the generations of a
Puerto Rican family, citing Puerto Rico's Indian, Creole, African,
Spanish, French, and American ties, among others. The student, recognizing some stereotypes that Ferré plays off in the novel, also drew in
the idiosyncrasies, or variations on the themes, which might have been
or still be possible in such a landscape.

A portfolio not only reflects culture; it indeed composes culture
(Sunstein 1994). It defines the culture to which its keeper belongs.
With writing invitations that evoke the students' own topic choices,
the portfolios in the case of my students in Puerto Rico reflect, shape,
and imaginatively foreshadow an emerging cultural, social, economic,
and political identity.

REFERENCES

Ferré, Rosario. 1995. *The House on the Lagoon*. NY: Penguin.
Qualley, Donna. 1997. *Turns of Thought: Teaching Composition as Reflexive Inquiry*. Portsmouth, NH: Boynton/Cook.
Sunstein, Bonnie. 1994. *Composing a Culture: Inside a Summer Writing Program
with High School Teachers*. Portsmouth, NH: Boynton/Cook.

8

DIGGING IN!
Dynamics of Assessing General University Competencies by Portfolio

MARILYN R. BARRY AND YASO THIRU

Only a few years ago our acquaintance with controversy involving artifacts had more to do with archeology than writing. As an eastern Washington resident, Marilyn had followed in the local news a fracas over who was entitled to excavate an apple orchard cache of Clovis tribe utensils. The adversaries—an anthropologist from a regional university, another "expert" on Clovis peoples from back east, and local Native American tribes—vied for the right (or not) to interpret the significance of the find. Unable to agree, they haggled in and out of court until the disgusted orchardist brought in a front loader, reburied the find, and planted the area in Grannie Smiths.

Artifacts, and their location within a discovery site, are means by which archeologists can hypothesize about otherwise lost cultures represented by the artifacts. To the Clovis people, the objects hadn't been artifacts but items integral to daily living. Researchers can't ask tribe members about their lives, and inferences will always be incomplete, no matter how expert the interpretation.

Because for the past four years we have been deeply involved in developing and administering a university-wide portfolio program, we now more commonly use the appropriated term *artifacts* to refer to work that students include in portfolios, selected by them to demonstrate mastery or competence of some kind. The archeological metaphor is useful for clarifying work with portfolios in some ways; not, in others. Artifacts of both sorts must be interpreted in the context of identifiable cultures. We diverge from the model in archeology that these products be interpreted and assessed by specialists alone. As with many other portfolio programs, what our students have to say about their own work is central to our assessment of their growth and accomplishment.

The need for students to self-assess grows out of a conceptual approach to portfolios that values equally the formative process of self-assessment and the summative assessment of the artifacts by experts. We see conversations between student and faculty evaluators as a way of negotiating the differences in our respective assessments and of moving students forward in their programs.

PROCESS, PRODUCT, AND TRANSACTION

Descriptively, process may be regarded as a series of steps culminating in a product or effect: writing instructors are familiar with the variously identified stages of student writings, which issue in a finished piece. But the concept of process may also be regarded evaluatively, as does de Chardin (1965), esteeming it as an act of creation—dynamic, ongoing; a means for acquiring knowledge and developing insight, for becoming more fully human.

Though writing teachers may disagree on the extent to which "process" ought to be the focus in composition courses, one goal for portfolios in writing classrooms is that students continue to work on pieces of writing as their capacity to explore subjects insightfully becomes more sophisticated over the course of a term. Versions of the same piece may be viewed as artifacts of process. At term's end, selected pieces become elements of yet another process, of reflection and self-assessment. Unlike accomplished writers and artists, who typically offer their work as its own justification, students are expected to explain the reasons for their selections. Their assessments can provide crucial information for the instructor, not only of the significance of the artifacts but also of the students' grasp of the cultural norms and of their achievement in relation to those norms.

Just as an archeological artifact needs to be understood in relation to the culture that produced it, portfolios need to be viewed in relation to articulated cultures: the one into which the student is attempting to be accepted and the one(s) from which the student comes. Laudable as specific goals for assembling a portfolio may be, confusion resulting from the intersecting of differing cultures may short-circuit the goal of fair and comprehensive assessments.

Archeologists work backward from the artifact to speculate on a specific culture, doing so on the basis of professional training that provides a context for interpretation. With careful attention to the item itself, investigators move forward and backward through the millennia, reinterpreting and often restructuring earlier paradigms to accommodate new findings.

As interpreters of student artifacts, we advocate a similar model of being investigators and learners, not merely assessors. Unlike archeologists, however, who can interrogate only the artifacts in attempting to interpret significance, we can easily consult the students who produce them. To fail to do so diminishes the value of the portfolio experience for both student and evaluator.

THE SPECIFIC CONTENT OF ONE PORTFOLIO PROGRAM

As developers of a university-wide portfolio program for a small, private institution, a group of faculty and students have found ourselves shuttling between theoretical notions and our ground-zero experiences as coaches, gatekeepers, learners. As ideas keep shifting about how to improve the process of the portfolio, so does our understanding about what constitutes our institutional culture and, therefore, what constitute legitimate artifacts and how and to what end we offer appropriate assessment.

We have come to believe that our portfolio must be valued first as a transactional process, continuously evolving, for student and faculty alike. This paradigm of ongoing self-assessment reflects the values of an academic culture that programmatically encourages students to take increasing responsibility for setting their own goals and for designing courses of action that will prepare them for lifelong learning.

Until four years ago graduating students had been required to pass comprehensive exams intended to evaluate general and program-specific competencies. In January 1995 our campus welcomed a new president, chosen in the aftermath of a difficult institutional reorganization. Alert to turmoil on many fronts, one of his first official moves was to respond to student dissatisfaction with the senior comps. He announced that the comps, as well as the traditional junior year writing competency exam, would be replaced with a "Junior Portfolio" program that would allow students to choose materials on which to be evaluated. The question of which competencies were to be assessed remained open.

The proposal struck the faculty as perhaps a fairer way to assess student achievement, but we weren't exactly sure how this was to be different, in purpose, from their taking and passing courses or, in form, from the CAEL-based (Council for Adult and Experiential Learning) portfolios (Lamdin 1997) some students assembled to apply for credit for workplace experience. An ad hoc committee spent a good bit of time trying to figure out just exactly what "portfolios" were, as if there were a Platonic version tucked away somewhere, familiar to other users of the term but hidden from us in the far north. We were spurred on, however, by the eighteen-month goal we had been given for developing and implementing a portfolio program. That faculty was given full professional responsibility for carving out the process appears to have contributed to its success (see Murphy 1997).

The portfolio was one of many changes in a radically revised curriculum that freed students to choose more courses that would meet personal goals. Overall, the curriculum was altered to include experiential learning components in many existing courses and to emphasize students' taking responsibility for doing independent work, including practica and full-scale senior projects. The portfolio was envisioned to function in part as a stock taking before the greater freedom of the senior year.

The president invited students to offer their views on what competencies were important. Faculty also began discussions, initially thrashing around, trying to articulate values shared in common with respect to Alaska Pacific's academic culture. The skills and understandings to be assessed needed to be more comprehensive than ones which might be developed in specific courses. Departments drew up wish lists of desirable *competencies* and came up with qualities as divergent as *grace* and *ability to use spreadsheet programs*. Besides a finite list, criteria also needed to be drawn up for assessing whether appropriate levels of mastery had been achieved. The focus continued to be on a final product that would change the form of "our seal of approval," marking that students met institutional standards for being "well-educated" or at least "well-enough-educated" to proceed with the senior project.

Unable to reach perfect consensus, the faculty nevertheless adopted the current published list with the caveat that it was open to future amendment. In this regard, our faculty is probably not much different from faculties elsewhere. This suggests that the notion of *culture* as a bundle of features needs to be considered in dynamic terms as well.

DEFINING THE PURPOSE

For some years earlier, the term *portfolio* had been identified with our "Credit for Prior Learning" program.[1] Students prepare autobiographies, chronicle significant learning experiences, and line out goals, as

---

[1] CAEL-based work is now identified as a sub-component of the General University Portfolio, renamed the Documented Experiential Learning (DEL) Folder to distinguish it from the more broadly based University Portfolio.

well as collect materials to document their competence in response to the requirements of a specific course, explaining in a reflective narrative how the included artifacts demonstrate those accomplishments. The format adopted for the university portfolio includes similar features of initial documentation.

The functions of the two kinds of portfolios, however, appeared to be significantly different. The purpose and process for evaluating the CAEL-based portfolio were well established: each is evaluated by the subject-specific instructor, rated credit/no-credit, a summative judgment. If the university portfolio were modeled along similar lines, reminiscent of the senior comps, it was unlikely that it could be used effectively for definitive assessment of a student's competencies across the board. An alternate model was that drawn from the writing classroom. The narrative reflections of the keeper of the portfolio could be used in conjunction with stated goals and selected artifacts to form the basis of ongoing discussions with advisors. As the focus shifted to a process that would evolve over several years, the committee set aside the term *Junior Portfolio* and instead adopted *University Portfolio*.

GOALS FOR STUDENTS AND FACULTY

Just as students needed to line out their educational goals in the portfolio, the committee laid out its goals for the project.

Goals for students included personal growth through reflection and self-assessment; increased independence while charting and carrying out plans for individualized learning; awareness that education is a process that occurs within and outside of the classroom; opportunity to demonstrate degree of mastery of university-designated competencies; introduction to the ongoing process of developing and updating a professional portfolio, which might later be used for purposes of employment or graduate applications.

Goals for faculty included increased sensitivity to different learning styles and needs; tool for more effective advising; a more comprehensive basis on which to assess mastery of competencies; foundational information for program assessment.

THE COMPETENCIES, CRITERIA FOR ASSESSMENT, AND DEMONSTRATION METHODS

The General University Competencies are ones developed by formal and experiential learning of a variety of sorts. Recurrent discussion among students and faculty about what should constitute the competencies has already led to changes in the originally adopted list. For instance, although course work in physical activities and health is no longer generally required, the addition of an *understanding of the value of wellness* reflects its importance to this particular culture. A large number of APU students come to Alaska to test their physical mettle, and our outdoor program is a major draw.

The *Portfolio Development Guideline* publishes the list of General University *skills* and *understandings*. In addition, each department publishes, and its students address, a list of competencies expected of majors. *The Skills* include demonstrated ability to communicate effectively in speech and writing; to analyze qualitatively and quantitatively; to be computer literate; to organize and carry out a project; to lead. *The Understandings* include those of self; of society; of the natural world; of ethics and religion; the humanities and the arts; of the importance of wellness.

Each of the named skills or understandings is accompanied by a description of the criteria to be used. For instance, *to analyze qualitatively* is described as "to demonstrate principles of logical deductive and inferential reasoning; demonstrate ability to think critically, formulate and solve problems, take apart and construct arguments."

All competencies require evidence in the form of an essay and documentation pertinent to the emphasis area. The essay is expected to include an explanation of what the student understands a particular competency to involve; a description of what has been done to achieve it, including formal course work and experiential learning; a candid assessment of what the student considers to be strengths and weaknesses with respect to fulfillment of the competency; and a description of what is included in the documentation section as evidence of fulfillment. Oral presentations may be appropriate to demonstrate particular skills or understandings, although this is included as an optional demonstration method and ordinarily is considered supplemental to a written presentation. Documents may include previously submitted or newly composed papers, video and audio performance tapes, photographs, letters. When support materials include nonprint materials (as, artwork, videos, Websites), "flat" copies (photographs or descriptions) are included. Transcripts and/or grade reports verify course work.

The following excerpt comes from Josh's *understanding of wellness* section:

> . . . this has come through my experience running a dog team. Mushing with a team of dogs is largely a psychological feat, far more so than physical. The major tool used to do the job is one's own spirit. This then requires the deliberate, conscious awareness of one's own state of mind, and the deliberate, conscious manipulation of that state to achieve a goal.

In the process of doing this, I have learned first hand the body/mind connection: the link between emotional states such as patience and good humor, and physical states, such as hunger, cold, tiredness, and sleep deprivation. I have learned how to set up conditions for a good attitude.

Josh offered as documentation two Websites that he had constructed, with hard-copy printouts and on-line addresses, one on mushing and another devoted to dogs that had been leaders of winning Iditarod teams. Also included was an essay from a seminar in philosophy about sled dogs and Zen, as well as his autobiography and the reflective essay on *understanding of self*, both of which spoke to his activities as a wilderness guide.

ASSESSING THE COMPETENCY STATEMENTS AND ARTIFACTS

The competencies are basic, not exotic. Still, because readers are likely to understand or value somewhat differently each of these criteria, every student portfolio is reviewed by the advisor and another member of the major department, and often by a third reader from outside. Juniors who address the General Competencies and submit the portfolio for formal review are not expected to be able to address all the general and major requirements. The resulting conversations are intended to issue in a mutually acceptable plan for completing the student's program, including plans for a junior-level practicum and senior project. Assessment is a matter of dialogue and advising, not of opening gates or, conversely, of affixing padlocks. As students complete the remaining competencies, they update their portfolios. The senior project is included as the last item.

When Jessica was stalled on designing a practicum and senior project, she and her advisor looked over her initial materials, revisiting early goals. Those included wanting to "to get one or two art classes back in the curriculum. . . . I would like a career that allows for a lot of creativity. . . . In order to carry this out I will have to believe more in myself and my work, something that has been difficult for me." A year and a half later she wrote of her senior project, a multimedia art show: "Whether art remains a hobby or I find a way to merge creativity with a career does not have great importance anymore. I have come to accept and be comfortable with the fact that fundamentally I am an artist . . . Whatever else I choose to do or pursue, art will be my comfortable companion, something I can go to for release and expression. This acceptance is a milestone for me as I never considered myself remotely qualified or talented to call myself an artist."

LEARNING FROM OUR STUDENTS

New students begin the portfolio process in a required orientation class. Here they assemble the initial documentation, constructing a cultural context for themselves and their readers: where they're coming from, hoping to get to, and how. Students are also advised to set aside materials each term that might document their achievements related to the competencies. As they become juniors, continuing students may proceed to "address the competencies" on their own, working from *The Portfolio Development Guide*, or may enroll in "Portfolio Development" if they want more direction. Just as students initially contributed ideas about what should be included as competencies, they have continued to help us understand what we we're seeking.

The pilot course was team taught by the CAEL-program instructor and Marilyn. When students were asked to write autobiographies, Marilyn suggested that they recall the previous exercise, which involved assembling a chronology of significant learning experiences, but assured them that they could write about whatever they wanted their readers to know about them. The veteran instructor had clearer expectations about what would be produced, based on long experience in giving such assignments. Marilyn, on the other hand, liked giving students a free hand and did not have clear expectations.

One junior creative writing major turned in what might have passed for a well-constructed short story—scene, narrator, characters, dialogue. The more experienced instructor refused to accept the piece, writing in her evaluation that she didn't understand what it had to do with the assignment. Marilyn, familiar with the student from other classes, found the story revealing, especially if viewed in the context that students were trying to introduce themselves and their interests to their advisors.

The three of us talked about our differing expectations. The student explained that the piece was part of a larger, semi-autobiographical novel he was working on. He saw the exercise as a chance to introduce himself as a writer and storyteller. However, he decided that he would offer a supplemental, more conventional autobiography to meet the expectations of readers who might not appreciate the subtlety of his intention. The other instructor acknowledged that the story, once explicated, helped her to appreciate the student's writing talents. Marilyn realized that she had overlooked a crucial principle: that the portfolio had multiple functions, including one which was rhetorical, and that we need to convey what the base-line expectations are, as well as encourage students to exercise individuality. We could also see a potential bucket of iceworms re-form itself into the tentative possibility that we were, indeed, moving forward in our understanding, thanks to the creativity of students who took us at our word: we were experimenting as we tried to find our collective ways.

TRAINING FACULTY AS ASSESSORS

A few faculty worked intimately with the portfolio the first year, but it was clear that more were needed to spread the load around. When Yaso was asked to take over the Portfolio Development classes she took the adventurous trip of putting together her own portfolio: the goal statement, significant learning experiences, and a narrative/reflective essay for a hypothetical accounting course. She wanted to be able to model the process for her students but was surprised at the effect the exercise had on her. It now seemed that learning was possible only through intentional reflection of the learning process itself. She felt it was not enough for students merely to come to class and turn in assignments. What gives meaning to learning is the reflection that puts the classroom experience in the context of the students' goals and their relationship to the world. This potency of reflection is noted elsewhere, notably in Yancey (1995). Yaso saw the selection of artifacts for the portfolio, then, as an attempt by the student to articulate this meaning.

The rest of the faculty has been slowly pulled into the world of portfolios by their advisees. To assist our colleagues, we developed assessment rubrics and evaluation sheets and put together special advising handbooks. We've offered workshops, visited department meetings, and made ourselves available as mentor readers. Recently other faculty presented a colloquium on ways they'd found to foster portfolio activities.

Administrative leadership has played a supportive role. The incorporation of experiential learning into our courses has allowed us to increase credit hours from three to four, thus reducing the number of course preparations faculty must undertake. Part of the savings in prep time goes toward overseeing experiential learning, but another portion is intended to be invested in the portfolio effort.

ONGOING REFLECTIONS

Commitment to the portfolio program is altering the way APU delivers other parts of its program as well. Writing courses have routinely asked students to be self-conscious about their writing abilities, evaluating achievements, strengths, weaknesses. Now, the word has spread about the need to incorporate student self-assessment in classes across the curriculum. Faculty report increasingly that they discuss the portfolio in connection with their courses and find themselves configuring at least some assignments that might be appropriate for inclusion. Danesa, a psychology major, addresses the *writing* skill:

> A use for personal narrative is in writing a self-assessment. Because I have had so much practice . . . it is easy for me to produce an honest evaluation of my work. Acknowledging a weakness is necessary to improve it. I've used self-assessment in [three courses]. My greatest strength as a writer is using my personal life as a baseboard for interpreting and understanding my education.

New questions pop up; others continue to nag. Asking students to prepare materials as extensive as the ones required by this program imposes a hefty, noncredit graduation requirement. It's vital that we continue to question whether the value to students and faculty alike is sufficient to justify the investment of our joint efforts.

Students say they like the idea of assembling a portfolio. Meagan writes:

> When first organizing for the portfolio, I was skeptical about the purpose of doing it. I did not see the merit in organizing material from four years of schooling at four different institutions. In my mind, it was more of a hassle than anything else. After collecting material, organizing, typing, formulating, and presenting . . . , I see new merit in the purpose of requiring this for graduation. This portfolio has allowed me to collect samples from each class I have taken so that I can look through the portfolio and see my progress through the last four years. . . . More importantly though, this project has given me the chance to plan more effectively for my immediate future so that I can graduate with a clear vision of what I want to do, where I want to go, and how I am going to do it.

Advisors who have worked with portfolios say they appreciate having more information about advisees and opportunities for interaction that go beyond signing student registration forms each term. While not all faculty are equally enthusiastic, the ones with reservations admit they have had relatively little experience yet with portfolios.

Two recent developments will likely impact on the success or no of the program. The first was the decision by the Faculty Review Committee last spring to ask faculty to prepare academic portfolios as part of the contract renewal and promotion process. One rationale for this development grows out of work with student portfolios: faculty are more likely to be effective mentors for students if they are actively engaged in the process themselves. The second is a university-wide drive to develop more rigorous program evaluation tools. Portfolios will provide one means to collect information about program outcomes. "Foundational information for program assessment" had been one of the original goals for using portfolios, but the institution is only now beginning to focus on how they can be used to realize that goal.

Time will test the merit and practicality of the undertaking. All of us together may decide the presently operative program involves too much duplication of effort, and bring in our own front loader to bury the project. For it to remain viable, it must continue to be flexible, responsive to any change in university goals as well as to the changes that routinely accompany the induction of new faculty and students. We are confirmed in our early decision that the project must be viewed as dynamic—a process that tries to hold in tension the combative flux of cultures, that fosters students' growth, and that encourages our own evolving selves. The process is changing whatever culture it is that we share.

REFERENCES

de Chardin, Teilhard. 1965. *Building the Earth*. Denville, NJ: Dimension Books.
Lamdin, Lois. 1997. *Earn College Credit for What You Know, 3rd ed*. Council for Adult & Experiential Learning. Dubuque, IA: Kendall/Hunt.
Murphy, Susan. 1997. "Teachers and Students: Reclaiming Assessment via Portfolios." In *Situating Portfolios: Four Perspectives*, ed. Kathleen B. Yancey and Irwin Weiser. Logan, UT: Utah State Press.
Yancey, Kathleen B. 1995. "Reflecting on Reflection: Notes on Developing a Reflective Frame of Mind." In *Assessing Portfolios: A Portfolio, Iowa English Bulletin*, 43: 9–16.

9

ARTIFACTS—DIFFERENT KINDS OF FACTS
How Material Culture Shapes the Researcher Portfolio

ELIZABETH CHISERI-STRATER

Nestled among the fond memories college students hold of their high school, of marching band and football games, of proms, graduation, and senior skip day, is a more bittersweet scene from the English classroom: that of the junior-year research paper and its companion of neatly stacked note cards. Students remember recopying their scrappy library notes onto skinny lined index cards and recoil at the frightening emphasis placed on citation format for them. Students are often amazed and relieved to learn that no such exercise will take place in their college writing classes, that research papers assume many shapes across the disciplines and bear little resemblance to the high school version. They also learn that index cards, while respectable enough for some kinds of library work, are not the only possible displays of documentation. And luckily, college writers take easily to another process of documentation—the researcher portfolio. In fact, students come to value the portfolio far more than the actual paper that accompanies it. Both students and teachers may discover that collecting artifacts into a researcher portfolio proves a liberating process which encourages a richer source of material culture than does documentation based only on paper note cards.

The researcher portfolio is described in *Fieldworking* (Chiseri-Strater and Sunstein 1997) as housing both the process and product of a research project. The student submits a final documented paper alongside a collection of all the reading, writing, and artifacts; in short, all the "material culture" that supports the written report. While the research portfolio sometimes resembles a scrapbook, it is far more focused and more reflective. Elliot Eisner offers a fine metaphor about the selectivity involved in the research process:

> But selectivity, although partial and framework dependent, is a way of giving point to observations and thereby helping others learn to see. Only the less competent try to attend to everything. . . . The skilled teacher knows what to neglect. The competent student knows what to focus upon. The expert chess player knows what patterns on the board count. . . . The making of a fine meal does not require the use of everything in the pantry. (Eisner 1991, 90)

The skilled portfolio keeper has a full kitchen from which to choose what she will display and highlight from her writing; she does not present a five-course meal, nor does she offer only snacks. Instead she selects from her rich store of textual and material artifacts to serve what are the richest meats of her project. Knowing that a selection of data will be required encourages student researchers to locate a much wider range of sources than only library materials, although libraries have now taken on the responsibility for making students aware of the vast array of information available to them through Web searches. Because every research project will include its own array of material culture, it is hard to make a definitive list of potential sources for the portfolio, but here are a few powerful ones:

Websites
historical archives
personal writing such as journals, logs, daybooks, and diaries
maps, both professional and amateur
photographs
videotapes and film
interviews and stories
direct observations of places, people, and events—field notes
material cultural artifacts
journal and newspaper articles and books
surveys, questionnaires
government and related public documents
phone conversations
drawings and sketches

This list of data sources suggests that research papers may take on a different look than traditional research papers and that the place where that evidence will best be found will not be in the bibliography but in the researcher portfolio.

The researcher portfolio, of course, is first cousin to Ken Macrorie's well-known I-Search paper, thoughtfully described in his book, *Searching Writing* (1984). Here Macrorie stresses making a personal connection to a research topic as the critical component of "I-searching" which, he says, stimulates a lifetime habit of curiosity. He also anticipates the power and joy of the World Wide Web when he suggests investigating real life issues such as finding out about a career, planning a trip, or buying a house—all topics that are easily accessed on-line. The four short sample papers in his book share a kinship with the researcher portfolio in that they include a narrative of the researcher's journey, what my co-author and I call the "twin tales" or the story behind the research process (Chiseri-Strater and Sunstein 1997). The difference between Macrorie's I-Search approach and the researcher portfolio is that the portfolio does not stand alone but accompanies a fully documented research paper. Macrorie's work often includes more about the research process and less about the formal findings. Since the researcher portfolio contains both the story of the research process and a collection of print and nonprint artifacts from the investigation, it is a very distant relative of the note card/outline system.

This chapter describes researcher portfolios that accompany a specific assignment given in a particular course. Along with many teachers, I have learned that another value of portfolios is that they often are developed to support and highlight particular course projects or goals for the purpose of meeting short-term standards. You will see how these students met (and exceeded) the course and project standards in different ways and that the real evidence of their hard work is most clearly shown in their portfolios, not necessarily their final papers. The first time I experimented with a researcher portfolio was in a master's program designed for adult working students who signed up for a course I taught titled, "Family Stories, Oral Histories, and Interviews." This course proved the perfect testing ground for the research portfolio: since then I have adapted this documentation process for more traditional, researched papers and projects in freshman writing courses. Because the entire course was devoted to writing a longish (12–20 pages) paper based on ethnographic field research, students' portfolios provided all the evidence for the entire investigative process. In creating guidelines for their portfolios, the students and I decided that while some artifacts could lie flat and fit into a folder, scrapbook, or accordion file, other nonprint artifacts also need to be displayed as rich sources of fieldwork. Some of these works were submitted in cartons, plastic bins, and shopping bags. Any container that enclosed the full range of the project's material culture would suffice.

Nonprint artifacts involved the most innovative and unusual data sources that students found and contributed to their portfolios. We most often associate ideas about cultural artifacts with archeologists and anthropologists who explain how artifacts are loaded with history and meaning that represent a culture's worldview. The most familiar cultural artifacts are quilts, baskets, pottery, religious and burial ceremonial objects as well as the tool and technological innovations of any particular culture. But as documentation sources for a field research project, artifacts represent different types of facts. Unlike facts written on an index card, the very tangible and material quality of artifacts collected into the researcher portfolio make them convincing sources of evidence for students' papers.

TRANSCRIPTS AS ARTIFACTS

Many of the participants in this course were interested in writing about their relatives—aunts, uncles, grandmothers, grandfathers, cousins, mothers, and fathers. Their researcher portfolios included the expected print artifacts of family trees, maps, letters, diary and journal entries, newspaper clippings, and interview transcripts, along with some analysis about the overall meaning and support these gave to their final papers. For example, Gwen wrote an oral history about her cousin's experience of being the first black salesperson at a prestigious Southern department store which had previously hired blacks only as maids or janitors. Gwen's primary documentation sources in her portfolio were the transcripts of her interviews with her cousin, along with photographs of her, the store where she worked, and company newsletters about its employees. Gwen searched the archives of local newspapers to try and locate a story about her cousin's integration of the department store staff to no avail. Seeing her cousin as the object of discrimination and oppression had shaped her interview questions yet she found no data in her transcript to support this interpretation. In fact, a review of her interview transcripts revealed a counter example. In one moment in the interview, Gwen's cousin tells a story about when the Klu Klux Klan came to town. Her cousin hid with all the other white employees under merchandise tables while the Klan swept through the store. Gwen's desire to tell the heroic tale of her cousin integrating a racist establishment turned out to be the "twin" tale she reflected on in her researcher portfolio. Even though it became only a small part of the actual oral history of her cousin, Gwen's portfolio included a great deal of self-reflexive analysis about the research process. The researcher portfolio, then, provides a space for the researcher to juxtapose the original transcripts against the final written version of the oral history and to see both documents as artifacts of the encounter between the researcher and her informant, between self and other.

Suzanne interviewed her grandmother and wrote an oral history of Esther called "Pity My Shoe" which comes from a road sign in the small North Carolina town of her grandmother's childhood. The road was named when a woman got so stuck in the mud there that her shoe was sucked under, causing her to remove it from her foot, saying,"Pity my Shoe." Suzanne's oral history of her grandmother's wonderful stories was distinctly different from the video she shared with the class and wrote about in her researcher portfolio. Suzanne had used a series of artifacts to prompt her grandmother's storytelling—a doll bed, a miniature wood stove, and a Bible helped shape the interviewing process. However, Suzanne also compiled a series of family photographs into a memory scrapbook which she took to Wal-Mart to have arranged and set to music. This videotape became an important gift that she gave to relatives for Mother's Day that year—to her grandmother Esther, her own mother, and her aunt. Suzanne's researcher portfolio includes both the transcripts of her audiotaped interviews as well as the family photos used to compile the videotape footage. Both print and nonprint artifacts were important to the way Suzanne chose to write the oral history of her grandmother, a woman who lived all her life in one house, surrounded by her relatives and the artifacts that represented her small town Southern culture. One of the key functions, then, of the researcher's portfolio is for the writer to analyze and reflect on the material artifacts that are collected there in order to explore the role of the researcher in the process of conducting interviews and turning these conversations into oral history.

HISTORICAL AND ARCHIVAL ARTIFACTS

For our course, Dick interviewed two surviving members of the WASPS, women who served as Airforce service pilots in World War II. These women ferried B-17, B-26, and B-29 bombers from American manufacturers to Europe during the war in a civilian capacity while following military training and rules and regulations. Although they lost thirty-seven members of their group who are now memorialized in Sweetwater, Texas, the WASPS were never considered part of the U.S. Military and therefore are not eligible for veteran's benefits, a source of contention among many military women and some supportive men. Much of Dick's preparation for his interviews involved background reading about the history of women in aviation as well as actual visits to air museums in North Carolina and Ohio. Dick's index to his portfolio (see Section III) reveals a wide range of print-based artifacts he gathered for this project: books and newspaper articles, historical documents such as training schedules and flight logs, and photographs of the early aviators as well as photographs of the Women's Air and Space Museum itself. The reflective letter that accompanies Dick's portfolio describes the importance of this range of documents. Dick's background reading included some military magazines that could only be accessed through archives such as *Naval Aviation, Retired Officers, Airman,* and the *Magazine of the American Airforce.* Overall Dick's researcher portfolio included forty-five pages of fascinating artifacts, ranging from a program for the 1996 National Conference on Women Airforce Service Pilots held in Anaheim, California, and the official insignia for the WASPS created by Walt Disney—Fifinella, a lady gremlin with goggles. Dick's researcher portfolio was far more interesting than his actual interviews with the women pilots, who were elderly and not entirely forthright. The strength of the portfolio is that he has now accumulated a wide range of cultural artifacts about this part of aviation history that he would not have gathered from just doing the interviews and has thereby created a rich resource for other researchers who might be interested in this topic. Since he is retired, Dick may also have opportunities to locate and interview other retired pilots or their relatives and can use his researcher portfolio to extend and expand such interviews. In this way his portfolio has a much richer future use than would a collection of interview transcripts.

ELECTRONIC ARTIFACTS

Lorraine is a columnist for a local newspaper who created a researcher portfolio, wrote a feature article for the newspaper, and created an electronic Website for her project in this course (http:www.greensboro. com/nronline/projects/eastmarket/index.htm). The topic of Lorraine's research was an African American neighborhood which flourished in Greensboro, North Carolina during the Second World War when the city was the site of the O.R.D.—the Overseas Replacement Depot, the main processing center for troops on the East Coast. This community included over a hundred small black-owned businesses. But in the late 1950s, the city decided that the neighborhood was a slum that needed to be torn down to make way for a highway project. The businesses and homes that were part of this black community were then demolished and residents relocated in the name of "urban renewal" into housing which is now referred to as "the projects." Lorraine's researcher portfolio and her electronic scrapbook re-create the original neighborhood through old photographs and interviews with those who lived there or knew relatives who once were part of East Market Street. Like Dick's portfolio, Lorraine's is a remarkable compendium of diverse documents, revealing wide-ranging researcher skills. She includes interviews, some taken on napkins and scrap paper, with over twenty-seven former residents or store owners from the area. Her portfolio includes city maps from 1945, showing the area marked for demolition as well as pages from a 1945 phone book, listing the fifty-eight black businesses to show how abundant they were: Meares' Tailor Shop, Rose's Beauty Salon, Ethel's, Harris's Bakery, Cox's Furniture Shop, Colonial Ice House, Ralph John's Clothing Store, Palace Theatre, two black dentists, six black doctors, and the list goes on. She found the original newspaper articles declaring the neighborhood a "blight" and the official city document proposing an urban renewal project, a slick brochure with pictures and text stating that the area was a "breeding ground for crime, disease, juvenile delinquency and other community problems." Her interviews reveal that during the Second World War, when Greensboro was an Overseas Replacement Depot in the segregated South, this neighborhood was the only place where a black soldier could get a haircut or have his uniform cleaned. In 1944, the East Market Street area built its own USO Club which served 18,000 officers in the first month. In spite of testimonies about the viability of the community and to guard against taking too romantic or nostalgic a view of the neighborhood, Lorraine located a black photographer who had shot many street scenes of the area and who suggested that in addition to the thriving businesses, there was also deplorable poverty in the East Market.

Lorraine's researcher portfolio contributed both to her feature article, "Ghosts and Good Intentions: A Walk Down Old East Market Street" (*Greensboro News and Record*, February 19, 1997) and to the creation of a permanent community scrapbook where residents can add their own photographs or written memories to the archive about this bygone era in the city's history. The Website features a street corner in the neighborhood from the heyday of the 1940s drawn by a local artist. Readers can point and click on selected features in the drawing to locate different pages in the scrapbook that highlight old family photos and memories in former residents' own words.

In addition to the rich sources of documentation which explore the larger historical, political, and social implications of her study, Lorraine's portfolio also includes the twin tale of her research process, of her own understanding and involvement in the oral history project she created. She reflects on the role of the reporter as outsider, as reporting what is most often considered the objective source of news and wonders if revisionist history is the only way to offer the full story of any set of events. In her portfolio she writes: "Can reporters be a product of their time, but also transcend their time? And is each of us serving a life sentence inside our own skin, or can we occasionally step outside and see ourselves and the world from the perspective of the "other"? Her reflection on trying to be both insider and outsider, on stepping in and stepping out of a culture or subculture was the point of the entire course and Lorraine's portfolio, not her news article or Website, was where she was most able to discuss that idea. She writes further about this insight in a final essay for her master's program:

> "I've heard people on deadline say that there is no such thing as the truth, and I know what they mean. There's no perfect, ultimate, complete story—even 20 years after the fact, even in book form. But there are true stories all around. At an overcrowded school, I met a teacher who held classes in the locker room. I knew a Montagnard boy who was orphaned in the last days of the Vietnam War, and was raised in the jungle. I met a mother so engulfed by crime and drugs that she bought burial insurance for her teenage son. And the final tragedy was, she ended up using it to bury him.
>
> This is their story, told in their voices and their words. According to them. . . .

SHARING THE RESEARCHER'S PORTFOLIO

Rather than turning in a stack of note cards as evidence then, students share and critique each other's collections of material culture at several stops in the fieldwork project. Early on I like to hold a festival of data in which students select their most useful, interesting, or telling facts or artifacts to share with our group. Students present this information on posters or newsprint so that we can easily read it as we spend time walking around the room, learning about each other's projects before each researcher talks about her data. These artifacts might be a blowup of either an interview transcript or a poster of actual field notes, or a picture of the fieldsite or the key informant, a Website or library source—whatever data has been key to the researcher's project. At a later point in the research process, I ask students to pair up as portfolio partners and again share their collected artifacts and print resources with one another as well as write a response to their partner's research questions and data sources. This data festival and sharing helps prepare students for the same process at the end of the semester when their written projects and portfolios are completed.

REFLECTIONS

All of these studies discussed in this article are focused on fieldwork projects, research on people, places, and subcultures, but the researcher portfolio itself is easily adaptable for any type of research project. In freshman courses where students are beginning to use library source materials, I ask students to evaluate several Web sources about the same topic. Students go on-line and print two or three Web sources about a topic such as raves or Civil War reenactments or Animal Rights debates and then analyze which source is more *authoritative* for their project and why. Some subcultures, such as raves, exist just as much on-line as they do in the dance clubs where these events take place, making the Website a critical source of information and one that invites scrutiny. Overall the portfolio concept of documenting source materials encourages a very different type of library and field research that ultimately leads to a better understanding of both facts and artifacts and how they are joined.

Students who get hooked on topics of high interest to them are eager to retrieve their research portfolios from me because they often plan to continue with the investigation. Anthony, who researched Civil War reenactments, wrote further on this topic in his second-semester composition course, building his research portfolio even more. Many students who compiled a research portfolio far exceeded my own research standards and expectations for the course as they collected and organized material culture for their projects. They learned the kinds of research skills that will serve them well in college and beyond. They now own skills for researching family, local, and historical archives as sources of material culture for self-designed projects. They can now see artifacts indeed as very valuable kinds of facts.

REFERENCES

Chiseri-Strater, Elizabeth, and Bonnie Stone Sunstein. 1997. *Fieldworking: Reading and Writing Research.* Upper Saddle River, NJ: Prentice Hall.

Eisner, Elliot, W. 1991. *The Enlightened Eye: Qualitative Inquiry and the Enhancement of Educational Practice.* New York: Macmillan.

Macrorie, Ken. 1984. *Searching Writing: A Contextbook.* Montclair, NJ: Boynton/Cook.

II

A STANDARD SET FROM
THE OUTSIDE

10

THE CONNECTED "I"
Portfolios and Cultural Values
DANLING FU

When I first came to this country, as an outsider, I tended to constantly label everything I saw people do here as "the American way," but as I mingled with more and more people of different occupations and professional backgrounds, I concluded that "the American way" is to be different, and that being unique is highly valued by this culture. Standardized tests and portfolio assessments, to me, represent different social and cultural values. As a student and educator in two countries for many years, I can't avoid comparing and contrasting Chinese and American education. I have noticed the vast difference in the two educational systems with their contrasting cultural values, and also striking similarities in teaching practices and assessments.

Now I have been an educator in this country for many years; I spend a lot of time in classrooms every week. I can call myself both an insider and an outsider of this culture. What I have noticed in many classrooms has come to puzzle me more and more, making me question the true values of this country. Initially I believed that being unique and creative was highly valued, but seeing the teaching in elementary and secondary schools, I find there is a disjunction between the cultural values this nation claims to honor and the teaching practices it allows to take place, especially in the area of assessment. As an individual growing up in an educational system which stressed nothing but standardized tests, I do not have test phobia. However, I question whether the standardized tests given in this country at present are testing what we want our students to learn, or are reflective of the values this country claims to honor.

In China, I found it much easier to prepare for standardized tests since everything is standardized there: the textbooks, the teaching approaches, the curricula for every grade level all over the country, and even the opinions that teachers are supposed to hold and pass on to their students. Memorizing book knowledge is the key in learning every subject. Uniformity is highly stressed in Chinese cultural values. To conform to a standard is the way the Chinese people live. And standardized tests, which represent its cultural value, have been used for centuries to select people to go on with their education, to confirm the people who will learn the same things the same way, and to weed out the learners who are different. Students in China are standardized before they enter kindergarten. When I read Lois Lowry's novel *The Giver*, it reminded me of my growing-up experience in China during the Cultural Revolution. Everyone was pressured to dress the same, wear the same hair style, talk and walk the same way.

But in this country, little is standardized in life. From a young age, children are encouraged to be individuals and to be respected as individuals. When they start to school, they are encouraged to be creative. It is not a surprise to see two teachers next door to each other having different teaching philosophies and using different approaches and different reading materials. But even though it seems that the teachers in this country have more freedom, they are also bound by standardized tests. It seems that this country uses standardized assessments to standardize teaching and learning that values diversity and individuality. This is a discrepancy between teaching and learning and assessment. It must pass on a very confusing message to the children: *Can you really be creative or diverse when your learning achievement has to be assessed by a certain set of standards?*

MARTIN: A LEARNER CONTROLLED BY TESTS

I have seen so many children in elementary and secondary schools in this country who are victims of assessment, which proves nothing but failure for them as learners. Martin was one of those students, a test-proved failure. The assessment shows that he is below grade level, can't read and write well like others, and doesn't have language skills like other children his age. His mother is a nurse in a local hospital. She is a single mother of two children, and Martin is the younger one. She works hard and cares very much about her children's education. When she works the night shift, she calls to check about Martin's homework, asking him to leave it on the table for her to check before she goes to bed. When Martin got his test scores, she heard him crying:

> It made me feel really bad when my son didn't pass the reading test. He was crying. His ITBS scores went down from last year. He was in the average range last year. Now he is in the low range with a lot of stuff. He is in third grade, already he often breaks out in tears over tests. I notice some nights he doesn't sleep well before tests, and I can't get him to go to bed. I wish I knew how to help him, or what was included on the test. I could help him over the weekend or the night before a test. Maybe I can help ease him and calm his discomfort.

Like Martin himself, his mother is frustrated with the test and doesn't know what she might do:

> I don't know, I don't know. All I know is that I am working so hard that my son shouldn't fall through the cracks. I am trying to do everything I can. I don't want him to feel like a failure. I don't want to compare him with others. Every child is different. I know he loves to learn. He is not afraid of learning. I don't want him to lose his love for learning.

From his mother's words, we can tell she is quite worried about the damage a test might do to Martin as a learner. Even though he can't pass the writing test, he is not afraid to write. He loves to write to communicate, as his mother observes:

> He likes to write me notes. Like sometimes, he would leave for the bus before I come home from exercising. It is like I am not going to know where he is, so he writes, "Mom, I've left for the bus. I'll see you when I get home this afternoon." Even when I'm in another room doing something, he goes to his friend's house and leaves me a note: "Mom, I went to Brian's house." I have no problem reading his writing.

His teacher, too, talked about Martin as a learner. She knows he is a hard worker and a learner who is different from others, who needs a lot of time to think about his work. She knows that it is hard for Martin, or anyone who learns this way, to do well in any test which requires its takers to think and act quickly.

> Martin, darling Martin. He tries soooo hard. He sits and thinks. He has to think about everything. You can tell. He sits for a long time before he'll put something on paper. You can tell he is not avoiding or daydreaming; his mind is working. He's sitting there trying to organize. He's not good at organizing on paper. He doesn't want to do prewritings like bubble sheets, flow charts, or power writing things. That is not his thing. He wants to sit there and think it through. And then when he's ready, he will start writing—from beginning to end. He's fun to watch when he writes, but it doesn't always come out the way he wants. He's got more inside here (points to her head) than he can get from there to paper. . . .

He cried when he didn't pass the grade level test. He's worried that he can't go on to the fourth grade. He works sooo hard at everything. He cares and works so hard. That is why it is so sad. He's worked so hard and it's still not sticking. He's frustrated with that. I have seen a change in his attitude; he becomes more withdrawn as he realizes his own disability. When he failed the reading test he was just blown away. And those things happen to him, and then he's less willing to write. He doesn't want to put anything on paper, as he's afraid it is going to look so bad. It's a shame to see that.

Martin talked about himself as a writer, and I learned that even though he constantly fails tests, he is still confident in himself and tries to do his best.

I like writing because it is fun. I get to practice how to write words. When you write, you can work on hard words. You can try to sound out words. I like to write in a writer's notebook, because I can choose my own topics. I like to write in writing workshop, because I get more time to write, then I get a lot of thinking done. I like to have conferences with my teacher during writing workshop, as she helps me get lots and lots of details. In other writing (prompt writing) I don't have enough time and I hardly finish anything.

Now my writing is getting better. I can write on the lines. I say a lot. I put more ideas down. I can spell better. I don't have to erase a lot, as I know the words. I try to write the words by sounding them out or saying them aloud. I can write fast now because I practice writing letters fast at home. But I still have a hard time on words.

I try to do my best, try to make good grades. I practice writing fast at home. I would set the timer, and ask my mom to see how fast I can write down my ABC letters. I want to read more and do a lot more thinking. I want to learn more about animals and write about them.

Martin knows he's improved this year. But the test score can't show this. It is unfair. From what Martin himself, his teacher, and his mother observe about him as a learner, a thinker, and a writer, we've learned that he has improved a lot, works hard, loves to think, and cares about his learning. He is concerned and worried about the test. If Martin had a portfolio, it might consist of the writing he took the time to do in his writing workshop, the notes he wrote to his mother at home, and even the "ABC letters" he practiced writing fast to improve himself as a writer. A portfolio would present how he learns, what he tries to do, what he can do, and what he uses writing for. His work as well as his self-assessment and his teacher's and mother's assessments about his learning could prove Martin's growth as a language learner and writer in his own way.

But the assessments given by his teacher, his mother, or Martin himself were not counted in when he was diagnosed and ranked. Their assessment is considered "too emotional," too subjective or "romantic," not scientific enough as it would be if shown with senseless numbers. I don't believe there can be a pure science in the field of social science. Human science cannot be free of cultural values or political beliefs. We know every student possesses a portfolio like Martin would have—if he had one. It depends on us, the educators, to give it a place in the curriculum. We must make the invisible portfolio visible, to value it in school learning, if we invite individuality to enter school life.

As Martin's mother said, we all know that children are different. The portfolio is an approach which acknowledges difference and celebrates diversity. It presents what this nation claims is its cultural values:

- It gives learners *freedom* to select their products to demonstrate their learning and growth.
- It highlights the *individuality* of each learner.
- It values all learners *equally* and respects the difference in their linguistic, social, and cultural backgrounds, and in their learning abilities and styles.
- It lets learners take *control* of their own learning and assessment of their progress.

Portfolios are not simply an alternative assessment tool, but they reflect a teacher's beliefs and practices. If we don't give students freedom of choice or we don't allow their individual voices in their literacy learning, then portfolios have no place in our curriculum. If learners can't see themselves in their reading and writing activities, then their portfolios, like themselves, will remain invisible in school learning.

TEACHING CHILDREN OF IMMIGRANTS

Usually students with learning difficulty are given less choice in their school learning. Endless worksheets suppress their creativity and identity. I saw this happening in a seventh grade classroom in an inner city school with 90 percent of the student population of new immigrants.

As a staff developer, one day I was led into this seventh-grade classroom when the teacher was working an A letter worksheet for handwriting with the class. She showed the class, with a transparency, how to write upper and lower case A and then circulated from seat to seat to check up on the students' work. I sat by a boy at the back of the room. It took twenty minutes for the teacher to come to him. He had filled up his worksheet with big and small A's, even with arrows to show how the lines should go. The teacher then said they had to write each letter only five times, so he began erasing all the letters he had written on the page. He had much time left, and so he drew pictures until the teacher came to check. She was not pleased with his hand-writing nor was she pleased with those arrows he drew. She showed him how to write big and small A's and asked him to redo his work. I waited patiently for this to end; twenty-five minutes of class time was gone and I wanted to see what the teacher would do next with her students. Finally, after she'd circulated through them all, she returned to the front of the room. She stood by the overhead projector, distributed another worksheet, and said "Okay, we are now going to work on the letter B. I thought I'd faint. I stood up and left the room. Those students, however, had to stay.

I have rarely felt so heavy, sad, and angry. I wonder if we should label our teaching, our tests, and our curriculum disabled before we dare to diagnose our students as disabled. I felt that those students were not being treated as intelligent human beings. I have visited many classrooms at different levels in many states in this country, and I've never seen anyone, kindergartners or high schoolers, practice letter writing for fifty minutes. We are cheating these students. We are wasting their lives and their time. We are *keeping them* on the margins for life. I know their families and they have sacrificed a lot for better educational opportunities. They don't know how demeaning this treatment is.

I think to myself, "from the early Pilgrims to the recent refugees and immigrants who gaze at the Statue of Liberty, all newcomers to this country are inspired to feel spiritual liberty, a sense of freedom, a feeling of self-worth. Every one of them knew that it was not easy to leave everything behind and start all over again in a strange land, but they were willing to make those sacrifices for democratic values and for the chance that their children might have a better life than they had before." Educational sociologists Treuba, Lila, and Kirton state:

> Immigrants and refugees come to America searching for economic opportunities and political and religious freedom, "The American Dream." No one else knows better than the immigrants and refugees the meaning of freedom and democracy, and no one is willing to pay a higher price in order to achieve The American Dream. Therefore, they endure hardships and drastic social and cultural changes unbearable for others, and they buy into American ideals and social, economic, and political participation, and of educational opportunity accessible to all. (1990, 1)

As well as I know how much trust those children and their parents have placed in our educational system and as much as I believe that schooling will help their children realize their American dreams, I am ashamed by what I see happening to these children in our schools. I wonder if they will really have a better future than their parents if they continue to be bound by senseless worksheets, or if they will truly be allowed to become literate in this culture.

Portfolios are no place for worksheets, letter drills, uniform friendly letters, or standardized book reports. Both Martin and those seventh graders knew a lot, could do a lot, and had many stories to tell. Instead of letting them say what they could and wanted to say, those worksheets prevented them from speaking and from preparing for the culture and the world they are here to join. In those worksheets, they don't exist as unique beings.

NATIONAL VALUES AND TEACHING PRACTICE

This nation is supposed to stand for individuality, equality, freedom, and justice for all. In theory, we believe literacy education is to enable our children and young people to discover, to experiment, to search for possibilities. We want them to be critical thinkers, to create and re-create the world, to find meaning in it.

I wonder just how many teachers in this country have full control of their teaching and can have their students read and write for self-discovery and for an understanding of the surrounding world. Every year, I begin my language arts course for prospective teachers with a survey of students' "literacy history," and repeatedly I hear the same story from the majority of the class: "I don't remember ever writing for myself until I took freshman writing in college." "I never remember ever being taught to write until high school, and then it was the five-paragraph style essay, the book report, or the library research paper." Unfortunately, these preservice teachers often witness the same language or writing instruction they experienced in the schools where they do their teaching practica. Still they see language instruction taught with an emphasis on isolated skills. Scripted programs, which demonstrate little individuality in either teachers or students, are used in many schools because raising test scores is the most important concern. It seems few teachers can afford to have students read and write for themselves—or have their own voices in their reading interpretation or writing expression. In basal or textbook-dominant classrooms, neither teachers nor students have a voice or require creativity. Rather, both must conform linguistically and write with predetermined tone, vocabulary, form, and genre. Hence I find a wide discrepancy between what values the American nation claims to be based on, and the classroom instruction practiced in many of our elementary and secondary schools.

In the Chinese culture, education is believed to mold people's minds. Teaching is for transmitting knowledge. It is believed that knowledge resides in books. The more one can memorize, the more one learns. To learn is to memorize; to write is to master certain sets of forms and language, and creativity means to follow and imitate tradition in a personal way. Conformity is stressed, and individuality, to a Chinese person, is a strange concept, sounding either too selfish or damaging to the communal values emphasized so heavily in the culture. These traditional values are reflected in what Chinese students learn and how their learning is assessed. Standards are important at every level in education. There are national, regional, district, city, and school standards. The quality of teaching is demonstrated—and measured—through and by the students' test scores.

This scenario doesn't sound too strange to American education when we look at what and how we teach our students, and the dominant ways we assess our students' learning. In theory, the Chinese and American educational systems should be polarized. But in teaching practice, there seems little difference between the two systems. I believe that nothing in our teaching is neutral politically or culturally. In teaching, we constantly pass on our beliefs to our students: our views of the world, our attitudes about life, our moral standards. We pass on our values to our students, too, through the materials we read to them or choose to have them read, through the ways we train them to be readers and writers, and through the ways we evaluate them. I wonder what kind of values teachers pass on to their children in those basal-controlled programs with preset unified standards. But of course, those values come from the textbook companies and not the teachers who use them. Maybe.

TWO LAYERS OF VALUES:
THE DEMOCRATIC AND THE CAPITALIST

When we find a discrepancy between the values the American nation claims to be based on and the values practiced in classroom instruction in many elementary and secondary schools, how can we explain this strange social phenomenon? I see this country having two layers of values. One is based on the founding principles of the nation, written into the Constitution, reflecting the democratic features Americans hold dear: freedom, individuality, equality, and justice. The other is based on commercial values that represent the American capitalist system, striving for accountability and immediate profit. In American literature, we learn the legacy of democracy. But in the life of schools, we see the public asking many administrators to search for quick ways to raise test scores, publishing companies pushing commercial textbooks into the classrooms, private companies trying to sponsor public schools, politicians pressing for teacher accountability. In short, these people strive for "capital" rather than fighting for individuality, equality, and justice for all Americans.

To me, this discrepancy between democratic principles and capital-controlled reality is causing problems and confusion in American education. Since I began teaching in this country, year after year, I've heard preservice teachers ask, "Why can't we see practices in the real classroom like what we've learned from our books?" When they see what the classroom teachers have to do for survival at their jobs, they start to question the practical values of what they have learned from the books and in their colleges. Soon they learn to believe that what they learn in the literature or in their teacher preparation programs is simply too ideal, too beautiful for the real world. I continue to see "at-risk" children like Martin and new immigrant children like those seventh graders (who believe that education will help them "make it" in this democratic world) being isolated from the others and kept on the margins culturally and academically with endless worksheets which make little sense to them. I wonder. How long will this nation keep its legacy when its people have trouble seeing its values practiced in everyday life? How can our young people value individuality, freedom, and equality if they have rarely experienced those privileges in their own schooling? Is there a connection between our teaching beliefs and the cultural and social values carved out for us? We need to ask ourselves, "under what system do we operate in our teaching?"

We are carriers of the torch for the future. We want to make sure this nation continues to hold its founding principles. Many of us are progressive teachers. We are the minority, but we represent an undefeated force as we quietly question the status quo and slowly push our society forward. No matter how frustrated we are and how much resistance we may meet with, we have made the difference. Our children are reading more and more real literature, their learning involves more personal "making of meaning" than ever before. They do write more. More and more teachers are working with writers' workshop approaches, giving their students freedom of choice in reading and writing, and using portfolios to assess and to teach. With today's technology, the world is much different than when we were children, and today's children are different too.

We push the system to adjust to change in the world, to change in the children, and to change in the country. We may represent a dissident voice, but it is a voice that always speaks. If this voice did not exist, the world would stand still. China is still backward, I believe, because its dictator system didn't allow for dissident voices. Nobody could question the status quo, nobody could express an opinion different from the authority's. When the world moves forward and one country tries to stand still, it moves backward without realizing it. The United States of America can be advanced and a leading power because it has a force that won't allow a chance to move backward. It can only move on toward real democracy. This is the principle of dialecticism: The world is constantly moving along with contradictory parts that co-exist, have conflicts, and push each other to adjust to changing conditions. The world depends on the conflicts of these parts to move on and on. Only a democratic country can allow the existence of a dissident force, which sees beyond the present and has a vision for the future. And we represent just that.

However, the world never moves in a straight line. It moves in curves and is recursive, back and forth. It is like the curved movement of the stock market; some years it goes straight up, sometimes it drops down. We are at a low in education. We shouldn't be discouraged, but rather stand and support each other. We can't give up what we have believed or achieved. We need on the one hand to understand the natural law of movement: When we want to make a fundamental change, we will encounter a strong resistance. That is what we face now—a resistance from the opposite view. We need to understand that the opposite force in this movement will try to use misconceptions to condemn our beliefs and practices. Instead of trying to understand us, they associate whole language, for instance, with "no phonics" and "no direct teaching"; writing process approaches with "no quality products"; reader response with "pure personal interpretation out of the context of literature." Under the banner of "compromise" or "finding a middle ground," they advocate standardizing portfolios, for example, with a Step 1,2,3 formula. I believe portfolio assessment and standardized assessment represent two different philosophies and two different value systems. Like all contradictions, they may co-exist, but there is no middle ground.

Education suffers because, like this country, it is caught between two value systems: the democratic, human values system and the economic, marketing values system. As the editors of *Language Arts*, Curt Dudley-Marling and Sharon Murphy point out on their editorial page, "If educators and the public capitulate to an agenda that privileges the needs of the economy over the needs of individuals as social beings within communities, then we should not be surprised if questions of social justice and human rights are taken up in the contexts of profits and losses. . . . Schools are about much more than employability. They are about cultivating a way of thinking about the world and one's place in it. Educators must lead the way in renewing the valuing of education as broadly defined so that today's students are truly prepared to encounter the world of tomorrow" (1998, 88–89).

We are in the business of education, and that means working with children, educating their minds and characters and preparing them for a future life in the world. We have to hold more human values than capital ones as we make sure this world is a good place for them to live. We search and explore the best ways to educate them, to assess their learning.

And so we need to work together to uncover the invisible portfolios from the students who are at the margins and give them a place in their literacy education. However, we don't want to stress individuality in portfolios without common human bonds. In its social and cultural dimensions, portfolio keeping is connecting learners with learners, learners with teachers, and teachers with teachers by sharing their individuality and their uniqueness. Only when each individual is valued can a community be a place for every member. Standardized assessment, because it is a non-dimensional measurement, appears to uniform the learners. In essence, it weeds out the differences, and encourages competition which separates learners and singles out teachers.

Standardized assessment, then, links itself with our American marketing values: it strives for efficiency, immediate profit, and standard products. Portfolio assessment represents the human values we associate with American democracy: freedom and control to the learners, equality and justice for all. I hope we can be proud of our dissident voices, of the constantly moving dialectic that is progress. I hope, too, that my idea of "the American way"—not the "one American way" I saw when I first came here, but the culturally diverse and fiercely unique "American ways" I learned about the longer I lived here—will help us keep portfolios in schools as a constantly speaking opposite kind of assessment to help us continue to move forward not backward.

WORK CITED

Dudley-Marling, Curt, and Sharon Murray. Editors Pages. *Language Arts*, 75, 1998, 88–89.

Trueba, H., J. Lila, and G. Kirton. 1990. *Cultural Conflict and Adaptation: The Call of Hmong Children in American Society.* New York: Falmer Press.

11

FROM QUEEN OF THE CLASSROOM TO JACK-OF-ALL-TRADES
Talking to Teachers About the Kentucky Writing Portfolio

ELIZABETH SPALDING

In March 1997, Emma Garland and I sat in an empty classroom talking about portfolios. By empty I do not mean devoid of students. By empty I mean devoid of furnishings, ceiling, flooring, and fixtures: Oak Bridge High School, a suburban/rural school on the outskirts of Lexington, Kentucky, was in the midst of a major renovation. Emma and I sat on chairs we had dragged in from another classroom. A tape recorder was perched on a stool between us. Our conversation, occasionally punctuated by the drilling of jack-hammers, echoed weirdly in this dim and barren space.

As a twelfth-grade English teacher, Emma is responsible for helping her seniors compile the writing portfolios required by the state's assessment and accountability system. She reflected on how the 1990 Kentucky Education Reform Act has affected her work:

> We did away with tracking here at the high school . . . [and] it has caused teachers to become jacks-of-all-trades. . . . I was used to being a queen . . . [but] I'm pretty comfortable now with being a jack-of-all-trades. I see it as being very positive. . . . Unfortunately, we still have . . . a lot of kings and too many people who think they're aces too!

With very few exceptions, all twelfth, seventh, and fourth graders in Kentucky public schools produce writing portfolios. As Emma's metaphor suggests, one result of this statewide mandate has been the democratization of the writing curriculum. While, to paraphrase Mel Brooks, it may be "good to be da queen," many Kentucky teachers of English language arts abdicated their thrones with the passage of the reform act.

The use of portfolios for large-scale assessment and accountability purposes continues to be hotly debated. One side of the argument might be summarized as, "If you mandate it, they will teach it" (Resnick and Resnick 1992; Wiggins 1992; Wolf, LeMahieu, and Eresh 1992). Another side argues, "If you mandate it, they will resist it" (Huot and Williamson 1997; Wile and Tierney 1996). I had heard these arguments and more during four-and-a-half years at the National Council of Teachers of English where I worked on the development of national standards for English Language Arts and the development of an English Language Arts portfolio assessment system for the New Standards Project.[1] As a new faculty member in the College of Education at the University of Kentucky, I was eager to see for myself how teachers implemented the writing portfolio and to hear their own views on its benefits and limitations.

In this chapter, I introduce three twelfth-grade English teachers— Emma Garland, Martin Sterling, and Kate Worth (all pseudonyms)— who shared their perspectives on Kentucky's required writing portfolio. Fortunately, I work in a field-based secondary teacher education program which allows me to spend much of my time at Oak Bridge High School (also a pseudonym), where they teach. In the spring of 1997, they generously allowed me to sit in their classrooms; to interview them at length about their views of English teaching, the KIRIS writing portfolio, and the Kentucky Education Reform Act; and to construct their stories here.

But first, a few words of caution about these stories. I caught Martin, Kate, and Emma during a school year when block scheduling was being implemented for the first time and classes were being carried on over the din of drills and heavy machinery. Today, the renovation is a memory and block scheduling seems like a natural way to organize the school day. In the daily life of schools, concerns come to the forefront, then fade into the background as good teachers work together to find solutions. I don't know what story Martin, Kate, or Emma would have told five years ago. I don't know what story they will tell five years from now. I guess we'll just have to keep talking.

---

[1] New Standards has largely discontinued its portfolio assessment efforts and concentrates principally on developing "reference examinations" in English language arts and other subjects.

THE 1990 KENTUCKY EDUCATION
REFORM ACT (KERA)

In order to understand the stories of Emma, Kate, and Martin, it is necessary to know a few facts about the history and progress of educational reform in Kentucky. This state has historically "stood at the bottom of nearly every measure of educational and economic success" (Holland 1997, 265). In 1985, sixty-six poor school districts filed a lawsuit "claiming the way Kentucky funded public education was inadequate and unequal" (Bishop 1998). The Kentucky Supreme Court agreed with them, declared the whole public school system unconstitutional, and in 1989 ordered the Kentucky General Assembly to establish a more equitable system and to "monitor it on a continuing basis so that it will always be maintained in a constitutional manner" (Rose versus the Council for Better Education, Inc., 1989, quoted in Guskey 1994, 1). The 1990 Kentucky Education Reform Act was the legislature's response.

KERA is "one of the most comprehensive pieces of educational reform legislation ever enacted in the United States," addressing nearly every aspect of public education "including administration, governance and finance, school organization, accountability, professional development, curriculum, and assessment" (Guskey 1994, 1). The reform was funded by a $1.3 billion tax increase and by changes in how property taxes were determined (Holland 1997).

The aim of KERA is "to see that all children learn and that they learn at a high level of academic knowledge and skill" (Prichard Committee for Academic Excellence 1995, xiii). Since a twenty-year time line was envisioned for the transformation, the Kentucky Instructional Results Information System was established to provide the public with clear evidence of progress toward this distant goal.

THE KENTUCKY INSTRUCTIONAL RESULTS
INFORMATION SYSTEM (KIRIS)

KERA outlined six broad learning goals for Kentucky students. From these goals, seventy-five "academic expectations" were identified and became the basis for developing an assessment system which was primarily performance-based.[2] Developers concluded that no existing,

---

[2] The assessment and accountability system has undergone many changes since its inception. In 1998, KIRIS was abandoned and replaced by the Commonwealth Accountability and Testing System (CATS). Multiple choice items have been added to this system and the writing portfolio, after heated and lengthy debate, remains a part of it.

norm-referenced, multiple-choice test could measure "proficiency" in KERA learning goals. In addition, they hoped that "an authentic, performance-based assessment system would compel educators at all levels . . . to focus instructional activities on the kinds of higher level skills that will be essential for success in the 21st century" (Guskey 1994, 3). KIRIS is high-stakes: teachers in schools whose students perform well receive financial rewards; schools whose students fail to improve or whose scores decline are sanctioned. The media avidly publish school scores.

Schools, not individuals, are held accountable for showing improvement. In the spring of 1992, KIRIS developers used a variety of measures to establish a baseline, or accountability index, for each school and to calculate the amount of progress each school would be expected to demonstrate every two years. The accountability index weights heavily progress toward KERA's cognitive goals as measured by KIRIS, although noncognitive indicators, such as attendance and retention rates, are also part of the formula (Trimble 1994). The original accountability grades were four, eight, and twelve. Developers envisioned that voluntary continuous assessment would occur in the "off-year" grades (Kifer 1994). Over the years, the accountability grades have been changed and distributed more evenly across the years of schooling.

The twelfth-grade KIRIS writing portfolio is only one of many statewide assessments Kentucky students complete. For example, eleventh graders take tests which include open-ended response items in a variety of subject areas (e.g., social studies, math, science, arts, and humanities). Reading is assessed through constructed responses to reading passages. Writing is assessed through response to an on-demand writing prompt. Originally, twelfth graders completed both a math and a writing portfolio, but the mathematics portfolio has been removed from the accountability index (Jones and Whitford 1997).

THE KIRIS TWELFTH-GRADE WRITING PORTFOLIO

In the late 1980s, Kentucky educators were already exploring the idea of developing a statewide writing assessment. With the support of the Kentucky Writing Program, many teachers were familiar with direct writing assessment and holistic scoring. A state-level writing assessment advisory committee was developing and piloting tasks. Even though this committee recommended that any move toward portfolio assessment occur in a "slow and methodical fashion," KIRIS developers moved forward "at an incredibly quick pace" (Lewis 1993, 9). Developers intended the writing portfolio to encourage more writing across the curriculum and to promote "process-guided instruction" (Callahan 1997a, 59).

In October 1991, teachers received content requirements for writing portfolios, which were to be completed by April 1992. In March, teachers were trained to score the portfolios, and in April they completed the scoring (Lewis 1993). Callahan (1997a; 1997b) has given an ethnographic account of the intense response of one high school English department during the second year of portfolio implementation. Negative reactions to this unfamiliar form of assessment were widespread, and many teachers perceived as whimsical or punitive the frequent changes in requirements and scoring procedures, as state department personnel worked to refine the system while implementing it.

In 1996–1997, the twelfth-grade writing portfolio consisted of seven items: (1) a table of contents; (2) a letter to the reviewer; (3) a piece of personal expressive writing (e.g., personal narrative, memoir); (4) a piece of imaginative writing (e.g., short story, poem); (5–7) three pieces which accomplish one or more of a variety of purposes (e.g., predict an outcome, solve a problem, defend position).[3] Two pieces must come from content areas other than English (Kentucky Department of Education 1996).

Twelfth-grade writing portfolios must be completed by mid-March. Teachers score their own schools' portfolios. While in most high schools English teachers do the bulk of the scoring, some schools are recruiting teachers from all subject areas to participate in the process. In this way, teachers of subjects other than English come to understand what qualities characterize "proficient" writing and which content-area writing assignments are working and not working for students. Procedural details, such as who scores which portfolios, how many times a portfolio is read, and when and where the scoring occurs, are left up to individual schools, but the state audits the process by re-scoring both random and targeted samples of portfolios.

Portfolios are scored holistically and characterized as "novice" (lowest), "apprentice," "proficient," "distinguished" (highest). In assigning a holistic score, readers consider the following dimensions: (1) purpose/audience; (2) idea development/support: (3) organization; (4) sentences; (5) language; (6) correctness (see Figure 11–1). Schools report scores, which are factored into the school's accountability index, to the state. Twelfth graders must complete the portfolio in order to graduate; a few districts require a minimum score of "apprentice" for graduation.

---

[3] Since then, portfolio content requirements have changed slightly. The pieces formerly referred to as "purpose pieces" are now called "transactive." Students have somewhat more choice as to the number and type of pieces.

KENTUCKY WRITING ASSESSMENT
Holistic Scoring Guide

NOVICE	APPRENTICE	PROFICIENT	DISTINGUISHED
• Limited awareness of audience and/or purpose • Minimal idea development; limited and/or unrelated details • Random and/or weak organization • Incorrect and/or ineffective sentence structure • Incorrect and/or ineffective language • Errors in spelling, punctuation, and capitalization are disproportionate to length and complexity	• Some evidence of communicating with an audience for a specific purpose; some lapses in focus • Unelaborated idea development; unelaborated and/or repetitious details • Lapses in organization and/or coherence • Simplistic and/or awkward sentence structure • Simplistic and/or imprecise language • Some errors in spelling, punctuation, and capitalization that do not interfere with communication	• Focused on a purpose; communicates with an audience; evidence of voice and/or suitable tone • Depth of idea development supported by elaborated, relevant details • Logical, coherent organization • Controlled and varied sentence structure • Acceptable, effective language • Few errors in spelling, punctuation, and capitalization relative to length and complexity	• Establishes a purpose and maintains clear focus; strong awareness of audience; evidence of distinctive voice and/or appropriate tone • Depth and complexity of ideas supported by rich, engaging, and/or pertinent details; evidence of analysis, reflection, insight • Careful and/or subtle organization • Variety in sentence structure and length enhances effect • Precise and/or rich language • Control of spelling, punctuation, and capitalization

INSTRUCTIONAL ANALYSIS

Examining instructional strengths can assist in improving writing and learning in your school. Student portfolios can provide evidence of instructional practices. This section of the Holistic Scoring Guide is provided to assist teachers in identifying sustained evidence of instructional practices through examination of student products. When scoring a student portfolio, scorers may identify <u>any number</u> of the instructional strengths listed below.

The sustained performance in this portfolio demonstrates that the student has applied instruction in the following areas:

- ○ Establishing focused, authentic **Purposes**
- ○ Writing for authentic **Audiences**, situations
- ○ Employing a suitable **Voice and/or Tone**
- ○ Developing **Ideas** relevant to the purpose
- ○ Supporting ideas with elaborated, relevant **Details**
- ○ Organizing ideas logically
- ○ Using effective **Transitions**
- ○ Constructing effective and/or correct **Sentences**
- ○ Using **Language** effectively and/or correctly
- ○ Editing for correctness

COMPLETE/INCOMPLETE PORTFOLIOS

A portfolio is <u>incomplete</u> if any of the following apply:

- • Portfolio does not contain required number of written pieces (6)
- • Portfolio does not contain Table of Contents or Student Signature Sheet
- • Portfolio does not contain number of pieces required or allowed in each category
- • Portfolio does not contain at least one (for grades 4 & 7) or two (for grade 12) piece(s) from a content area other than English/language arts
- • Table of Contents does not contain required information (Title, Category, Study Area, Page Number) for each piece
- • One or more entries are plagiarized (plagiarism must be proven)
- • One or more entries are different from those listed in the Table of Contents
- • One or more entries are written in a language other than English
- • One or more entries demonstrate <u>only</u> computational skills or consist of <u>only</u> diagrams or drawings
- • Portfolio contains a group entry

Revised 9/97   Division of Portfolio Initiatives,
Kentucky Department of Education

SCORING CRITERIA

CRITERIA	OVERVIEW
PURPOSE/ AUDIENCE	The degree to which the writer • establishes and maintains a purpose • communicates with the audience • employs a suitable voice and/or tone
IDEA DEVELOPMENT/ SUPPORT	The degree to which the writer provides thoughtful, detailed support to develop main idea(s)
ORGANIZATION	The degree to which the writer demonstrates • logical order • coherence • transitions/organizational signals
SENTENCES	The degree to which the writer includes sentences that are • varied in structure and length • constructed effectively • complete and correct
LANGUAGE	The degree to which the writer exhibits correct and effective • word choice • usage
CORRECTNESS	The degree to which the writer demonstrates correct • spelling • punctuation • capitalization

FIGURE 11–1

OAK BRIDGE HIGH SCHOOL

Oak Bridge High School serves a predominantly (95 percent) white student population of approximately 1,200 in grades 9 through 12. Although Oak Bridge increasingly attracts suburbanites who commute to nearby cities, the community's economic base is agriculture, horse farming, and light industry. A number of the teachers, like Martin Sterling, live in Oak Bridge and have taught there for over twenty years. While there are occasional serious disruptions to the pleasant, orderly atmosphere, the principal himself jokingly confesses to sometimes napping in his office. When results of the 1996 KIRIS tests were released in December 1997, Oak Bridge High School narrowly missed being ranked among the "top ten."

In August 1996, Oak Bridge High School adopted a block schedule, consisting of four ninety-minute class periods each day. Teachers teach three blocks per day, and students take four courses per semester. Students take English during either the first or second semester (except for senior Advanced Placement English, which extends over the entire year). This means that some twelfth graders compile their portfolios from September through December, while others complete them from January through March.

In January 1997, Oak Bridge began a schoolwide renovation project. No one escaped its consequences. Kate Worth, for example, was teaching in three different classrooms and had trouble keeping track of which files were stashed where. When old ceilings were removed so that new ceilings could be installed, the gaping empty space allowed sound to travel unimpeded from classroom to classroom. The library was closed for most of the second semester and only a few computers were operational. The school was literally being deconstructed and reconstructed over the heads of teachers and students. Nevertheless, portfolio production carried on.

MARTIN STERLING: MASTER GARDENER

Martin Sterling has been teaching English at Oak Bridge High School for twenty-five years. When portfolios were first implemented in the 1991–1992 school year, Martin became the school's coordinator of training and scoring and has held this position ever since. In the spring of 1997, Martin was teaching one class of Advanced Placement English and two classes of "regular" senior English. Tall, athletic-looking, and distinguished by his neatly styled gray hair and wire-rimmed spectacles, Martin is respected for his high standards for "quality writing."

Martin describes English teaching with a metaphor from agriculture.

He compares himself to a "master gardener" who has the skill and experience to cultivate a "quality garden." A master gardener can endure the tedium of weeding, the discomfort of the heat, and the long hours of laboring in the soil because he knows the rewards of the harvest to come. The student, as "helper" to the master gardener, sees only the hard work at hand. It is the job of the master gardener to pass on his expertise and vision of a quality garden to the student. "Quality" is a word Martin uses often, and many of his concerns about KERA and the writing portfolio arise from his commitment to this standard.

In Martin's view, the requirement of a writing portfolio at the twelfth grade is a case of too little too late:

> I think if we required each class—the freshmen, the sophomores, the juniors, and the seniors, of course—to do the portfolios, scored them, gave them feedback . . . that would be big help. The students would understand, the teachers who have all these students would start to understand more about what is required in the portfolio. Then if we can require the students to score an "apprentice" before they graduate, it makes the student accountable, and without that everything else is more or less for naught as far as I'm concerned.

The requirement that two portfolio pieces come from content areas other than English is a shared concern among the senior English teachers at Oak Bridge. Martin said, "Students who are capable should be producing quality pieces in every class . . . in every grade [there should be] twenty to forty top-notch, quality pieces from history, math, chemistry" and other subjects. Slowly, teachers from other departments at Oak Bridge are getting involved in portfolio scoring. In spring 1997, ten teachers from other departments volunteered to be trained to score portfolios, but portfolio production at Oak Bridge is still perceived as primarily the responsibility of the English department. In fact, Martin, fully conscious that his decision will probably cause scores to go down, has finally resolved that he will not help students produce or revise the pieces required from content areas other than English.

Despite these and other concerns about the portfolio, Martin called it "by far the best thing to come out of KERA." Students benefit by getting experience with a variety of genres:

> [T]he student isn't locked into just writing short stories, or just writing poetry . . . but that student also needs to be able to write a good letter . . . a good analytical paper . . . to critique a movie. . . . [Mechanics] can be fixed much easier than purpose, voice, connecting with an audience, using language in a sophisticated way. . . . And some of those in the past were just ignored. In the real world, that stuff counts.

According to Martin, the portfolio allows teachers, not just English teachers, to "get at the core of their subject":

> Without the writing, a teacher can go through a whole course and give fac-
> tual tests, where the students just simply have to regurgitate facts, informa-
> tion, not using it for anything. The portfolio forces the student to think
> critically, analytically, to use information . . . to solve problems. And the
> teacher becomes a part of that.

After six years of working with portfolios, Martin's learning curve has
leveled off: "We haven't had a change in the format of the portfolio,
the requirements, the grading criteria or anything." Because he has always emphasized writing in his classes, he doesn't believe his practice
has changed dramatically because of the KIRIS portfolio:

> I was doing basically [writing] before [the portfolio] came along with my ad-
> vanced classes. . . . I've got examples in my files that the students had writ-
> ten, years ago, long before KERA and the portfolio ever came along. . . . I
> did not do it necessarily with every student I had. . . . If I had a low level
> class, I usually didn't attempt that with those students. . . . [Now] they have
> to analyze, evaluate, critique, explain a process. So I guess it has forced me
> to address those students at the lower end of the scale and try to move them
> into that type of writing. . . . Before with the lower level students, I would
> tend to write letters.

Even though Martin does not perceive much change in his practice, he
seems to be moving toward becoming a jack-of-all-trades himself.

KATE WORTH: ANIMAL TRAINER

Unlike Martin, Kate Worth had no pre-KERA teaching experience.
Four years ago, she was hired to teach senior English at Oak Bridge
High School—her first full-time teaching position. Even with four
years' experience, Kate believes she still has a lot to learn about teaching. She often refers to teaching English as "hard work," comparing her
job to that of an "animal trainer." Here in the Bluegrass, where thor-
oughbred training is a science and trainers are highly skilled professionals, that metaphor is not as odd as it may seem to someone unfamiliar
with horses.

Kate is well aware that teaching seniors, in large part because of the
writing portfolio, is not a coveted position at Oak Bridge. Nevertheless,
she enjoys working with twelfth graders:

> I just remember my senior year in high school being a really good experi-
> ence and I wanted it to be that way for them. . . . I like seeing them gradu-
> ate. . . . That's just one of the best feelings in the world—to see that they've
> made it. . . . And, yeah, they need my class. . . . They're there because they
> have to be, not because they want to be. But at the same time, they have to
> have it, so I feel like I'm giving them something they can use.

Since senior English is not tracked at Oak Bridge, Kate's students span the spectrum of skills, interest, and aspirations: "I have kids that have IEP's on one end and kids who should be in the AP class but maybe they didn't want to put that much effort forth." She estimates that about 70 percent will immediately go on to post-secondary education. About 30 percent will enter the work force or the military. Perhaps because of the diversity of her classes, Kate has a very practical goal for her students: "I want them to be able to communicate clearly, especially in writing."

Practicality characterizes much of what Kate does in the classroom; even her simple pageboy and conservative attire bespeak no nonsense. She tries to show students how reading, writing, and speaking connect to their lives and are valued in the workplace. She teaches her students to write resumes and cover letters and has them research careers. She is frustrated by the fact that British literature is the focus of senior English, "which is pretty difficult for high school seniors and so I try to pick out things that are manageable for them . . . as well as meaningful for them." In her teaching, she integrates "writing, literature, and grammar," assigning writing pieces that go along with the literature but that are also designed to fit the portfolio requirements.

Kate likes to write with her students and to share her writing with them. When teaching the "Letter to the Reviewer," for example, Kate brought in a paper from her undergraduate days in which she described her writing processes. She also distributed to students sample letters from exemplar portfolios, which are provided to teachers by the State Department of Education. On this particular spring day, however, students are reluctant to work on this piece and instead pepper Kate with questions and complaints about procedural issues:

Does the Letter to the Reviewer get scored?
Will we find out how we did?
Does it have to be typed?
Does the whole portfolio have to be in the same font?
Do we have to have a cover page?
As long as we complete it, we can graduate—we don't have to pass it?

Kate answers their questions patiently and matter-of-factly, finally quieting them with a hint, "Okay, guys, it's time to work. This time next week, we might just be havin' a little party."

A post-portfolio party is one of Kate's motivational techniques, and motivation coupled with a lack of student accountability, as she sees it, is the biggest problem with the writing portfolio:

I've got kids here that have been in school for twelve years. Some of them could care less. You know, I'm dealing with some really apathetic students and trying to get them to work is very hard sometimes and they're extremely apathetic about portfolios . . . so then I'm struggling with that, trying to get them to do that when the only thing that comes back to them is maybe the grade in my class. . . . . [T]here's absolutely nothing on the students' part to hold their feet to the fire.

Kate becomes more efficient each year at getting the portfolios completed and scored. In her first year at Oak Bridge, she recalls having two days of released time during which she, Martin, and Emma together scored some two hundred senior portfolios. Now, most of the English department participates in the scoring—but Oak Bridge no longer gives released time for this work. Kate took twenty-five portfolios home to score and brought portfolios about which she was unsure to an after-school scoring resolution meeting. Kate, Martin, and Emma try to avoid scoring their own students' portfolios, but this is almost inevitable in a small school like Oak Bridge.

Portfolio completion and scoring create stress for Kate. She reminds her class, "This is serious stuff for you guys. I'm stressed because I'm worrying about you. I want to see you . . . on May 30 [graduation], having fun." She told me, "I'm worried that a kid's not going to turn one in, and even though it's not my fault, I'm still going to feel bad." During her brief career, Kate has had to deal with two separate cases of portfolio plagiarism—an offense which can prevent a student from graduating. In one case, Kate had to testify before the Board of Education and defend the department's decision: "I worried about that. . . . I know [the student] said evil things about me and evil things were said about me—the fact that she didn't get to go through the graduation ceremony. That hurt me. . . ."

If Kate harbors doubts about the value of the writing portfolio, she didn't express them to me. Perhaps one reason for this is that Kate herself keeps a teaching portfolio, as required by her district. In college, she compiled portfolios to demonstrate her competence in both journalism and in secondary education: "What's amazing is when I came in for this job, I was the first teacher with a portfolio and they were quite impressed, because they hadn't seen that [before]." For Kate, the KIRIS writing portfolio is simply a fact of life.

EMMA GARLAND: PUZZLE SOLVER

Before coming to Oak Bridge six years ago, Emma taught English in Texas for five years. Last year, she was recognized as Oak Bridge High School's "Teacher of the Year"; seniors often mention her name in their portfolio reflective letters. She has been teaching senior English for the past four years and will take over as portfolio coordinator and AP English teacher when Martin retires next year. Emma's son attends Oak Bridge High School and she has two children in elementary school, so she has had the opportunity to observe the impact of KERA as a parent: "My elementary children are both very aware of audience and purpose. . . . and I think that is a direct result of KERA . . . I'm thinking we're going to see better writers [in the future]."

Emma compares teaching English to "working on a puzzle of 500 pieces:"

> You see what the picture can be. You have to constantly look at the box picture . . . and sometimes the pieces that fit the sky are awfully hard to put together because they're all blue. . . . And sometimes you try pieces that don't fit at all, but it's worth the effort to keep fitting the pieces and trying the pieces until they all fit so that you're left with a completed really pretty picture at the end. And I think that's how really *each kid is*. Some kids come to you with 300 pieces instead of 500, and so they're not going to be a completed picture, but you have to do what you can do to get the picture to come out as best you can. . . . Puzzles are hard, but I think a lot of times it can be the English teacher that is able to put the pieces together because so much thinking is involved in our discipline . . . [T]hinking to know someone's heart or soul, I don't think that can come anywhere but in an English class.

Emma's gentle demeanor—with her bobbed hair and petite frame, she looks like a cross between Dorothy Hamill and Mary Lou Retton—is undergirded by iron convictions about the teaching of English. Her goals are "to help the kids be good readers . . . [and] to see that from the reading they can form ideas about what they've read and express those ideas themselves in writing. . . . I see myself as a task master with skills as well . . . The concepts can't come until some of these fundamental skills are mastered." She attributes the fact that an increasing number of students arrive in her classes lacking mastery of "the fundamental building blocks" of reading and writing partly to the times and partly to KERA, which has been "more forgiving of that kind of student."

Having taught English at every level at Oak Bridge, Emma can clearly describe the developmental differences between ninth and twelfth graders. She characterizes "the senior writer" as "able to synthesize ideas . . . to draw his or her own conclusions . . . more sophisticated in expression . . . a more serious writer . . . better able to deal with audience and purpose." Because of her concern about development, Emma questions whether Oak Bridge's move to block scheduling is wise:

> I don't think block is good for writing because writing is like any kind of sport. You have to work at it for so long before you reach your stride, running, or

swimming, or anything . . . And I feel like many of our writers are just now reaching their stride where writing's not so painful. That, "Yes, I can say this better than I really thought I could say it." That, "There's lots of writing techniques that I wasn't aware of." But English is over. And I think that's going to be bad for our portfolios and just for the development of the writer in general.

Like Martin and Kate, Emma is troubled by the lack of a schoolwide effort to contribute to and support the writing portfolios. Recalling her experience in Texas, she wishes Oak Bridge had "an instructional administrator," who could help teachers across the content areas with curricular issues. Emma compares herself and her colleagues to mice in a maze: "We've got teachers who know what the problems are, but we don't have the manpower and at the end of the term we don't have the will power . . . So I just think we're all in a maze. I think . . . we sense issues . . . and we're all heading toward 'Out,' but we're not pooling our efforts."

Emma is clearly someone who senses the issues and has specific ideas for school improvement. For example, she would like to use Extended School Services money (another result of KERA) "for students who've been targeted as being on the line, whether it's the novice/apprentice line, or the apprentice/proficient line, or the proficient/distinguished line. I'd like to use ESS money to target those writers and ask them to come in voluntarily and work with some of us . . . to help get some of those borderline pieces up to snuff." But most of Emma's ideas for improvement are aimed at herself.

Each year, Emma sets personal goals for her teaching. For example, each semester she strives to have her students produce fifteen to twenty pieces: "Anything contrived, anything false, anything unreal to the kid will be less than good. And not all pieces can be real to every kid, that's why you have to do many pieces . . . At the end of the semester, they can look through those . . . and think, 'Okay, these were eight really good ones.'" In addition, after assessing where students are in their writing at the beginning of a semester, she sets goals for their portfolios:

My goal is usually pretty high, and I had set a goal for myself of five novices this year. I was disappointed we had nine. . . . Of those nine, two were novice writers. There wasn't going to be any way they could be beyond novice without more than teacher conferencing on my part. Now, if I wanted to be dishonest and less than true, I could have no novice writers. So seven of the kids fell down for various reasons . . . but could have been apprentice.

Like Martin and Kate, Emma blames lack of student accountability for most poor scores: "The majority of our students could be apprentice writers . . . and I think if we placed the accountability of the writing portfolio on the students themselves, instead of on the school, then I think we'd have a greater number of apprentice portfolios."

Emma sums up the role of the portfolio in her teaching: "It drives the curriculum." Over her years of working with the portfolio, Emma has changed her approach to both the portfolio and to assigning and assessing writing. Early on, she realized she had to "give [the portfolio] credence if the kids were going to do good work." She carefully lays the groundwork at the beginning of the semester by likening the writing portfolio to the senior picture portfolio:

> I say, "Your portfolio as a senior is much more interesting to a viewer if I can
> see you in jeans, or in skirts, or in a dress, or in a robe, because those are all
> sides of you. Your writing portfolio is the same." . . . You know you've made
> a hit when a kid comes up and says, "Now I know I need a piece that kind of
> livens it up because I'm too boring, you know. This piece from earth science
> is pretty boring, because it's about, you know, water."

Every writing assignment Emma makes can potentially become a portfolio piece, and she has changed the nature of her assignments. In pre-KERA days, she had students write an analysis of conditions of Packingtown after reading *The Jungle*. Now, they write letters to the editor expressing discontent with Packingtown conditions, proposing a solution and a method of implementation. In the past, students wrote analytical papers after reading *Of Mice and Men*. Now, they research resources for migrant workers in the community and write a speech to the city council for or against providing services for Mexican agricultural workers. Emma formerly required another analytical response to *Cry the Beloved Country*. This year, a student suggested choosing characters from the novel and writing dramatic monologues for them. In addition, Emma now allows any student to rewrite a paper "as often as he or she wants to until he or she is satisfied with the grade." As to assessment, Emma said, "I don't ever assign a piece that will work in the portfolio that I do not assess. . . . And every piece includes a rubric. . . . [S]ometimes my categories are "not yet," "getting there," and "there" rather than an ABC grade."

Letting the writing portfolio "drive the curriculum," however, has its down sides. This year, in order to focus on producing and polishing portfolio pieces, Emma abandoned the lengthy research project she has traditionally required of her seniors. But ever the problem solver, Emma said, "My biggest dilemma this summer will be, 'How can I bring back the research without diluting the importance and quality of the writing portfolio?'" More serious is her concern that:

> English may dissolve into strictly a composition course and you might pick
> up a piece of literature on the side. It just seems like—for those of us who

truly love literature—that this is what has changed. You know that piece that we could just die for—A *Tale of Two Cities*—I live and breathe that. Well, get real! Get real! I can teach "sacrifice" in a short story. So if I can teach sacrifice in a short story, then I'll teach it in a short story . . . but I've had to give up the words of Dickens to do it. And that's a hard pill to swallow for some people. . . . I had to ask myself, "Who's benefiting from this [e.g., reading Dickens]—myself or the kids?"

After four years of working with the portfolio, Emma has developed a sort of wish list for it. First, she'd like to see what she called a "personal piece": "a piece that showed the writer, 'This was the moment when I arrived' . . . you know, kind of a cathartic moment. . . . Many kids can tell you what piece it was in which they reached their stride." Then, she'd require a reflection upon this piece "separate from the letter to the reviewer." Third, she'd require "a piece that reflects . . . progress" together with "a reaction from the writer": "No one has taken into account [that] a writer can make progress and still be on that same step, but we don't reward that writer." In other words, the portfolio system does not reward the student whose writing progresses from "low apprentice" to "high apprentice."

Emma increasingly incorporates reflection on writing into her teaching:

For instance, the dramatic monologue, I said—now react to that piece, reflect, tell me what I need to be looking for when I read this dramatic monologue. . . . Then they said, "I really want you to notice, between lines two and four, that I have a shift in the character, because this word right here is showing how his feelings are changing."

While, in Emma's view, many "sticky wickets" remain in the implementation of KERA and the writing portfolio, her outlook remains positive: "I just think we get better every year."

WHAT CAN WE LEARN FROM THE STORIES OF MARTIN, KATE, AND EMMA?

Martin, Kate, and Emma identified many of the issues that make Kentucky's writing portfolio so controversial—stress on teachers, unethical practices by students (and teachers), lack of student motivation, the reluctance of subject departments other than English to contribute to the portfolio, the effect of block scheduling on equitable writing opportunites, the danger that twelfth-grade English may metamorphose into a "composition course."

Too often, debates about the merits and limitations of educational reforms swirl about in a level of the stratosphere far removed from the daily lives of teachers and students. My work with Martin, Kate, and Emma showed me that there is not one, monolithic KIRIS portfolio which has been imposed upon the teachers and students of Kentucky. Rather, each of these teachers viewed the portfolio from his or her perspective as an English teacher. Martin, the most experienced and perhaps the most traditional of the three, might ask, "How does this portfolio fit with my personal definition of quality writing?" Practical Kate, who had no pre-KERA teaching experience to recall, might ask, "What's the most efficient way to get these portfolios done?" And Emma, the reflective, problem solver, might ask: "How can I best use this portfolio to help my students find their voices as writers?" They have shaped their instructional and assessment practices around these questions: Martin now goes beyond "letter writing" with his "low-level" students; Kate, perhaps emulating Emma, allows rewrites on all assignments; Emma spends her summers figuring out how to help her writers move from the "novice" to the "apprentice" level.

The mandated writing portfolio has not caused a swift and final revolution of writing instruction in Kentucky, as some may have hoped. The cases of Martin, Kate, and Emma show that change occurs over time and in small increments: three social studies teachers volunteering to score portfolios one year and a math and a science teacher coming on board the next; moving from teacher-centered writing assignments to opening up to students' suggestions; having students reflect regularly on writing rather than hastily crank out a "portfolio roll call" in the form of the letter to the reviewer. Given the fact that most of these changes originate with individual teachers and classrooms, since much of professional development offered by the state concerns scoring and procedural issues, these shifts in practice are even more remarkable. None of these teachers has yet developed what Yancey (1992) calls a "portfolio pedagogy," but Emma, for one, seems to be moving in that direction.

As Emma put it, teachers "sense" the issues, but often lack the "manpower" or the "willpower" to address them collectively. Martin, Kate, and Emma concurred on the two greatest barriers to their ability to implement the portfolio as effectively as they could: lack of student accountability; and lack of schoolwide support for the portfolio. Most experienced teachers know the herculean efforts required to keep high school seniors academically engaged when spring rolls around. But possibly only Kentucky teachers know what it's like to accomplish this when their own—not the students'—reputations, and even jobs, are on the line. These three teachers were unanimous in their practical solution: hold students accountable.

Martin is retiring; but I wonder how long Kate, Emma, and others like them will have the willpower to press on in the face of student apathy. Likewise, Martin's suggestion for "continuous assessment" by portfolio makes sense. In the ideal world, the elementary portfolio would follow the student to middle school, the middle school portfolio would be passed on to the high school, and the high school portfolio would have some value to colleges or employers. Each year students would compile and receive feedback on their cumulative portfolios.

In reality, many twelfth graders still arrive for senior English with empty folders, chagrined to discover that they will be expected to write rather than coast. The "content" pieces are especially problematic. Even after six years, writing across the curriculum—at least writing that passes portfolio muster—has not taken root at Oak Bridge. When I try to "walk a mile" in others' shoes, I imagine my former English teacher self being told that I would have to infuse mathematics in my curriculum—and not just simple computations, but sophisticated, polished solutions to complex problems! How eager would I be to embark on this strange course? While Martin's, Kate's, and Emma's frustration is understandable and may build a certain sense of solidarity *within* the English department, it hardly enhances collegial relations with other departments. Unless the state takes seriously the practical knowledge and dilemmas of teachers, it may sabotage its own reform effort.

Clearly, there are many valid criticisms of the KIRIS portfolio, but I think the cases of Martin, Kate, and Emma show that good things *can* happen when instruction, assessment, and accountability converge on a worthy goal: improving writing instruction for all students. My experience with the teachers at Oak Bridge suggests that they, as Emma said, *will* get better every year—if they receive the support, resources, and professional development they need.

The flaws these teachers identified are serious and not to be ignored; yet, I keep coming back to a day I sat in Martin's classroom perusing some finished portfolios. He handed me the portfolio of a twelfth grader who had spent most of her academic career in special education classrooms. In the letter to the reviewer she noted that this was the first time she had done any writing in high school and that she was proud of her portfolio. As I read her short but moving narrative on the death of a pet, I was proud of her too. Her portfolio affirms KERA's principle that, given the opportunity, all students can learn. Without the state's directive, would Martin have decided on his own to extend opportunities for "quality writing" to *all* his students? Would Kate dredge up pieces from her own college portfolio to share with her students? Would Emma be puzzling over ways to encourage students to be more reflective about their writing? Would kings, queens, and aces choose to become jacks-of-all-trades? Perhaps. Perhaps not.

We need to study the effects of educational reform in many contexts (e.g., classrooms, departments, schools, districts, communities) and from the perspectives of many stakeholders (e.g., teachers, students, administrators, parents). Each pass with a different lens gives us another "piece of the puzzle." Emma's metaphor for teaching English might apply to educational reform in Kentucky as well: "You see what the picture can be. . . . And sometimes you try pieces that don't fit at all, but it's worth the effort to keep fitting the pieces and trying the pieces until they all fit so that you're left with a completed, really pretty picture at the end."

REFERENCES

Bishop, B. 1998. "Equality Was Heart of Reform." *Lexington Herald-Leader*, February 15 F1, F3.

Callahan, S. 1995. "Portfolio Expectations: Possibilities and Limits." *Assessing Writing*, 2 (2): 117–151.

———. 1997a. "Kentucky's State-mandated Writing Portfolios and Teacher Accountability." In Kathleen. B. Yancey and Irwin Weiser, eds., *Situating Portfolios: Four Perspectives*. Logan, UT: Utah State University Press.

———. 1997b. "Tests Worth Taking? Using Portfolios for Accountability in Kentucky." *Research in the Teaching of English*, 31(3): 295–336.

Guskey, T. R. 1994. "Introduction." In T. R. Guskey, ed., *High Stakes Performance Assessment: Perspectives on Kentucky's Educational Reform*. Thousand Oaks, CA: Corwin Press.

Holland, H. 1997. "KERA: A Tale of One Teacher." *Phi Delta Kappan*, 79(4): 264–271.

Huot, B., and M. W. Williamson. 1997. "Rethinking Portfolios for Evaluating Writing: Issues of Assessment and Power." In Kathleen B. Yancey and Irwin Weiser, eds., *Situating Portfolios: Four Perspectives*. Logan, UT: Utah State University Press.

Jones, K., and B. L. Whitford, (1997). "Kentucky's Conflicting Reform Principles: High-stakes School Accountability and Student Performance Assessment." *Phi Delta Kappan*, 79(4): 276–281.

Kentucky Department of Education. 1996. *Kentucky Writing Portfolio Grade 12 Teacher's Handbook*, 2d edition. Frankfort, KY: Author.

Kifer, E. 1994. "Development of the Kentucky Instructional Results Information System (KIRIS)." In T. R. Guskey, ed., *High Stakes Performance Assessment: Perspectives on Kentucky's Educational Reform*. Thousand Oaks, CA: Corwin Press.

Lewis, S. 1993. "KY Writing Portfolios: A History." *Kentucky English Bulletin* 43(1), 9–11.

Prichard Committee for Academic Excellence. 1995. *Keepin' On: Five Years Down the Road to Better Schools*. Lexington, KY: Author.

Resnick, L., and D. Resnick. 1992. "Assessing the Thinking Curriculum: New Tools for Educational Reform." In B. R. Gifford and M. C. O'Connor, eds., *Changing Assessments: Alternative Views of Aptitude*. Boston, MA: Kluwer.

Trimble, C. S. 1994. "Ensuring Educational Accountability." In T. R. Guskey, ed., *High Stakes Performance Assessment: Perspectives on Kentucky's Educational Reform*. Thousand Oaks, CA: Corwin Press.

Wiggins, G. 1992. "Creating Tests Worth Taking." *Educational Leadership*, 49(8): 26–33.

Wile, J. M., and R. J. Tierney. 1996. "Tensions in Assessment: The Battle over Portfolios, Curriculum, and Control." In R. C. Calfee and P. Perfumo, eds., *Writing Portfolios in the Classroom: Policy and Practice, Promise and Peril*. Mahwah, NJ: Lawrence Erlbaum.

Wolf, D. P., P. G. LeMahieu, and J. Eresh. 1992. "Good Measure: Assessment as a Tool for Educational Reform." *Educational Leadership*, 49(8): 8–13.

Yancey, K. B. 1992. "Teachers' Stories: Notes Toward a Portfolio Pedagogy." In Kathleen B. Yancey, ed., *Portfolios in the Writing Classroom*. Urbana, IL: National Council of Teachers of English.

12

IDENTITY AND RELIABILITY IN PORTFOLIO ASSESSMENT

JAMES D. WILLIAMS

Since the mid-1980s, portfolio assessment has become a widespread means of evaluating writing. Peter Elbow and Pat Belanoff (1997), for example, characterized portfolio assessment as an "explosion" that "has gained steady strength" (21–33). This explosion is readily seen in colleges and universities that have adopted portfolio assessment for their writing programs, as well as in states such as Vermont and Kentucky, where portfolio assessment has become an integrated part of public education in K–12.

Like other popular movements in composition studies, such as sentence combining, writing workshops, and holistic scoring, portfolio assessment evokes a range of issues associated with implementation, pedagogy, and outcomes. Some of these issues are theoretical—others are political—and it seems that a decreasing number are pedagogical for many teacher-scholars. For example, Elbow and Belanoff argued for portfolio assessment because they saw it as a means of subverting more traditional methods of evaluating writing, including holistic scoring, which they claimed is "inherently untrustworthy" because it calls for "only one piece of writing" (25). Likewise, Brian Huot and Michael Williamson (1997) and Pamela Moss (1194) argued that validity and reliability are undesirable factors in evaluation and claimed that portfolio assessment offers a viable alternative because it resists standardization. In this vein, Sandra Murphy (1997) claimed that "highly standardized portfolios may restrict opportunities for teachers and students to demonstrate individual initiative and ingenuity" (72–88). According to Huot and Williamson

(1997), standardization is undesirable not only because it homogenizes heterogeneous classrooms but also because it proposes that "the ability to write is a universal, identifiable human trait that can be measured accurately and consistently" (46). Huot and Williamson, following Wiggins, recognized that *standardization* is not the same thing as *standards* (Wiggins 1993, 47), but they ignored the fact that standardization is a necessary factor in establishing standards because it allows for the comparisons that underlie all standards. Rejecting standardization, therefore, commonly results in a failure of standards, which Williams (1998) described as the "postmodern position" vis-a-vis assessment: "When students cannot reach the pre-established standard, the problem does not lie in the students or the instruction they receive; it lies in the standard" (265).

Without standards for implementation and outcomes, students are likely to suffer as assessment becomes whimsical, capricious, or influenced by factors unrelated to the quality of the writing. In fact, portfolio assessment, as well as holistic scoring—upon which portfolio assessment methodology is based—was developed as a means of reducing the subjectivity associated with evaluating writing, and it can meet that goal convincingly, provided that administrators follow standard protocols (see White 1986; 1993; 1994). However, conflicting perspectives on the goals of assessment and the role of standards and standardization make it highly predictable that there will be little consensus among teachers on how to implement and use portfolio assessment, even after they have been trained in standard procedures. Lack of standardization is likely to be unfair because it increases the subjectivity teachers bring to evaluation. In such an event, students find that their writing is judged on the basis of a given teacher's personal preferences and idiosyncrasies rather than on the quality of the writing.

With these factors as guides, the study reported in this chapter was conducted to examine how a group of public school teachers implement portfolio assessment. One goal was to assess the effectiveness of implementation. Equally important, however, was the goal of comparing teachers' assessments against an external evaluation of portfolios. The final goal was to determine what role, if any, demographic variables play in teachers' assessments of student portfolios. An initial hypothesis was that few teachers would implement portfolio assessment effectively. An additional hypothesis was that, of the demographic factors studied, ethnicity and IQ would most influence assessment outcomes.

PROCEDURES

One hundred teachers from public schools in the South and the Midwest volunteered to participate in the study. All the teachers were at schools where portfolio assessment had been adopted in language arts classes, and all had been formally trained by their districts on how to implement and conduct portfolio assessment. In all cases, teachers were in their second or third year of implementation. From the initial group of 100, 50 teachers in grades 5–12 were selected at random to participate in the study. The total number of students was 1,824; they were divided into two groups by grade level. The first group was in grades 5–8, whereas the second was in grades 9–12. This grouping was predicated on the perception that student writing clusters along these divisions with respect to topic, maturity, length, and genre.

Data were collected throughout an entire semester. Demographic data for students and their families were collected from school records; additional information was collected via questionnaires that teachers and parents completed. The student data included age, IQ, parents' educational background, socioeconomic status (SES), gender, and ethnicity; the teacher data included age, length of teaching experience, level of educational training, and ethnicity.

The teachers were interviewed for the study and were told that for the purposes of the investigation all writing assignments had to be written rather than oral. In addition, the teachers agreed to allow research assistants to observe each portfolio assessment at the participating school. The research assistants were trained in portfolio assessment and in observing and making a log of their observations. After each assessment, the teachers gave the student portfolios to the research assistants, who made photocopies for later analysis; the portfolios then were returned to the individual teachers. There was a total of 128 individual observations, or an average of 2.6 portfolio assessments per teacher during the semester of the study. A second interview with 30 participating teachers was conducted after the data were analyzed. Participating principals were also interviewed at this time.

When students submitted their portfolios for assessment, each student received a general rubric (with a 6-point scale) that was developed for this study. Research assistants explained how to use the rubric, and then students recorded (on a 3×5 card) what they believed was an appropriate grade (on a 6-point scale) for the papers in that submission. These student scores were collected by the observers for later evaluation.

External evaluation of the portfolios was conducted by evaluators who had received training in both holistic scoring and portfolio assessment. Training also included a discussion of how demographic factors, such as ethnicity and gender, had the potential to influence evaluation. These evaluators were college composition instructors, some of whom had teaching experience in the public schools. The external evaluators were divided into two groups by grade level, with one group assigned to evaluate students in grades 5–8 and the other assigned to evaluate students in grades 9–12.

Training followed standard procedures. Prior to each scoring session, the evaluators were socialized to a rubric to ensure reliability. Each portfolio was read twice, with the first score being masked during the second reading. Scores were checked periodically to assess accuracy.

Budget and time constraints precluded external evaluation of all portfolios, so assistants selected students at random (but grouped by teacher) and photocopied their portfolios before they were assessed. Each portfolio contained student submissions and the corresponding writing assignments; in some cases, they also contained rubrics that the teacher had developed for a given assignment. The external evaluators examined two portfolio submissions per student, and the total number of portfolios assessed was 600, or 300 from each group.

The external evaluation was conducted in two stages. The first followed standard protocols with readers using an age-appropriate general rubric (with a 6-point scale) developed for this study. Whenever a teacher's rubric was part of the submission, features from that rubric were incorporated into the general rubric. This stage was intended to assess the overall quality of each portfolio.

The second stage also followed standard protocols, but the readers assessed the portfolios using a primary-trait rubric that identified 10 demographic variables, shown in Table 12–1 below. During a pilot study, these variables had correlated significantly with a representative demographic database. The primary-trait rubric provided a Lichert scale for each variable, with 5 being high and 1 being low. This assessment was intended to determine to what degree student portfolios reflected identifiable demographic features related to ethnicity, gender, and SES. Black English Vernacular (BEV) verb forms, for example, could range from "none" (1) to "numerous" (5). Thus, primary-trait scores could range from a low of 10 to a high of 50; these scores were subsequently averaged for each portfolio, resulting in a demographic score.

The data from the questionnaires were tabulated, and each observation log was read and matched against standard protocols for assessment. Each portfolio had four sets of scores. The first three sets were defined by group: teacher scores, students scores, external scores. In addition, each portfolio had a demographic score based on primary-trait assessment; these scores ranged from 1–5. The demographic score was calculated as the mean of the primary-trait scores. Because a large number of the participating teachers did not use numeric scores when grading the portfolios, letter grades were converted to numeric scores ranging from 1 to 6. The raw data then were analyzed using SAS. Tables 12–2 and 12–3 below show the aggregate demographic data.

TABLE 12–1   Demographic variables

Variable	Description	Measuring
Handwriting	Palmer method	Gender
Topic	What the paper was about	Gender, ethnicity, SES
BEV verb forms	*Be* as aspect maker, etc.	Ethnicity
Omitted suffix on present-tense verbs	E.g., "He talk pretty fast."	Ethnicity
Been as a past-perfect marker	E.g., "They been told us to leave."	Ethnicity
Double negatives	E.g., "He ain't never goin' to stop."	Ethnicity
By strings	A *by* prepositional phrase functioning as a nominal cluster in the subject position: e.g., "By many children being sent to school where there aren't enough books. The children face a major difficulty."	Ethnicity
Possessive designated by prepositional phrase	E.g., "This is the book of my brother."	Ethnicity
Topicalization	E.g., "The party at Buggsy's, it got way out of control."	Ethnicity
Reference	Specific reference to idease, events, or places	Gender, ethinicity, SES

RESULTS

Evaluation of the observation logs showed that 42 of the 50 teachers failed to follow standard protocols when conducting portfolio assessment. For example, these teachers did not team with other instructors for grading but rather graded their students' papers themselves. They generally did not develop rubrics for each assignment, nor did they individually read portfolios holistically; instead, their grading can best be described as the application of traditional assessment techniques to papers submitted in a folder. That is, these 42 teachers tended to read and edit each paper, making copious corrections for spelling, punctuation, word choice, sentence structure, and so forth. They also provided terminal comments of one kind or another that justified the grade. All of these teachers used letter grades rather than numeric scores for assessment; they then averaged the individual grades on student papers to arrive at a portfolio grade.

TABLE 12–2   Aggragate demographic data for students

Total students:	1824
Number in grades 5–8:	892
Number in grades 9–12:	932
Gender:	52% female; 48% male
Ethnicity:	46% white; 20% black; 22% Hispanic; 11% Asian*
Parents' education:	31% with BA or BS
	12% with MA or MS
	4% with Ph.D., M.D. or other terminal degree
SES (annual household income):	<$25,000 (12%)
	$26,000–$50,000 (31%)
	$51,000–$75,000 (11%)
	$76,000–$100,000 (37%)
	>$100,000 (9%)

*1% of the students were classified as "other."

TABLE 12–3   Aggragate demographic data for teachers

Total teachers:	50
Number in grades 5–8:	25
Number in grades 9–12:	25
Average age:	41.5
Average length of experience:	10.3
Gender:	89% female; 11% male
Ethnicity:	64% white; 32% black; 4% Hispanic
Degrees:	26% held a master's degree; 80% of the secondary teachers held a degree in English
Number with formal training in portfolio assessment:	100%
Average class size:	36.5

The high number of teachers who did not follow standard protocols motivated separate follow-up interviews with school principals and 30 of the 50 teachers to obtain information that would shed light on their reasons for using portfolio assessment. The principals' responses fell into two major categories. Those principals who did not appear to be well informed about portfolio assessment indicated that their goal was to follow district guidelines. Principals who were better informed about assessment indicated that their goal was to implement a more effective assessment technique. These responses, however, showed no correlation with teacher responses.

The teachers uniformly stated that they did not follow standard protocols because they did not believe such protocols were important in assessing writing, even though they all had been trained in portfolio assessment prior to using the approach in their teaching. When questioned about the need for reliability, the teachers stated that reliability was not an important factor in the assessment of public school children. Moreover, many stated that they were sufficiently qualified to recognize good writing and that the training they had received in portfolio assessment was unrelated to this ability. Sixty-three percent of the teachers stated that they felt that standard portfolio assessment was unfair because it rank-ordered students on the basis of ability and gave teachers too little freedom to use grades as motivators and tools for building self-esteem. Approximately 76 percent of the teachers stated that they did not believe grades should be used exclusively as a measure of achievement, and of this group, 97 percent stated that they believed that the most important use of grades was to enhance students' self-esteem.

At this point, it seemed reasonable to ask the teachers about their reasons for using portfolio assessment. They identified several factors, but five were cited most frequently, irrespective of grade level; these factors are ranked below by frequency:

1. Desire to reduce time spent on grading
2. Administrative pressure or requirement to implement portfolios
3. Desire to empower students
4. The influence of a journal article or a former teacher
5. Desire to try something new

When the interviewers pointed out that portfolio assessment reduced the time spent on grading papers only when it was conducted properly, the teachers disagreed, claiming that it saved them time because it reduced the number of papers that they read compared to the traditional approach. Having learned during their training that portfolios typically have three or four papers for each submission, the teachers had reduced the number of writing assignments to three or four. Thus, instead of having students submit what they thought was their best work, teachers uniformly had students submit all of their work. When the interviewers suggested that reducing writing activities missed the point of portfolio assessment completely, a majority of teachers disagreed, arguing that portfolios were intended to help them better organize writing and writing evaluation, which it did.

Analysis of variance indicated that the portfolio scores varied significantly by scorer group for all grade levels. (Significance was set at .001 for all analyses.) Overall, teacher evaluations differed from external evaluations by almost 2 points. Student evaluations were significantly closer to the external evaluations and differed from teacher evaluations by more than a point. (Interrater reliability for the external evaluators was .87, using Cronbach's alpha.)

In addition, demographic scores correlated positively with the tabulated demographic data obtained by questionnaire. A separate analysis of variance, as well as regression analysis, was used to examine holistic scores and demographic scores. The results showed several differences across all grade levels. First, there was a significant difference between teacher scores and external scores; this difference increased as the demographic score increased. Second, there were individual differences for each teacher. That is, portfolio scores decreased as demographic scores increased. Differences for each external evaluator, on the other hand, were measurable but not significant. Overall, teachers rated portfolios with high demographic scores almost 2 points lower than papers with low demographic scores.

Factor analysis indicated that the greatest differences occurred among papers oriented strongly toward the following rank-ordered clusters:

1. SES
2. Ethnicity
3. Gender
4. IQ

High SES correlated positively with high portfolio scores from the teachers, whereas low SES correlated positively with low scores. Ethnicity, however, was inversely related to portfolio scores: High ethnicity correlated positively with low scores, whereas low ethnicity correlated positively with high scores. The most significant loadings were for BEV verb forms and omitted suffixes on present-tense verbs for African American students and double negatives and topicalization for Hispanic students. Handwriting, an indicator of gender, loaded high for girls but low for boys—that is, handwriting characterized by smooth, flowing cursive (Palmer method) with large loops and swirls was strongly associated with higher portfolio scores among teachers.

When the influence of the demographic variables was factored out of portfolio scores, the assessments converged significantly, with the notable exception of IQ. In other words, the writing abilities of those with high demographic scores and those with low demographic scores moved toward equality (although they never reached it) when the demographic factors were removed from the assessment.

The findings with respect to IQ were interesting for a couple of reasons. Within the range of 100 to 115, IQ did not exert a significant influence on portfolio scores. Outside that range, however, IQ was significant for both teacher and external evaluations. Analysis of variance indicated that the biggest differences were for those students with IQs below 100. Their portfolio scores were well below those of students with IQs of 110 and higher, regardless of all other factors. That is, IQ was controlling even when other demographic factors were positive. Closer examination of the writing in this group showed two characteristics that appeared to offset positive demographic variables: a very high number of errors in sentence structure, word choice, and punctuation, as well as an absence of content. Between the range of 115 to 125, IQ scores exerted a significant influence on portfolio scores, but above 125 this influence was measurable but not significant. In fact, the influence of IQ on portfolio scores was the same for students with IQs of 135 (95th percentile) and 150 (99th percentile).

Because parents' education background correlated highly with SES and IQ, it was not surprising to find that this variable also correlated with portfolio scores. However, the influence of educational background was not particularly robust.

CONCLUSION

Given the way in which participating teachers mixed elements of portfolio and traditional assessment, it was unlikely that teacher evaluations of their students' writing would match the independent evaluations. Two different procedures were at work, so it did not come as a surprise that teacher scores and external scores differed by almost two points on the 6-point scale. Such a difference frequently separated a passing paper from a failing one. In addition, the finding that the student evaluations of their own writing were closer to the evaluations of the external readers clearly merits additional research.

The difference in scores between the teachers and the external evaluators, however, cannot be explained entirely on the basis of procedural differences. Although the results reported here are largely correlational, factor analysis suggests a level of causality that is hard to ignore. It clearly appears that demographic factors had a significant negative effect on teacher assessment. Analysis showed that this effect occurred among all teachers in the study; it was not limited to white teachers unconsciously responding to racist or sexist impulses. Indeed, demographic factors for SES and ethnicity influenced black teachers more than it did for any other group. The black teachers, for example, showed much less tolerance for BEV than did their white counterparts.

The influence of SES on portfolio assessment was of particular interest for two reasons. First, one of the initial hypotheses was that, if demographic factors exerted any effect whatsoever on assessment, ethnicity would dominate owing to school-grammar notions of correctness and the prevalence of BEV among student subjects. Second, when the influence of SES was examined in light of the demographic data, it suggested a disturbing trend. The income data were largely bipolar: A large percentage of students came from households with low incomes, and a large percentage came from households with high incomes. Missing were those in the middle. Only 11 percent of students came from households with incomes between $51,000 and $75,000. This finding is congruent with Census Bureau data showing a significant decline in the middle class, data that have led various social commentators to suggest that we are moving toward a two-tiered society. The question to be asked, however, is why teachers, whose average salary was $45,000, would penalize students whose writing reflected a low SES background.

Although this finding is congruent with research conducted many years ago by Loban (1976), it may have broader implications. The participating teachers, as mirrors of our increasingly two-tiered society, may have been so uncomfortable with socioeconomic limitations that they unconsciously discriminated against those students from families of modest means. If there is growing intolerance nationwide for those who are not on the socioeconomic fast track, we should expect to see its influence in our schools. In this study, it was clear that those students from privileged homes were rewarded not only for their ability to write but for how much their writing reflected the success and values of their parents.

A related issue appears to be students' right to their own language, which has been debated for about three decades now. The findings in this study suggest that there is little tolerance for dialects in our classrooms, calls from various education groups for greater tolerance notwithstanding. The participating teachers consistently gave lower grades to students who used nonstandard dialects in their writing. This result was expected, but it is worth noting that, as far as could be determined from examining course outlines and lesson plans, few of the teachers in the study provided explicit instruction to help students master formal standard written English. Moreover, the interviews with teachers and the review of their lesson plans and assignments indicated that their language—both spoken and written—deviates measurably from formal Standard English.[1] Students therefore were in a difficult

---

[1] It must be noted that neither the interview nor the writing samples were occasions for informal, conversational language.

situation. Their teachers expected students to use formal standard English *even though it was modeled neither at home nor in the classroom.*

Equally disturbing was the clear gender bias against boys in virtually every class. It has long been recognized that boys generally are at a disadvantage when it comes to cursive writing because their lack of fine-motor skills makes the task inherently harder for them than it does for girls, whose fine-motor skills are usually superior. Even so, the shift from printing to cursive is nearly universal in the third grade. It seems increasingly reasonable to challenge the value of cursive instruction, considering that cursive script does not exist anywhere outside the classroom, with the obvious exception of signatures. All texts are printed, and the wide availability of computers means that students now have the ability to print their papers. Personal letter writing, which in theory might provide an occasion for cursive, has all but disappeared, having been replaced by the telephone, the fax machine, and email. Nevertheless, large numbers of language arts teachers resist this technology in their classes. Among the teachers in this study, 73 percent stated that they prohibited submission of writing assignments done on computer.

The findings in this study offer yet another reason to abandon cursive writing. The boys consistently were penalized for their difficulties with script. When this variable was factored out of the analysis, the gap between teacher scores and external scores narrowed significantly. The negative influence of this demographic variable meant that the boys were not being assessed on their writing ability but on something over which they had little or no control. Allowing (and encouraging) students to use computers for the majority of their work would have alleviated the existing bias.

Given the high number of participating teachers who did not follow standard protocols, it is tempting to generalize, but certainly these findings may not be representative. Many schools have implemented portfolio assessment effectively, providing regular monitoring to ensure that standard protocols are in place and followed closely. Nevertheless, the findings do suggest that many of our teachers may not understand or invest in portfolio assessment even after they are trained to use it. Particularly troubling is the fact that a majority of the teachers in this study rejected the need to adhere to standard protocols. There is no way of knowing how many teachers nationwide would do the same when dealing with portfolio assessment, but this study indicates that the number may be high. Certainly, proper monitoring procedures may have enhanced implementation in the subject schools, but it seems unlikely that external control would bring the teachers to accept the validity of the premises that underlie the protocols. Thus, rejecting the idea of adhering to standard protocols suggests that any slackening of external monitoring and control may have disastrous consequences for assessment fairly quickly because the teachers would be inclined to deviate from the established protocols whenever they saw fit.

Although effective monitoring and leadership generally have a positive influence on the outcome of portfolio assessment, there were two obstacles that made such monitoring and leadership problematic for the teachers in this study. Follow-up interviews with school principals revealed that most knew very little about portfolio assessment or the inservice workshops that their teachers had attended. Many expressed a condescending attitude toward what they characterized as a "fad" that was getting in the way of "real teaching." In such an environment, the teachers' inclination to deviate from established protocols was implicitly endorsed by leaders who had no commitment to the new assessment program.

One of the arguments for portfolio assessment is that it empowers teachers, allowing them to move away from standardized tests.[2] Although there is merit in this argument, the teachers in this study found it misleading, for they interpreted "empowerment" as meaning that they could exercise their own judgment regarding how to implement portfolio assessment. The teachers assumed that they could recognize good writing when they saw it, and the empowerment message associated with portfolios led them to conclude, incorrectly, that their own expertise justified abandoning standard protocols.

Part of the teachers' rationale for ignoring their training was the widely held perception that standard assessment procedures are unfair because they rank order students. Portfolio assessment indeed identifies outstanding papers and ranks other papers against them. Thus, rank ordering can work to the disadvantage of students with lower abilities, especially in heterogeneous classes such as those in the study, because such students must compete with those who have greater ability. For example, IQ scores among the students in this study ranged from a high of 150 to a low of 70, with students mixed indiscriminately in all classes. Grades and teacher reports showed, as would be expected, that students with low IQs could not perform at the same level as students with high IQs. Nevertheless, the assignments and, to a certain degree, teacher criteria for what constituted success on the assignments did not take into account the significant differential in performance associated with wide gaps in intelligence. However, during their interviews, when asked what factors assessment should be based on if not rank ordering,

---

[2]None of the schools in this study, however, used standardized tests to measure students' writing skills. Standardized tests were used at the district level to collect aggregate data.

the participating teachers' most frequent response—"effort"—failed to provide an acceptable standard since, on the basis of effort, bright, capable students would receive lower grades than slow ones because they generally expend less effort on tasks. The other two most frequent responses—"motivation" and "self-esteem"—seemed to be based on poorly understood concepts from motivation theory and increasingly indefensible notions of social promotion and "feel-good" pedagogy.

Overall, the results of this study suggest that writing teachers and administrators need to be very careful when implementing portfolio assessment. During the past decade, we have witnessed the transformation of "process" from a pedagogical tool to a political position. A similar transformation appears to be occurring with respect to portfolio assessment, and it threatens any benefits that might accrue to teachers and students by confusing the issues. Portfolio assessment was developed with the goal of making the evaluation of classroom writing more objective, more fair, and more realistic. Yet this goal is seldom articulated in current discussions of portfolio assessment. Perhaps if the teachers in this study had been trained with this goal in mind, they would have been less confused about the need to follow standard protocols.

This study suggests that any efforts to make assessment more subjective are likely to penalize students, but a more important interpretation is that teachers and administrators must be proactive in guarding against even the unconscious application of gender, ethnic, and socioeconomic biases when grading student writing. Adopting a proactive stance, fortunately, is not particularly difficult, as training of the external evaluators illustrates. It requires a candid discussion of the potential influence of demographic factors and close adherence to a pre-established rubric. These steps will not eliminate biases, but they go a long way toward reducing their influence.

REFERENCES

Elbow, Peter, and Pat Belanoff. 1997. "Reflections on an Explosion: Portfolios in the '90s and Beyond." In *Situating Portfolios: Four Perspectives*, ed. Kathleen Yancy and Irwin Weiser. Logan, UT: Utah State University Press.

Huot, Brian, and Michael Williamson. 1997. "Rethinking Portfolios for Evaluating Writing: Issues of Assessment and Power." In *Situating Portfolios: Four Perspectives*, ed. Kathleen Yancy and Irwin Weiser. Logan, UT: Utah State University Press.

Loban, Walter. 1976. *Language Development: Kindergarten Through Grade Twelve.* NCTE Research Report No. 18. Urbana IL: National Council of Teachers of English.

Moss, Pamela. 1994. "Validity in High Stakes Writing Assessment: Problems and Possibilities." *Assessing Writing* 1: 109–128.

Murphy, Sandra. 1997. "Teachers and Students: Reclaiming Assessment Via Portfolios." In *Situating Portfolios: Four Perspectives*, ed. Kathleen Yancy and Irwin Weiser. Logan, UT: Utah State University Press.

White, Ed. 1986. Teaching and Assessing Writing. San Francisco: Jossey-Bass.

———. 1993. "Holistic Scoring: Past Triumphs and Future Challenges." In *Validating Holistic Scoring for Writing Assessment: Theoretical and Empirical Foundations*, ed. Michael Williamson and Brian Huot. Cresskill, NJ: Hampton.

———. 1994. "Issues and Problems in Writing Assessment." *Assessing Writing* 1: 11–28.

Wiggins, Grant. 1993. *Assessing Student Performance*. San Francisco: Jossey Bass.

Williams, James D. 1998. *Preparing to Teach Writing*. Mahwah, NJ: Lawrence Erlbaum.

13

INTERPRETING TEACHER AND STUDENT PORTFOLIOS AS ARTIFACTS OF CLASSROOM CULTURES
A Descriptive Assessment

JULIE CHEVILLE, SANDRA MURPHY, BARBARA WELLS PRICE, AND TERRY UNDERWOOD

W hen the Iowa Writing Project (IWP) received a grant from the Roy J. Carver Charitable Trust to underwrite an initiative entitled "Writing to Learn, Learning to Transform," one stipulation of the grant was that an independent review be conducted of the project's success. The IWP Steering Committee and Advisory Board, with director James Davis, recommended placing the review in the hands of professional colleagues. Barbara Price, an assessment specialist, was appointed to chair the review and convened a panel of professional educators with varied experience in writing and portfolio assessment to design and conduct a descriptive assessment of portfolios submitted by teachers and students participating in the IWP initiative. Project planners believed the best structure for the review was one in which assessors could act as colleagues, offering participants feedback about a small sample of their work and the work of their students. Accordingly, the descriptive assessment would involve several features (see Figure 13–1).

The IWP leadership and Barbara Price felt that the review should provide responsive feedback that could not be reduced to statistics. As Fran Claggett (1996) has pointed out, the Writing Project experience has taught writing teachers to be leery of reductive testing. Iowa Writing Project director James Davis initiated the IWP Descriptive Assessment with letters of invitation to school sites already participating in the Carver initiative. He invited IWP site directors at each location to identify five teachers for involvement in the descriptive assessment and

FIGURE 13–1   Features of the Descriptive Assessment

The review would

- offer participating teachers a new source of information for reformulating instructional theories and practices, as well as pose practical and theoretical questions which might initiate teacher reflection and dialogue
- be conducted in accord with IWP principles
- model practices and theories that the IWP had long encouraged
- recognize portfolios in the context of the classrooms and interactions which produced them
- qualitatively describe, not quantify, those teacher and student portfolios submitted for review
- detail the process and outcome of the descriptive assessment for the granting agency and IWP membership

---

to submit the portfolios of those teachers and their students, along with their own.

BARBARA PRICE: DESIGNING THE DESCRIPTIVE ASSESSMENT

In designing the review of the IWP initiative, I believed the most important principle was that it not take the form of an outside prescription but be a truly collegial activity. James Davis and I decided upon a review that would support participating teachers' reflections upon their classroom work, as well as the work of their students. We hoped the review would offer teachers new information or evidence that they might use in reformulating the theories they were already and continuously forming. As project designers, we had no desire to impose our own thinking or theories on participating teachers and assessors. As Donald Graves (1992) notes, "Most evaluation structures do not inform teaching. Rather than set benchmarks, research ought to reveal potential for more effective teaching and learning" (10). As project director, my goal was to develop an evaluation structure that could support teaching and learning (see Figure 13–2).

When assessors Julie Cheville, Sandra Murphy, Terry Underwood, and I met during the first summer of the review, we started not by drafting our own definition of what a portfolio is, which would surely have produced attendant expectations for what a "good" portfolio should be expected to contain and what it should look like. Instead, we agreed that assessors should begin by taking a careful look at the collected portfolios and proceed by describing, as thoughtfully as they could,

FIGURE 13–2   Descriptive Assessment Structure

Fall 1995:   Invitations Sent to UWP Site Directors

James Davis, IWP Director, sends letters of invitation to school sites already participating in the Carver initiative. IWP site directors at each location are encouraged to solicit the involvement of at least five teachers and their students and provide minimal instructions for portfoliokeeping.

Spring 1996:   Site Directors Submit Portfolios

Twenty teachers representing five sites submit teacher and student portfolios created during the 1995–96 school year. Participation ranges from one teacher at one site to five teachers and the site director at another.

Summer 1996:   Descriptive Assessment Begins

Barbara Price, project director, and James Davis, IWP director, select and familiarize assessors with the "Writing to Learn, Learning to Transform" initiative. Assessors convene in Iowa to negotiate a review protocol for the assessment phase, to describe and interpret sets of teacher and student portfolios, and to draft summary documents for participating teachers, the granting agency, and IWP membership.

Fall 1996:   Written Review Disseminated

The IWP leadership disseminates results of the descriptive assessment to participating site directors and teachers, as well as to its membership. Each participating teacher receives a copy of "Themes and Promising Practices" and a personal letter, in which one reviewer, speaking on behalf of the panel, describes and responds to the teacher's set. The document is also offered as a supplement to the report to the granting agency and, at the fall IWP conference, as a starting point for negotiation of the assessment project.

Assessors report on their review at the fall IWP conference and meet with participating teachers who wish to provide feedback

New invitations are submitted to school sites and former participants are encouraged to continue.

Summer 1997:   Descriptive Assessment Continues

Assessors reconvene to revise the descriptive assessment protocol and to begin the second cycle of descriptive review. Former and first-year site participants are represented in the second review.

Fall 1997:   Written Review Disseminated

A summary document is presented to the IWP membership at the fall conference, at which Barbara Price reports on the second summer assessment cycle.

what they saw there. During this process, they found evidence that, in varying degrees, teacher and student portfolios shared enough similar features to warrant descriptive categories, or themes (see Figure 13–3). Within each category, assessors further described aims and practices that seemed explicitly or implicily clear in the portfolios of teachers and their students (Iowa Writing Project 1997). In the category, or "theme," of reflection, for example, assessors documented correspondences between aims stated in a teacher's portfolio and the evident

---

FIGURE 13–3   Themes Arising from the Summer 1996 Review

Reflection: Evidence that teachers created opportunities for students to reflect on their work, their learning, and their growth and progress as writers. Evidence that teachers were reflective about their own practices and the impact of their practices on students.

Individualized Instruction: Evidence that teachers highlight students' individual growth as writers; that they compare their performances with earlier performances rather than the performances of other students; and that the prevailing expectation in the class is growth toward individual goals and potentials rather than an artificial standard.

Dialogic Emphasis: Evidence that reading and writing occur in a social context; that students have opportunities to exchange ideas and work with a variety of audiences: teacher, other students, parents, siblings, friends, etc., at any stage of the reading or writing process.

Student Responsibility for Learning: Evidence that teaches encourage students to assume responsibility for documenting their learning; that teachers challenge students to set their own goals for writing and reading, to assess their own work, to select pieces for their portfolios, and to experiment and take risks.

Process Approaches to Literacy: Evidence that students have opportunities to learn effective strategies for managing writing processes. This may include evidence of prewriting activities, drafting and revising, obtaining feedback from readers, reflecting across drafts, assignments, and other artifacts. Evidence that writing and reading processes vary by the task, avoiding formulaic stages.

Writing for Varied Audiences and Purposes in Varied Contexts: Evidence that students have opportunities to engage in writing of many different sorts; that their writing is directed to different audiences, both familiar and distant, and that they write for many different purposes, such as writing to learn, discover, and entertain, as well as writing to communicate knowledge or information. Evidence that students have opportunities to engage in writing over various time periods—to write brief, informal pieces as well as engage in extended projects that may involve research, interviews, or collaborative work with peers.

practices appearing in that particular teacher's set of student portfolios (see Figure 13–4).

During the descriptive process, assessors experienced a number of tensions. For example, the range (number and nature) of artifacts across the classroom sets of portfolios was dramatic: from a single un-marked manila folder containing decontextualized samples of student writing on one extreme to a binder containing clearly annotated, var-ied, and expansive samples of both teacher and student work, along with abundant contextualizing information. As project director, I real-ized that another tension involved interpreting evidence gathered from classroom purposes within a larger investigation of the impact of the IWP. This suggested to me that to be most effectively received, teach-ers needed to shape their work specifically toward the purposes of the project review. This might mean something as simple as teachers pro-viding more contextual explanation of how their student portfolios demonstrate instructional purposes. For teachers accustomed to re-viewing their students' work and familiar with all the surrounding work not represented in the portfolio, contextualizing materials might not have seemed very important. For an outside reviewer who had only the portfolio from which to create understanding of student and teacher practice, however, those contextualizing devices were crucial.

While it would have been possible to have offered suggestions to site directors, teachers, and students, for making the portfolio easier for

---

FIGURE 13–4 Excerpts of Assessors' Description of Promising Practices —Summer 1996

Theme #1: Reflection

Stated Teacher Aim (teacher portfolio)	*Evident Practice* (students' portfolio)
• "to encourage writers to reflect on their work" ➤	• students (even as early as 1st grade) select pieces of work for their portfolio and explain why pieces were chosen • students question, "I can improve this piece of writing by . . ."
• to stimulate long-range reflection ➤	• students create a traveling folder that follows them across the years; revisit old selections to reflect; add new ones.
• to involve students in goal-setting and self-evaluation ➤	• students create reflective pieces that explain goals and evaluate progress

participants prior to teachers' and students' year of portfolio making, much would have been lost if James Davis and I had regularized the portfolio design. Mark Milliken (1992) has written of the need to "keep portfolios fluid, changing, and responsive—and to keep the students at the center"(44). This was the position that the IWP leadership and I endorsed.

SANDRA MURPHY: CREATING A DIALOGUE ABOUT PROMISING PRACTICES

> Keeping track is a matter of reflective review and summarizing, in which there is both discrimination and record of the significant features of a developing experience. . . . It is the heart of intellectual organization and of the disciplined mind.
>
> John Dewey, *Experience and Education*

A number of considerations influenced our decisions about which procedures assessors would use, and which we would avoid, in our review of the Writing to Learn, Learning to Transform initiative. We were aware, for instance, of the limitations of many traditional techniques in evaluation that compare evidence gathered in one situation with one set of individuals with evidence gathered in another situation with yet another set of individuals, or that measure evidence in relation to a predetermined standard. Traditional, positivistic approaches look for and measure what has already been defined and prescribed elsewhere. Although such approaches allow for comparisons of classrooms and schools, they are not designed to reveal new knowledge, new insights, or for that matter, new approaches to pedagogy. Thus, they cannot indicate the depth and range of the impact of a program of professional development that casts the teacher in the role of a "maker" of knowledge and of an "artist" of practice.

Instead of adopting a traditional approach, then, the assessors drew upon assumptions and procedures associated with the fields of anthropology and sociology. In the manner of Michael Agar's "professional stranger," we approached our data with an eye toward understanding their significance for local participants rather than evaluating their merit for a distant audience (Agar 1980). Instead of measuring performance against preset criteria or employing a priori analytic schemes, we focused on interpreting what we saw to create a portrait of existing professional practice.

Our approach was influenced as well by our desire to maintain "philosophical" continuity between the procedures of the evaluation and those of the IWP program. The Writing Project's teachers-teaching-teachers model of professional development places an implicit value on the conception of the teacher as a professional who is expected to engage in inquiry and curriculum development and to share his or her own expertise with colleagues. Accordingly, we thought of the review not as an end point, but as an opportunity for taking stock, which in turn could spark new dialogue, curricula, and instructional practices. We had in mind what Egon Guba and Yvonna Lincoln (1989) call a "responsive" approach to evaluation in which the questions asked and the information collected drive from stakeholder input. We also had in mind an interactive process that would involve the many stake holders in the evaluation in a kind of extended collegial dialogue, including the assessors, who became stakeholders themselves because their roles were public and they stood to gain from the process.

Two other important considerations were the goal and audience of evaluation. While we knew that information from the evaluation would be examined by the Carver Trust to determine the effectiveness of its philanthropical efforts, the teachers were our primary audience. Our goal, and the goal of the Carver Trust's grant, was to help the teachers develop more effective writing instructional practices. As a first step, then, we "published" an inventory of existing effective strategies derived from the data so that each of the teachers could benefit from what their colleagues were creating (Iowa Writing Project 1997). We believed that learning about their colleagues' innovations and "promising practices" might help all of the teachers see new possibilities. As a second, perhaps more important, step, we provided qualitative feedback to individual teachers about what we saw in their portfolios so that they could gauge their own progress toward transforming their classrooms into learning communities. In other words, assessors set the stage for evaluation to happen where it counts—at home. To borrow Dennie Palmer Wolf's (1993) phrase, we planned to make the evaluation "an episode of learning."

What did we learn? What might we do differently if we were to do this again? The original call for portfolios was open-ended, leaving decisions about portfolio design up to each teacher. While this allowed teachers to retain authority for their work and to decide how their work would be represented to external audiences, the resulting collection of portfolios assessors studied ranged widely in character and quality. Some teachers and students provided clearer portraits of classroom practices than others. For example, the portfolios from teachers who employed what we call "contextualizing strategies"—information about the students, about the teachers' instructional goals, about the classroom portfolio process, and about the school and district context—were more informative than portfolios that were simply collections of artifacts. Providing guidelines and/or examples of effective contextualizing strategies to participants might have increased the likelihood that classroom teaching and learning were more visible to people who had never been present.

Perhaps the most effective "contextualizing strategy" was professional reflection. Reflection, as Bonnie Sunstein (1998) defines it, is "the act of seeing one's own work and its relationship to the self and explaining it" (41). Portfolios from teachers who reflected on their purposes and practices, and who explained how those purposes and practices were revealed in their portfolios, were more informative and easier to interpret than portfolios from teachers who did not. Knowing that reflection is not an automatic skill, teachers support students by asking reflective questions that invite response. Providing similar kinds of questions for teachers asked to keep portfolios would support their efforts to communicate effectively their professional practice to others. In this way, assessors might also help teachers achieve a reflective stance.

In retrospect, it would have also been helpful to give the teachers opportunities for face-to-face dialogue with the assessors *during* the review. Several times during the review, one or more of us expressed puzzlement about the significance or appropriateness of particular portfolio artifacts. Face-to-face discussion of portfolio contents would have enabled clarification and reduced the possibilities of misinterpretation. More opportunities for dialogue after the review would also have been valuable. Although the external assessors attempted to establish a kind of collegial dialogue via the individual letters, in reality the exchange was fairly one-sided. Teachers had few opportunities for face-to-face discussions with the authors of these letters. (Some teachers had the opportunity to talk with the external assessors at a later conference, but many did not.)

More opportunities for dialogue would also have helped the stakeholders as a group, including the assessors, to develop a consensus about standards. The "promising practices" we identified were based on the assessors' interpretations of the goals and standards of good practice of the Writing to Learn, Learning to Transform initiative and the Iowa Writing Project. But as we all know, interpretations vary among and across individuals. Explicit discussion of the expectations in advance of each summer review could have helped the teachers create more focused and effective portfolios.

In sum, we adopted an approach which we believed would complement the philosophy of the Writing Project and provide teachers with responsive feedback on their teaching. On the whole I believe we were very successful. Along the way we learned some things that will help us do it better next time, but that is what one hopes for in a project of this kind. Reflecting on what one would have done differently prompts learning and transformation.

TERRY UNDERWOOD: HEEDING THE MIRROR

Before the Iowa review began, the IWP leadership made no list of promising practices for the assessors to see, thereby minimizing the twin problems of coercion and intrusion. For a practice to qualify as promising in the assessors' themed list, at a minimum it had to show up voluntarily somewhere in the work of an Iowa teacher. The assessment was as if a mirror was held up for Iowa teachers to view themselves.

But the assessors were not fooled by the ghost of neutrality. Chosen because of our credibility as educators, we were already aware that our backgrounds shaped our reading. We knew that our work could not be replicated as easily as one might replicate an analysis of, say, soil. Before going to Iowa, I understood the assessors' task: to examine artifacts of schooling as knowledgeable representatives of the writing community so that evaluative data could be stabilized and transported to a funding agency, and to Iowa teachers.

This mirror talked.

The Iowa portfolio review protocol that assessors created acknowledged our power to change teaching practices in Iowa for good or ill. As a result, the protocol required us to be professionally and rhetorically responsible. At the conclusion of the review, assessors wrote individual letters to teacher participants, a practice that made the portfolio review an example of classical Aristotelian rhetoric in two ways. First, the assessors had to consider their audience as they read the portfolios and wrote about what they saw. The letters were not boilerplate documents but were carefully crafted responses to what we had read and understood. Second, the assessors knew that the letters in the context of the list of promising practices could influence the thoughts and actions of their audience.

The rhetorical nature of the Iowa review distinguishes it from other review systems. Ordinarily, every effort is made to render invisible the relationship between the assessor and the assessed. The assessor is almost never named personally, and the report is attributed to a nameless and faceless entity purportedly neutral and objective. And, if the assessed is named, the name simply fills a slot that could just as easily be a number. In most cases, every effort is made to objectify assessment data to apply to anyone anywhere. Results are published in boilerplate documents, and the assessor takes no responsibility for changes in the thoughts and actions of the assessed. In the name of objectivity, the assessor is, indeed must be be, blind to these consequences.

Making visible the relationship between assessor and assessed in Iowa meant holding the assessor accountable for judgments. When Barbara introduced the assessors in her own letter to teacher participants, a letter which prefaced the list of promising practices, as well as the individually signed letters, she named the assessors and described their professional backgrounds. Later in this letter, she facilitated direct connection:

> We also enclose a self-addressed envelope, hoping that you will accept it as an invitation to write to any member of the committee. We welcome your response, questions, suggestions, reactions, musings . . .

The mirror listened.

An analysis of the assessors' letters to teachers showed that we sought to influence the thought and actions of participants through appeals to reason and emotion. The following excerpt came from an assessor's letter to a teacher whose student portfolios obviously had been constructed according to tight specifications from an externally designed, standardized portfolio system. This excerpt illustrates an appeal to reason:

> I wondered how helpful the portfolio evaluation system represented here actually is for the students. Clearly, putting together these portfolios represents much work. But the sense that I got from reading their entry slips was that the dominant motivation for them was to "make the grade" rather than to "understand themselves better as literate human beings." I wondered what the "portfolio evaluation forms" actually meant to Jennifer and Jessica when they got back their grades. Did they know why they received those grades? Did they gain any new insights into themselves that could help them grow as readers and writers? Or did they simply know that they had managed to jump through another institutional hoop?

Here, the implied argument of the assessor is that teachers ought to ask their students to do work of benefit to them as learners.

The following excerpt illustrates an assessor's appeal to emotion:

> It's a pleasure returning to [portfolios from your district] for a second summer. As I write, the temperature rises to what forecasters predict will be record highs. Your collection is like a reassuring, cool breeze on a day that promises to extinguish any-thing that grows. What I like so much about your portfolio is that it is—in the most conclusive, richest sense— a portfolio. During the course of the review (this year and last), I have found that many teachers use the words "folder," "collection folder," and "portfolio" interchangeably. I worry about this conflation because, if my sense for the history of composition studies this past twenty-five years is accurate, these words have evolved into practice from different perspectives.

In this excerpt the assessor uses analogy, as well as a conversational tone, to influence the teacher's self-perceptions of his/her work. The assessor also reveals a "worry," that is, an emotion, as a means of underscoring the teacher's impact upon her own professional thinking.

Assessors in the IWP portfolio review acknowledged that writing and the teaching of writing are complex human activities. We did so because such an assessment can only be done by human beings, by those with political and professional positions that must be made visible. In this particular review process, accountability and reliability involved both teachers and assessors, and validity was established case by case, not as an overall characteristic of a positivist system. Because the review was a necessarily rhetorical act, assessors had to write and read with greater responsibility, technical accuracy, and openness about their values and their biases. We had to appeal to the humanity and professionalism of teachers, rather than view them and their students as nameless, faceless, and anonymous entities who can be analyzed as objectively, and as coldly, as soil.

JULIE CHEVILLE: RESISTING STANDARDIZATION

As the multiyear Iowa Writing Project initiative concludes, I must admit that I remain hesitant about small-scale external assessments. I worry about several issues. First, external assessments have a tendency to obligate teachers within a department, a school, or a district to participate. In the case of the IWP assessment, site directors' enthusiasm and entreaties probably involved a range of persuasive appeals to teachers. In some cases during the review, I wondered to what degree the austere portfolios of certain teachers implied their level of investment. Beyond guessing at correlations, it seems important to think about the political dynamic shaping this review. Terry's right about the lack of overt coercion, but that's not to say pressures of an implicit variety didn't exist. Assessors were chosen because our conceptions of the portfolio, reflected in our professional writing, dovetailed with instructional principles of the IWP. That meant something not just to why we were hired but what we saw and who we validated. As paid consultants authorized not just with the task of providing formative, collegial support to teachers and students but with the task of gauging the link between participants' evident instructional practices and IWP principles, assessors experienced, in fact created, a political dynamic that I suspect was apparent to those teachers complying with the requests and deadlines of site directors.

So what does all that matter? In her analysis of a multi-year, small-scale portfolio assessment, Judy Fueyo (1997) acknowledges that external assessments, even those providing formative support to teachers and students, inevitably precipitate the standardization they are created to defy.

> The profession is not so much "doing portfolios" as doing them in. It's taken a potentially good thing and is specifying the life-force out of it. Why do I say this? The elementary classrooms I'm following are responding to school district directives to "do portfolios." This district has invited much input from classroom teachers and initially left many specifics open. Still . . . the portfolios are becoming more and more prescribed as we come upon the third year of the initiative. (69)

Ultimately, external portfolio assessments, particularly multi-year initiatives in which participants pass through a series of annual reviews, affect how teachers and students represent themselves to those beyond their classrooms. The problem, over time, is that such assessments reduce the likelihood that teachers and students any longer represent themselves to themselves. In an ironic turn, portfolios in such assessments grow standardized, evermore removed from the contexts in which they should be negotiated.

Another of my concerns emanates from perhaps the most painful story arising from the Iowa Writing Project assessment, the tale of a secretary in one school district's central office who, in the course of preparing her district's portfolio sets for mailing, balked at the prospect of printing and mailing so much material. Instead, she photocopied and sent to IWP headquarters only every fifth page of every student's and teacher's portfolio. In one fell swoop, a single individual located beyond the context of the classroom had made literate lives incomprehensible. What seems clear, regardless of the assessment protocol, is that once portfolios leave the context of a classroom, the risk of misinterpretation and misappropriation escalates. What this means to teachers, students. and their assessors can be devastating.

Several years ago James Berlin (1994) noted that elementary and secondary students who have passed through the nineties are "victims of one of the most test-crazed eras in the history of our country" (58). I agree, and again I wonder, is it possible for any assessment (large- or small-scale, quantitative or qualitative, arhetorical or rhetorical) to support teachers and learners? I leave the IWP review process as an assessor who has, in the rhetorical sense Terry describes, been transformed. I leave more fortified by the following convictions about portfolio keeping and descriptive assessment.

- No educator or student must ever be forced to create and maintain a portfolio.
- Educators, administrators, and assessors who ask students to create portfolios must do so themselves.

- Extensive time, display, and negotiation must be devoted to the process of portfolio keeping in classrooms.
- Educators, administrators, and students must teach, mentor, and model reflective strategies.
- Portfolio keeping must evolve within a rhetorical context in which students, educators, administrators, and assessors assemble, share, and revise their portfolios on a regular basis. Here, I think of what Patti Lather (1986) identifies as "face validity" and envision the interaction of portfolio keeper and reader-assessor in face-to-face discussions which "recycle analysis through at least a subsample of respondents" (67).

I still believe that multiyear, small-scale assessments offer the potential to transform teaching and learning, but I think the evaluative context must be one which (1) serves internal rather than external needs; (2) allows for frequent face-to-face validity; and (3) offers the same level of logistical and material compensation to all involved. To some, perhaps even many, such an evaluative context may seem impossible to achieve. But I believe it's precisely these criteria, these *priorities*, that may assist voluntary circles of teachers (across grade levels, subject areas, schools, or even school districts) to create and conduct their own descriptive assessments.

CONCLUSION

As Sandra points out, and Barbara and the IWP leadership understood, the basic anthropological question at the heart of the IWP portfolio review is important. "What is happening here?" As assessors entered into the portfolios of students, teachers, and site directors, they sought, as best they could, to *describe* the aims and practices evident in artifacts in terms of the diverse classroom cultures that had produced them. Looking back, we realize that we both succeeded and failed; inevitably, we affected teachers and students. Still, in the tradition of reflexive anthropology, project leaders and assessors created a protocol for descriptive assessment which may assist teachers to initiate their own voluntary projects, the kind of cyclical portfolio reviews that allow revolving teams of teachers to experience not only the role of assessor but the responsibility and delicacy of negotiation. It's this narrowing of the gap between those who assess and those who teach which seems the restorative ingredient necessary if portfolios are to resist standardization.

REFERENCES

Agar, Michael. 1980. *The Professional Stranger: An Informal Introduction to Ethnography*. San Diego: Academic Press.

Berlin, James. 1994. "The Subversions of the Portfolio." In *New Directions in Portfolio Assessment: Reflective Practice, Critical Theory and Large Scale Scoring*, ed. Black, Portsmouth, NH: Boynton/Cook.

Claggett, Fran. 1996. *A Measure of Success: From Assignment to Assessment in English Language Arts*. Portsmouth, NH: Boynton/Cook.

Dewey, John. 1916. *Democracy and Education*. New York: Macmillan.

Fueyo, Judy. 1997. "Dear Portfolio Explorers." In *Assessing Portfolios: A Portfolio*, ed. Bonnie Sunstein and Julie Cheville, Urbana, IL: NCTE.

Graves, Donald. 1992. "Portfolios: Keep a Good Idea Growing." In *Portfolio Portraits*, ed. Donald Graves and Bonnie Sunstein. Portsmouth, NH: Heinemann.

Guba, Egon, and Yvonna. Lincoln. 1989. *Fourth Generation Evaluation*. Newbury Park, CA: Sage.

Iowa Writing Project. 1997. "Themes and Promising Practices." Unpublished document. Cedar Rapids, IA: Iowa Writing Project.

Lather, Patti. 1986. "Research as Praxis." *Harvard Educational Review* 56(3): 257–75.

Milliken, Mark. 1992. "A Fifth-Grade Class Uses Portfolios." In *Portfolio Portraits*, ed. Donald Graves and Bonnie Sunstein. Portsmouth, NH: Heinemann.

Sunstein, Bonnie. 1998. "Searching under Surfaces: Reflection as an Antidote for Forgery." *The Clearing House* 72(1): 39–43.

Wolf, Dennie Palmer. 1993. "Assessment as an Episode of Learning." In *Construction Versus Choice in Cognitive Measurement: Issues in Constructed Response, Performance Testing, and Portfolio Assessment*, ed. Randy E. Bennett and William C. Ward. Hillsdale, NJ: Lawrence Erlbaum.

14

LATCHING ON TO PORTFOLIOS
Assessment Conversations in English Education[1]

JOE POTTS, RON STRAHL, AND DON HOHL

As educators, we are mere infants in the use of portfolios. Artists have used them for years as a means of representing the range and depth of their best and most current work. Only in the last five years have educators latched on to the portfolio as an alternative to evaluating the literate work of students, principally in the area of writing.

Donald Graves—"Portfolios: Keep a Good Idea Growing"

Nearly a decade after Donald Graves offered these words in *Portfolio Portraits*, portfolios have certainly evolved into legitimate and even preferred ways to assess students' competencies. Even more important, however, portfolios have gone beyond simple assessment as an end result to build bridges between what faculty do in the classroom and how students perceive their own learning. Portfolios have, at least in our case at CSULB, brought faculty closer together to look at the tangible results of their teaching. Since 1995 we have latched on to portfolios in our English education program, and they have opened up social spaces, or contact zones, that have provoked intellectual critique and professional conversation about content knowledge, literacy, teaching, learning, and our profession. In a department never known for its introspection or its water cooler debates over methodology, we have seen portfolios create conversation that resonates with reflection, inquiry, and energy.

---

[1]Portions of this article appeared earlier in Potts, J. 1999. "Cross Connections: Making Contacts with Portfolios in English Education." *Issues in Teacher Education* 8(1): 53–69.

THE BEGINNING

Because we are university educators who work for a public institution, we are bound to educational fiats and public expectations for teaching and student learning. In the early nineties, the California Commission on Teacher Credentialing required secondary teacher education programs to devise and implement content standards and an assessment program to evaluate student work in relation to those standards. Each student, *prior* to student teaching had to be evaluated and "certified" content knowledgeable. Grades in courses and the previous sole determiner of competency, the GPA, were seen as mere "formative" measures and were not to be regarded at all as "summative" assessment.

The commotion generated in the department drew faculty close as they railed at the bureaucrats for once again intruding into the teaching/learning transaction. They lamented the good old days when the classroom repelled transgressors and academic freedom was sacrosanct. But for a couple of colleagues in English education and the department of English, this latest fiat from state government hinted of possibility and opportunity. Could productive and professional conversations shape this new assessment program? Could the very act of being forced "to talk" about evaluation create impetus for curriculum reform in our program? Could this process of carrying out what the state demanded breathe some new life into a program that had functioned well but had never been particularly student-based or unified by common purpose? Lethargy would be too strong a word; benign passivity might better describe the program.

Nevertheless, the anger triggered by university faculty being told what to do created an energy that would, we were amazed, carry out the fiat and change our program—for the better. Eventually the shrillness of the conversation subsided and inquiry, however awkwardly, began taking shape: faculty began talking to each other about teaching. There was, all argued, a problem with grades and maybe another kind of assessment was in order. All reluctantly acquiesced, and the collective sigh was heard across campus. Work began. Now the early conversations did not exactly celebrate student competency. What propelled many in this endeavor was a belief that some of our students did not know enough and the assessment program, in whatever form it took, would get rid of the ones surviving as a result of inflated grades. A "we will get them now" attitude prevailed. Words such as "ownership," "reflection," "community," "voice," "mentoring," and "support" did not drive the conversation. The "contact zone" was not yet articulated; timing was everything.

For many of our faculty, and particularly for the more vociferous ones, the standards, or the expectations faculty had for each student, was the most important factor. How we assessed student competency was less important to many than what was to be measured: the old process/product debate reared its ugly head again. Curiously enough, the debate over standards was relatively swift; tweaking language took much longer than actually deciding substantive issues. The content of the various courses comprising the English education option had to be squarely represented in the standards, or in the "competencies" as they were to be termed much later. No one could be expected to teach anything different from what they had taught in the past. After all, this state mandate was not about faculty performance but about student performance. All agreed—"for now."

Clearly "more" was better, and the standards, as they evolved, became more rigorous, more responsible, and according to one professor, "more likely to get rid of those students who should never teach and there are lots of 'em." Whatever the motivation behind each faculty member's early work on the program, the final outcome still promised, for a couple of faculty, real reform. Once faculty interests were matched with obvious teacher expectations and also with the state framework for language arts instruction, the outcomes were formulated and some new bridges built between courses and faculty. At least the articulated standards hinted of a unified, purpose-based program. It was a beginning. In essence, each prospective English teacher in our program would have to meet the following standards:

Written Communication: Understands and demonstrates the composing process and is able to write effectively for different purposes and audiences using conventions of both standard and rhetorical discourse.

Reading and Literature: Understands and demonstrates fundamental literary concepts while interpreting, analyzing, and reflecting on literature as it relates to ethical, cultural, and political values of human experience, including women and persons from diverse ethnic groups.

Language Development and Linguistics: Understands and demonstrates the basic principles of first and second language learning and acquisition, particularly in written discourse, and the cultural and cognitive influences of language learning and development.

There was something in the standards for everyone —the respective faculty, the state, the community, and, of course, the students. The standards clarified what the students were expected to know, a simple but previously uncommunicated idea.

Round 1 ended. Many faculty, now assured that "what they stand for" was given tangible form, dropped out of the conversation. A decade after Graves declared that educators were "mere infants in the use of portfolios," political exigency was to give us the opportunity to use portfolios to shape and define our program. Round 2 was as blood-less as Round 1: no one could come up with a cost-effective, time-pleasing, low-energy way to assess these three gargantuan standards. Suggestions of a battery of tests, oral interviews, take home exams, and the GRE died quick and painless deaths. The committee became smaller; silence replaced complaint. The time was right. A decade after *Portfolio Portraits*, finally, humbly, with just a hint of sarcasm, the question was posed: "Why couldn't we ask students to submit a—what do you call it?—a portfolio?" And how faculty and students do "business" in the program was changed, almost immediately.

THE EMERGING VISION

Let's say up front that as a faculty we had no idea that portfolio assess-ment would change our program so completely. In the beginning, our intent was only twofold: to create a rigorous student-centered assess-ment program that would aid, rather than inhibit, a student's intellec-tual and professional growth by empowering rather than excluding; and to "soften" our English education program, to create more of a commu-nity by bringing faculty and faculty, students and students, and faculty and students closer together to join in a conversation about teaching. While these are certainly ambitious, some would say idealistic goals, the last few years have forcefully demonstrated a myriad of possibilities and actualities afforded by portfolio assessment. Our vision has been colored intricately by carefully cultivated as well as spontaneous out-comes. But first things first. Faculty members agreed that the portfolio should be "professional," attractive, substantive, and "owned" by the students; it was also hoped that the portfolio would be important enough for the student to carry to her job interviews. Rather quickly, we also envisioned the actual portfolio (a 2- or 3-inch binder), with cover (decorated creatively with a picture of the student), her data, and a title that best represented her education as a prospective English teacher), dividers separating the artifacts and each standard, and a table of contents was decided. Over the first couple of years, the portfo-lios became distinctive, creative, and very personalized. The students came to "own" them, as we had intended. More important, Round 3 comprised an agreement on what should go inside the portfolio. There was consensus almost instantaneously that two or three artifacts would demonstrate each standard, the number ultimately left up to the student. These artifacts could be a myriad of things: papers completed inside or outside class, book reviews, videotapes, audiotapes of presentations, graphic projects, bibliographies from courses, etc. The student was to choose what to include, but over time papers written for particular classes have far outnumbered other artifacts for the portfolios.

Debate became more animated when a faction argued for evidence of applications within each of the three standards. In other words, students would include in each content area (writing, reading, and language) a lesson or application that bridges content and methodology, even though the charge from the state focused only on content. Also, we decided to require students to include a philosophy of teaching statement to get a sense of how they were approaching teaching as a career. Most important, we wanted Dear Reader letters for each of the sections. These letters allowed students to (1) argue explicitly for their respective competency; and (2) reflect on their academic accomplishments, an essential aspect of the portfolio.

The last nuts-and-bolts aspect of the portfolio process was how students would present their portfolios, the actual evaluation, and any subsequent activity. In essence, students are made aware of the portfolio early in their matriculation, almost as soon as they declare themselves an English education major. As a result, they have, in some cases, over two years to collect pertinent artifacts, to make sure they are getting the kind of training needed to demonstrate the standards inside their portfolios.

All students are then required to submit a portfolio about halfway through their methods course, the final course prior to student teaching. They are then assigned a mentor teacher in the field, and the faculty recommend collaboration between the two. Mentors volunteer their time and assist their soon-to-be colleagues with organizing and reflecting on their portfolios. They also share wisdom and knowledge accrued through years of teaching experience. Since mentors have been recognized as exemplary teachers in their schools, they offer teachers-in-training useful ideas and suggestions before the student teaching experience.

They actual evaluation consists of students presenting their portfolios to a university faculty member and at least two English mentors during an hourlong session. While the intensity and tone of the "presentations" have varied, ultimately the portfolios have encouraged wonderful conversation between professionals—at times motivational, at times instructive, almost always genuine and sincere.

In the first year or so of the portfolio program, students were skeptical to say the least, some even cynical. Many saw the standards as another barrier placed in front of them. Words like "competency" and "standards" overpowered what we saw as the important words—"conversation," "empowerment," "student-centered," "support," "mentor," and "cultivate." Mistrust between university faculty and our students characterized the environment simply because there really had never been an engaging conversation about what "good enough" looked like inside a portfolio. Students had every reason to be skeptical.

After the first year, though, groups of students "latched" on to portfolios, viewing the process as a celebration of their undergraduate and graduate years of education. Crucial self-reflection multiplied in direct correlation to decreasing anxiety over the assessment process.

Nina, a preservice educator in our program, devoted hours to collecting, selecting, and reflecting what she would place into her portfolio. She used the three department-mandated standards as a guideline to help her determine content and locate gaps in her learning. As she sifted through the stack of papers and projects produced during her undergraduate career, Nina noticed that she had very few artifacts representing subject-matter knowledge in the third standard, Language Development and Linguistics. Nina noticed this gap, formed a goal, and then acted to acquire the knowledge she needed. During the conversation session that Nina had with her evaluation team as a celebration of her portfolio, she explained:

> I was a speech communication minor, majoring in English education. I didn't study language acquisition or first/second language development; therefore, I had some research to do on my own in order to show competence for that section of the portfolio. I spent a few hours in the library researching this topic, and then I ventured out into our public schools to observe classrooms in which teachers were working with second language learners. I got to see first-hand some teaching strategies that work with second language learners, visual aids in particular. Those are things that I don't think that I would have found out had I not completed research for my portfolio.

Nina was glad that she "latched" on to the process of developing her portfolio. The standards for her portfolio enabled her to identify strengths and to determine gaps in her subject knowledge. Portfolio work also prompted Nina to conduct research and make contact with public school teachers working specifically with second language learners.

Almost from the beginning, the real power of our portfolio assessment was predicated on self-evaluation, which was, we reasoned, the most lasting, the most meaningful kind of evaluation. It was our hope that the actual presentation of the portfolio would be student-driven, personal, rigorous, with the faculty and teaching representatives supporting our teacher candidates and offering resources and encouragement. Many students received the standards and portfolio specifications early in their class work and then have used their actual courses (as it should be) to create artifacts that would, quite intentionally, find their way into a portfolio perhaps a year or two later. Like Nina, many have recognized gaps in learning and have made self-prescribed decisions to learn and meet the standards on their own.

More than anything though, portfolios have been most productive, in our estimation, when conceptualized as a process that creates contact zones as social spaces where cultures meet, clash, and then grapple with each other's uniqueness (Pratt 1991). We—the faculty, mentors, and preservice educators—define a contact zone as a social and intellectual space prompted by portfolio development and energized by exchange among pre-service, university, and public school educators (see Figure 14–1).

In our program, then, the portfolio serves as an assessment and as a site where pre-service, public school, and university educators can meet to discuss and determine academic performance relative to the three competencies. As a site that promotes contacts, the portfolio engenders exchange and critique of ideas and beliefs about teaching, cultures, language, and learning. In our five years of work with portfolios, we have concluded that it is the professional contacts and conversations that preservice teachers have with mentor educators and univer-

FIGURE 14–1   Portfolio as Contact Zone

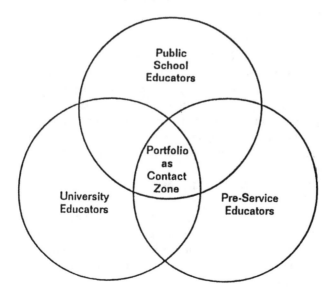

sity professors and, ironically, professors with professors, that make the portfolio a valuable process.

ASSESSMENT CONVERSATIONS WITH MENTOR EDUCATORS

Each semester university faculty pair teachers-in-training with mentor educators who teach English in secondary schools contiguous to our university. With years of classroom experience, mentors provide preservice educators seasoned perspectives about the rigors and demands, rewards and joys of teaching in urban contexts. Interaction promoted by the portfolio also encourages the preservice educators to ask practical questions about lesson design, philosophies of teaching, and assessment practices. In the past, mentors have also encouraged methods students to design and teach minilessons in their own classroom settings.

Julie, a mentor educator, and M'Liss, a student in the program, met several times during the semester to discuss M'Liss's portfolio. In the process of selecting and revising artifacts for her portfolio, M'Liss went to observe Julie in her classroom. There they often talked about lesson design, management issues, and unit projects. They also talked a great deal, however, about M'Liss's portfolio and possible artifacts to include in it. Julie, the mentor, starts a conversation with M'Liss after latching on to one possible artifact for the portfolio. In the following conversation here, Julie questions a paper that M'Liss has written which allows for a colloquial talk to follow:

Julie: "Winds of Change?"

M'Liss: Right, "Winds of Change" exactly. I responded in this paper that I wasn't seeing the winds change anything in the classroom. But I have seen it happen, and I know that teaching writing as a process and teaching in a writers' workshop setting can be successful. You know, I have been spending all of this time observing teachers, and I haven't seen the workshop happen. So I was a bit sarcastic in this paper, and I wrote, you know, it might be a slight breeze.

Julie: That's great.

M'Liss: Well, it specifically addresses process writing, and that's why I wanted to put this in.

Julie: It sounds like kind of an argument? A persuasive piece of writing?

M'Liss: Yeah, that's pretty much what it is.

Julie: You're starting with the "I," with a narrative. It sounds like you are starting off this essay by getting your plug in there.

M'Liss: Right, yes.

Julie: I haven't read one like that in the portfolios before. But you know the portfolio is all about you. It sounds like a great paper. You are writing a paper about process writing while demonstrating with several drafts of this piece your own writing process. That's great. You demonstrate understanding of what's in the first standard.

From this excerpt it is clear that Julie and M'Liss had both read Hairston's (1982) classic piece, "The Winds of Change," and understood M'Liss's angst about how little, from her perspective, the paradigm had shifted in the teaching of writing. Both also shared an understanding of the "process of writing," and appreciated M'Liss's play on words when she suggested that the "wind" propelling systemic change in the teaching of writing was actually a "slight breeze." Most important, perhaps, was that M'Liss articulated why she felt this piece was important and must be represented in her portfolio. Sensing M'Liss's conviction, Julie acknowledged M'Liss's ownership of her portfolio and concluded that selecting artifacts for the portfolio was entirely M'Liss's responsibility.

Preservice educators have benefited from their contacts with veteran educators in the field, but there are good reasons why mentors have latched on to the portfolio project, too. Don, a twenty-five-year veteran language arts teacher and adjunct professor at the university, has served as a mentor since the inception of the portfolio project. His participation in the portfolio process has become a source of professional growth for him, providing a contact zone for learning new ideas in education. Don mused after a day of conversations with preservice and university educators:

> I am thinking about the continual growth that we as classroom teachers need on a regular basis with our colleagues who also are committed to professional growth. In addition, we need contact with our mentors, our old, college professors, who, um, now see us more as colleagues than as students. This process, then, is truly collegial; it allows us to work with our new colleagues as well as interact with our old professors on a equal basis.

For Don, Julie, and other veteran teachers, the portfolio project has enabled them to make contact with university students and professors, who, in Don's estimation, are "listening."

What faculty had not anticipated, though, were contact zones that promoted collaboration among ourselves. The following is an early conversation, replicated from our memory, between two faculty who taught methods courses:

Ron: I need to know about one-pagers. I thought Susan took a real chance using a one-pager as one of her artifacts in her portfolio. It worked though . . . I was impressed with the risk as well as the writing.

Joe: I think that Susan did take a risk and that many more of our students in the future will select one-pagers for their portfolios . . . I learned about one-pagers from Bonnie Sunstein, who uses them in her classes to provoke students to apply complex reading material or to reflect on what they've read. . . . My students seem to like them, although they're a bit tricky to compose. Not as easy as we might think.

Ron: I would imagine. Actually they might be an alternative to all the journals my students do, and I'm really tired of reading those journals.

Joe: Try it. I have some one-pagers in my office if you want to read through them.

Ron: I like the possibilities. It's tough "to write short." I could use them to cover the reading that I don't get to in class.

The portfolio process has enabled faculty members to sit together and to consider their own classroom practices in light of the artifacts that students have included in their portfolios. Here Ron and Joe, two CSULB faculty members, shared ideas about a writing task, the one-pager, which Ron noticed as a result of reading and assessing a preservice teacher's portfolio. The preceding segment of dialogue is illustrative of the conversations—sparked by portfolios—that have led faculty members to collaborate, question curriculum, and imagine new possibilities for instruction.

CONVERSATION AND COLLABORATION IN PORTFOLIO GROUPS

As English education students develop their portfolios and reflect on their accomplishments, they also collaborate with their peers in groups of three or four. The professor responsible for the final methods course encourages the development of these groups. Portfolio groups serve to develop community among students, enabling them to share their portfolios and come to know each other as individuals. Because our university is a commuter school, students usually zip in to campus and then quickly drive away at the conclusion of class. Few have had opportunities to spend time together outside of the three hours that they meet in class; the groups provide an opportunity for additional contact with other prospective educators.

Martin, Gloria, and Andrea—preservice educators in one of the methods courses—met five times during the semester, sometimes spending as much as four hours per meeting working on their portfolios. When they met, they read and responded to each other's writings, edited for syntactical missteps, offered suggestions about artifacts to include, and imagined new writing activities that held potential for demonstrating subject matter competency. In one of those meetings held in the university library, they discussed the significance of their work together:

Gloria: We met every two weeks. This is our fifth or sixth time together, and we have met for more than four hours at a time. It has been very positive, very valuable because we have read each other's papers and that has helped us to correct mistakes. We learned from each other in terms of peer editing.

Andrea: Working in this group helped us to keep focused and to keep the process going. I know that it did for me. When we first started to meet all this stuff, it was like, I have all this stuff. Well, it was just pretty overwhelming, but everybody pitched in.

Martin: It's been helpful because everybody contributes something different. I mean, if somebody doesn't catch something, then somebody else does. It really helps for people to read your work several times because what one person doesn't catch, another person may be able to.

Andrea: We have also made suggestions. Each one of us feels that she is strong in one area. Gloria is really strong in language acquisition. Martin is strong in literature, and we complement each other. I'm the grammar police.

Martin: That's what has been so helpful. Because Andrea and I have a literature background, we might be able to help out Gloria with literature; and she will be able to help us out with more info about language acquisition because that's her background.

Gloria: We are very fortunate that we have everyone in different areas. We are mutually learning from each other.

This portfolio group discussed its joint efforts to learn from each other as they revised and developed artifacts for their portfolios. Members immediately "policed" artifacts for sentence-level missteps, but their collaborations stretched beyond error hunting into rich conversations about pieces of literature and theories of learning and development. Each person contributed to the discussion as members shared their individual expertise and experiences. Working together they "latched" on to significant connections and contacts with their portfolios. In Gloria's terms, it was a mutual aid society in which all of us ended up "mutually learning from each other."

The group also latched on to one another, forming a bond that served to provide moral support. Andrea and Gloria explained.

Andrea: We were able to help each other out editorially, pedagogically, and analytically; however, moral support was the number one thing that I got from the group interaction. I was able to take things that I wasn't sure about, like my rough draft for a language paper, ask the others, "Am I going the right way"? They would say that I was headed in the right direction, and I could finish the paper because I had confidence that I was going the right way.

Gloria: Yes, it, we became more than just a group. The portfolio became more a of personal mission for everyone. We had to complete this because we were all in the same boat. We stuck together because we felt comfortable with each other. We became friends. When we first met, I don't think that we were as comfortable with each other as we are now. We're tight, now.

Andrea: We were really nervous and stiff when we met the first time. By the second time, we were better. We had planned to meet only two hours the second time, but we ended up meeting for four hours.

Collaborative group work with portfolios places the focus on sharing and constructing knowledge. As members of this group shared, polished, and rehearsed ideas, they found themselves joining forces to document and demonstrate their literate achievements. Initially, each independent member sought assistance with his or her portfolio and came to the group anticipating some help. Something significant occurred, however, between the first and second meeting that transcended the initial reason for working together. By the conclusion of the second meeting, the group had found solidarity and developed a bond that caused them to latch on to each other and to become "partners" in the process. Members of this group moved from working independently with the portfolios to functioning interdependently with their peers.

A CONTACT ZONE FOR MENTORS AND PROFESSORS IN PORTFOLIO CONVERSATIONS

Each semester for one day, twenty mentor educators join preservice students and professors on our university campus to converse about artifacts, applications, and reflections—all linked together in the portfolio. In the first year, the faculty called this component the "interview" process; however, that term took on such a negative connotation (almost as if the originator of the portfolio was going to be required to defend his/her thesis) that we coined the interview/evaluation component a conversation between the originator of the portfolio and the evaluation team. Before the day of conversations, mentors travel to campus to read the portfolios and use a rubric to assess students' mastery (Tables 14–1–14–3). Portfolios in the program are assessed with a binary system: either the portfolio meets the standards, or it does not. On the designated day for the conversation, preservice students meet individually with a group of three mentors and a university professor. In a comfortable, nonthreatening forum, the hourlong conversation provides opportunities for mentor teachers, students, and university professors to make contact and to talk openly and directly about students' academic performance, goals, and accomplishments displayed in the portfolios.

Group conversations often lead to critical dialogue not only about academic standards but also about the rigors of teaching in urban schools where student populations are diverse and challenging. As the portfolio in the review creates a contact zone, a place for students and teachers to meet to discuss academic performance, it also represents a rite of passage. Cathy, a preservice educator who developed a portfolio, talked about her experience during her portfolio conversation:

> That was a good experience for me. It wasn't bad at all. I know that we talked in class before the team review about its being a conversation, but I think, um, because the conversation stayed anchored and focused on what I was thinking and what I had included in the portfolio, and my ideas and plans, that, um, it was a good experience. Also, I didn't feel that it was an adversarial relationship. Often when we confront a group who is assessing us there is a built-in sense of them versus us. In this conversation, I received a sense of assurance, that the members of the review committee were colleagues. These were colleagues welcoming me into the profession, rather than evaluators who were trying to keep me out.

The portfolio interview provided for Cathy another opportunity to make contact with colleagues. Unlike a jury or dissertation committee charged solely with tendering a verdict, the group of public school and university educators conversed with Cathy about her portfolio, enabling her to discuss ideas and plans with soon-to-be colleagues. She came away from the conversation with a sense that the committee members were four earnest professionals who wanted to know about her, her portfolio, and her career aspirations. In Cathy's estimation, the review team wanted to "welcome her into the profession" and were not aiming to "keep her out."

Some students in the program haven't been as successful as Cathy, and some have had to revise artifacts or to enhance and develop academic skills essential for teaching language arts. In many instances, students who are asked to revise artifacts in particular competencies add depth to their thinking and learning. Students whose portfolios have

TABLE 14–1   Compentency One: Written Communication

Competency One: Written Communication Skills	Exceeds the Competency
Understands and demonstrates the stages of the composing process, and is able to write effectively for different purposes and audiences using conventions of both standard and traditional rhetorical discourse.	
Meets the Competency	**Needs Revision**
• Shows evidence of the composing and revising processes • Adapts writing to a range of audiences (for example, self, peers, distant audience) • Adapts writing for a variety of purposes by using, for example, different voices, styles, and formats. • Transitions are smooth among sentences and among sections of texts • Uses, where appropriate, literature or public discourse as a resource for understanding significant ideas • Writings are of sufficient length and complexity to demonstrate mastery of standard English and traditional rhetorical discourse • Does not commit writing errors that divert attention or cause confusion about meaning.	In the space below, offer suggestions where appropriate for revision.
Artifacts and Applications	**Additional Comments**
Please write the titles or a description of artifacts and the application here:	

TABLE 14–2   Competency Two: Reading and Literature

Competency Two: Reading and Literature	Exceeds the Competency
Understands and demonstrates fundamental literary concepts while interpreting, analyzing, and reflecting on literature as it relates to ethical, cultural, and political values of human experience, including women and persons from diverse ethnic groups.	

Meets the Competency	Needs Revision
• Demonstrates mastery of fundamental literary concepts • Analyzes, interprets, and evaluates whole texts produced for a wide range of purposes and audiences • Make connections among parts of a text, across several texts, and/or between texts and personal experiences (For example, there is substantial evidence of extending /applying and of generalizing beyond tests	In the space below, offer suggestions where appropriate for revision.

Artifacts and Applications	Additional Comments
Please write the titles or a description of the artifacts and application here.	

TABLE 14–3   Competency Three: Language and Linguistics

Competency Three: Language and Linguistics	Exceeds the Competency
Understands and demonstrates the basic principles of first and second language acquisition, particularly in written discourse, and the cultural physiological, and cognitive influences on the evolution of standard English, including the language development of the pre-adolescent.	
Meets the Competency	**Needs Revision**
• Understands and demonstrates basic principles of first and second language acquisition and learning, particularly in written discourse • Identifies and analyzes theories of language learning and their relations to language acquisition • Shows understanding of an intercultural approach to language teaching and learning	In the space below, offer suggestions where appropriate for revision.
Artifacts and Applications	**Additional Comments**
Please write the titles or a description of the artifacts and application here:	

not passed the review have enrolled in independent study courses de-signed to enable them to build fundamental literacy skills essential for classroom success. A less-than-acceptable portfolio, determined by the committee, represents an opportunity for prospective teachers to iden-tify their specific goals and specific plans to build literate skills and strategies.

A CONTACT ZONE FOR LEARNING THROUGH THE PORTFOLIO PROCESS

What have we as a faculty learned about portfolio keeping since we latched on to them? A great deal, we think. We've discovered how portfolios can lead preservice, public school, and university faculty to work productively together in the process of building professional rela-tionships and determining subject matter knowledge. We've learned that conversations are much more productive and collaborative than are interviews. We've built relationships and a process that should re-main ongoing through the life of each educator connected to the port-folio and its conversation.

As a group we have developed coherent philosophy about portfolios constructed through actual experience, trial-and-error, revision, and conversation. As are portfolios, these elements are always under con-struction, always in process:

- Portfolios help us to make visible to students productive teaching and assessment strategies. To us, the entire portfolio is an artifact that represents a social and recursive process that is never fin-ished, that is always in progress, and that requires collaboration and interaction. When imagined as a tool to spark critical conver-sations about subject matter knowledge and pedagogy, we've dis-covered that the portfolio can become a site, a contact zone, in which professors, mentors, and preservice students can learn from one another as they assess their literate performances. This triad partnership of educators comes into contact with one another through the portfolio, grows and matures through collaborating with one another, and documents this growth in both the portfo-lio and its subsequent conversation.
- To understand a portfolio and appreciate its power for reflection, interaction, and assessment, a teacher must keep one herself and share it with her students. Each faculty member keeps and revises a portfolio that demonstrates to us, our students, and our col-leagues the qualities and dimensions of our literate and teaching lives.

- We've also come to believe that allowing students to choose pieces for their portfolio is critical to the success of the assessment process. The act of selecting artifacts for a portfolio involves analytical and evaluative skills that we, as professors, often give lip service to in our classrooms. However, in haste to bring a quick close to the democratic process of choice, we fall into the autocratic mode of demanding, requiring, sometimes selecting. If we would only remember that choice leads directly to ownership, and ownership leads to investment in the process.
- Finally, we've come to believe that a portfolio project is only as strong as its reflective and collaborative components. Without both, portfolios lose power and reveal themselves as mere collections of artifacts for display. Portfolios in our program represent and encourage more than public display of subject matter knowledge—though we are all interested in working with thoughtful colleagues who have ample knowledge of their subject matter. We've concluded that a portfolio cannot be done to students; it must be developed with them. It must be viewed as a site for conversation and inquiry, a contact zone, where students and teachers can latch on to knowledge and then discuss accomplishments and determine new possibilities for learning.

REFERENCES

Graves, Donald. 1992. "Portfolios: Keep a Good Idea Growing." In *Portfolio Portraits*, ed. Donald Graves and Bonnie Sunstein. Portsmouth, NH: Heinemann.

Graves, Donald, and Bonnie Sunstein, Eds. 1992. *Portfolio Portraits*. Portsmouth, NH: Heinemann.

Pratt, Mary Louise. 1991. "Arts of the Contact Zone". In *Profession* 91. New York: MLA.

Hairston, Maxine. 1982. "The Winds of Change: Thomas Kuhn and the Revolution in the Teaching of Writing." *College Composition and Communication*, 33(1) 76–88.

15

PORTFOLIOS AND THE POLITICS OF ASSESSING WRITING IN URBAN SCHOOLS

JOHN S. SCHMIT AND DEBORAH A. APPLEMAN

Assessment is a tool with a very sharp edge. In the hands of the well trained, it can cleanly separate good from faulty practice or sufficient from insufficient curricula. It can lead to greater accountability, more accurate diagnosis of ineffective methods, or better means by which to address the needs of students. Good assessment is a good tool.

In the hands of the untrained and uninformed, however, the tool may bring results varying between botched curricula and outright butchery. In the case of writing assessment, it can further separate the "successful" students from the "unsuccessful" students by driving the latter from our schools. This happens in a number of ways: the privileging of class dialects over cognitive abilities, of performance over competence, and of convention over imagination. Further, timed performance-based writing assessments encourage students to avoid risk, to focus on the superficial, to employ formulas—in short, to do all the things that good writing instruction teaches them not to do.

What should educators do, then, when faced with standardized writing assessment? Teachers who must prepare their students for writing assessments have a variety of choices available to them. They might tailor their teaching to the assessments, which is not a bad strategy if they can procure a test worth teaching to. They might fight for assessment reform, for instance through the use of portfolio assessment. Or, they might simply employ the best writing practice available and let the political chips fall as they may in the vast pastures where politicians choose to drop them. Implied within this last choice are two assumptions: first, that portfolios represent the best practice available and that their use offers significant hope for improved student writing; and second, that employment of portfolios in standardized assessment is more likely to undermine portfolio-based writing instruction than to improve standardized assessment.

The latest public outcry to improve schooling and make student learning (and teaching) more accountable has made even more relevant the thorny issue of writing assessment and the use of portfolios for both assessment and instruction. When we consider how best to implement assessment within the complex sociocultural context of urban schools, the issue becomes even thornier. We present here the case of one public school district as it attempts to better serve its increasingly diverse student population at the same time that it struggles to accommodate the state government's attempt to answer that public outcry to improve schooling. Might portfolios be the way to accomplish both, or would the use of portfolios for assessment turn a powerful pedagogical tool into a dull knife or even a blunt instrument?

MINNEAPOLIS: A CASE STUDY OF URBAN SCHOOLS AND WRITING ASSESSMENT

Minneapolis, Minnesota is one city facing the challenge of governmentally imposed writing assessment. As we anticipate the impending collision between the city's demographics and the implementation of statewide assessment, this challenge seems even more complicated than it might initially appear.

The Changing Face of Minneapolis

Over the past decade, Minneapolis has seen a large-scale shift in its demographics. This is particularly reflected in the school-age population, where the percentage of students of color has risen from 35 percent in 1983 to 68 percent today. The results of this population change are felt in three primary areas: the devastating effects of poverty and transiency, cultural difference and the politics of inclusion, and language proficiency.

The poverty rate among children has grown enormously. The Twin Cities have the highest minority poverty rate of any of the twenty-five core cities in the nation's most populous metropolitan areas. Forty-four percent of nonwhites in Minneapolis and St. Paul live in poverty. This compares with a minority poverty rate of approximately 14 percent in Los Angeles and San Diego and approximately 21 percent in New York and Washington, D.C., and poverty rates have risen in the Twin Cities over the past five years for African American, Asian American, and Native American residents.

The disparity between incomes in the Twin Cities and their suburbs mirrors the educational achievement rates. The poverty rate in Minneapolis is more than twice that of the seven-county metropolitan area, and the poverty rate for children is much higher than for adults. Sixty-two percent of elementary school children in Minneapolis qualify for free or reduced-price lunches; this number has risen from 33 percent in 1989.

In 1996, public school eighth graders were given math and reading basic standards tests. The results indicated a large disparity between students in the suburbs and those in the core city. The failure rate in Minneapolis was 63 percent, compared with a failure rate of less that 33 percent in the seven-county metropolitan area. The writing assessment is soon to follow, and there is little hope that the percentage numbers will be higher than these.

Because family income correlates closely with achievement on standardized tests, it is easy to predict that this assessment will most greatly affect low-income and Limited English Proficiency (LEP) students, two growing populations within the Twin Cities. Jay Simmons' (1992) studies on traditional writing tests from eleven New England school administrative units support this claim:

> Since SES [socioeconomic stratum] was directly correlated with test score, this means that poorer schools are hurt most by essay-only writing tests. Rich schools' test scores significantly surpassed those of low SES grade five schools, while portfolio differences for the same schools were only marginal. (112)

These data seem to provide powerful evidence of the potential harm done by traditional writing assessments.

As Minnesota prepares for statewide assessment, an even more important question is whether students from these growing populations will remain in school to take the tests we prepare for them. While it might be the case that successful assessment practice can improve teaching and learning, such improvements come at a high price: students who don't succeed don't stay in school. Over the past decade, the school dropout rate in Minneapolis has hovered near 50 percent. This compares with a dropout rate of about 30 percent for Hennepin county, where Minneapolis is located, and a statewide dropout rate of less than 20 percent in Minnesota. The dropout rate is also higher for students of color: in 1993–94 the Minneapolis school district dropout rate was 11.5 percent, but it was 14.8 percent among African Americans, 19.3 percent among Hispanic Americans, and 23.2 percent among Native Americans.

Clearly, these dropout rates precede the imposition of state standards, but this is not an area that standards are designed to address. The outcome of the Graduation Standard, not surprisingly, is better performance by those who graduate. The standards offer little if anything for students on the margin deciding to drop out or persist.

The Challenge of LEP Students

For LEP students the standards movement is especially threatening. The unsettling effects of relocation to a new country combine with the devastating effects of poverty to create a sobering challenge. The standards movement seems to contradict the needs of diverse student populations, but it will inevitably play a significant role in the future of Minneapolis' schools.

The number of students participating in LEP programs in Minneapolis has risen from approximately 1,600 in 1984 to nearly 5,300 in 1995, 8.5 percent of all children in the Minneapolis Public Schools. Eighty-four percent of these are Southeast Asian refugees, and 83 percent of all LEP students are classified as low-income. The success of these students will depend heavily upon the district's ability to couple school language with the language of the student's own experience.

In *Whole Language for Second Language Learners* (1992), Freeman and Freeman explain why this is the case:

> Cummins (1989) has shown that immigrants need about two years to develop conversational proficiency in a second language, but it takes five to seven years for students to develop academic language proficiency. These results are not surprising. New arrivals learn the language they need first. They have to be able to communicate messages orally. It takes longer for them to develop school language, particularly the language found on standardized tests. In part this is because they have less immediate need for such language and in part because test content often has little real connection to the world outside of school. (89)

For LEP students, the difficulties and the time required for gaining academic proficiency in a new language argue for alternatives to standardized assessment. Unfortunately, the needs of this growing population seem to be largely ignored as Minnesota forges ahead with its program of statewide assessment.

Literacy and Culture

Linguistically diverse students are not the only population whose educational gains may not be adequately measured by standardized testing. In Minneapolis, one of the challenges of creating a fair and effective system of evaluation of student performance will be to first understand the cultural identity of students within the school district and critically assess the means by which the district might best represent growth in student achievement. So long as literacy is measured in academic language, those with limited exposure to this medium will continue to show up under the labels of "underprepared" or "unsuccessful." As well, there must be a match between the expectations of the district for its students and the expectations of the students for themselves.

This lack of fit between expectation and experience is noted by Kutz and Roskelly (1991) in *An Unquiet Pedagogy*:

> The school population is increasingly diverse, and that means that teachers encounter students who have problems with Standard English, who come from cultures with ways of knowing and communicating different from those of the mainstream, those who, in earlier decades, would not have been in school at all. Such students enter the schools less prepared to achieve the literacy of the mainstream culture, yet they must achieve a higher level of literacy than most students of the past. (10)

Traditional means for assessing learning are not culturally appropriate for populations whose cultural identity differs significantly from those of the mainstream. Achieving the literacy of the mainstream culture is a special challenge for African American students, the largest single group among Minneapolis school children.

For African American students, standardized tests pose a particular problem. According to John Ogbu (1987), African Americans develop both an oppositional identity and an oppositional cultural frame of reference as a means of self and cultural protection. This cultural framework also brings about distrust: "they perceive inferior education as being perpetuated through many subtle devices like biased testing, misclassification, tracking, biased textbooks, biased and inadequate counseling, and so on, and because blacks doubt that public schools understand their children and their educational needs" (169).

Ogbu examines various types of cultural and language differences that can interfere with student performance. One type of difference calls into question the status and possibility of people from the nondominant culture, and this difference often creates difficulties for African American students. In response, African American students develop "a new cultural frame of reference, or ideal way of behaving, in opposition to the cultural frame of reference of their 'white oppressors'" (156–57).

The greater the reliance upon standardized assessment methods, the greater will be the perception that the needs of minority students are being ignored.

If proficiency in the academic language remains the benchmark, then learners from other cultures will necessarily be viewed as "deficient" in their ability to express themselves in educational settings. This is not to argue that we forego attempts to increase the abilities of all students in standard language. We must recognize, though, that those students who experience cultural difference will experience greater difficulty in the attainment of academic language, and therefore will be less able to demonstrate their academic growth.

MINNESOTA'S NEW GRADUATION STANDARDS

The standards movement is alive with a vengeance in Minnesota. At the same time that the student population has become both increasingly diverse and economically stratified, the state legislature has suspended the current graduation rule—which was based, as it has been in most states, on seat time and "Carnegie units"—and initiated the Minnesota Graduation Standard, a performance-based assessment system with basic skill tests. In order to graduate from high school, the class of 2000 must not only pass the basic skills tests but must demonstrate competence in several broadly defined areas of academic endeavor.

The new graduation rule mandates that student writing be assessed by means of a proficiency exam. This exam involves an isolated writing sample, generated without context in response to a single, uniform prompt. For example, a prompt cited as typical in the most recent Handbook for the Minnesota Basic Standard Test of Written Composition (1997) reads as follows: "Name one goal you would like to accomplish and give specific reasons why. Give enough details so that your teacher will understand your ideas." This prompt exemplifies the kind of writing exam that Simmons (1992) refers to as "less than shallow" (111). He adds that if such tests are timed, they wreak the greatest injury among the weakest writers: "Most students who score the lowest on timed writing tasks do significantly better when classroom writing is graded, while most average and above-average scorers do not" (111).

In Minnesota, as in many other states, the standards movement in general and the elements related to language arts in particular have created both fear and optimism. Teachers rightly worry about the influence of noneducators on the content and process of academic standards and the long-term effect mandatory basic achievement tests will have on urban schools and disadvantaged learners.

On the other hand, the mandate for performance-based assessment might be satisfied through systematic use of portfolios. If language arts teachers in Minnesota throughout the K–12 spectrum can focus on the demonstration aspect of portfolios and provide methods of providing holistic and longitudinal methods of assessment in student portfolios, perhaps the standards movement will enhance rather than deter the progress of our students' writing.

POSSIBILITIES FOR PORTFOLIOS

Portfolio assessments have been used successfully to meet state-mandated assessment guidelines, as Roberta Rosenberg (1991) demonstrates in an article that outlines the response of Christopher Newport College to a resolution from Virginia's state legislature. If Minnesota educators and legislators can follow the lead of states such as Virginia, Vermont, and Kentucky in using portfolios as an integral part of their statewide assessment, then the new standards may serve to support the learning of all Minnesota school children. For unlike the proposed standardized tests, portfolios are especially compatible with classrooms with diverse learners.

To illustrate this diversity, we provide here some brief descriptions of students in a class that Deborah recently taught in a Minneapolis high school. There were thirty-one students in the class, fifteen white students and sixteen students of color. The students of color included eight African American students, one Native American student, two Latino students, two Asian American students, one Hmong student, and two Vietnamese students. The class, a trimester-long English elective, included students from grades 9 through 12. Students ranged in ability from reading and writing far below grade level ability to college readiness. Below is a brief description of some of the students in the class:

> Terry is the daughter of two college professors. A senior, she has been accepted to Oberlin College and writes as well as most college juniors.
>
> Arnie is an alienated tenth grader who writes beautiful poetry but has never turned in a completed expository assignment.
>
> Darnelle is in ninth grade but reads and writes at a fourth-grade level.
>
> Dee is a motivated twelfth grader who would love to attend college but whose writing is around 8th grade level. He was recruited to play basketball.
>
> Chi-Lee is a tenth grader who learned English six years ago.
>
> Tom is an ninth grader who is a father of two and has never successfully completed an English credit. He hates to write.
>
> Roman is a bright tenth grader whose writing is strong and clear. His gang activities prevent him from focusing on his schoolwork as he would like.

The diversity of this classroom is not unique. As every Minneapolis teacher knows, this is now the rule, not the exception. This diversity does call into question the viability of standardized writing assessments such as those proposed for the Minneapolis Public Schools. It's hard to imagine all these students taking a single test, completing the same paper assignments or trying to proceed lockstep through traditional assessment material, but this will be the case.

How, then, do we respond? What kinds of assessment could be used to demonstrate improvement in the writing of all of these students? Portfolios could prove to be the a powerful tool, but should they be part of the assessment process?

THE CASE FOR PORTFOLIOS

Given the changing population that we see in Minneapolis, it would seem that portfolio assessment has never been more promising to urban schools. One might even go so far as to claim that the use of portfolio assessments in language-arts classrooms may be the single most effective instructional approach available to contemporary educators. The individualization of student assessment that portfolios make possible argues for an expansion of their use. They offer the ability to create a multidimensional portrait of a student's growth, to demonstrate longitudinal achievement rather than point-in-time snapshots of academic attainment, to focus on the student growth and progress, and to customize course content and accommodate individual difference.

On the other hand, should their use be expanded into the arenas of assessment? There is a case to be made for portfolios as an assessment tool. Porter and Cleland (1995), for example, in *The Portfolio as a Learning Strategy*, explain how portfolios provided the assessment tool they needed to chronicle the diverse and dramatic learning of their students. Confronted with the diverse learning needs of their students, they wanted to create a middle school learning environment designed to facilitate and encourage all student learning. They struggled especially with the issue of assessment: "Traditional assessment procedures simply did not meet the needs of our students" (7). Informed by recent literature on whole language learning, they concluded, "We now understood that assessment needed to match the beliefs we had about learning, which in turn was reflected in our classroom instruction and informed by the assessment instruments being used" (29). They make an eloquent case for portfolios to support learning, to provide formative rather than summative evaluation, and to accommodate the needs of diverse learners.

Still, portfolios are more than a tool for assessment: they are also a strategy for learning, and they accommodate a wide variety of learning styles. A portfolio is not merely a collection device; it is a learning tool because it requires that students actively reflect on and judge their own work. They also have control over the assessment, especially when they have input into the contents of the portfolio. The following table, taken from Dennie Wolf's (1989) "Portfolio Assessment: Sampling Student Work," (as quoted in Porter and Cleland 1995) lays out the contrast between what assessment has traditionally been and what it can be when portfolios are used:

Traditional Assessments	*Nontraditional Assessments*
focus on skill performance	focus on process
students acquire objective knowledge	students thoughtfully judge their own work
achievement matters	development matters
teacher's responsibility	shared responsibility
first and only draft work valued	multiple drafts valued
used to determine a grade	used by student and teacher to guide learning

One common theme among these nontraditional assessments is that they focus on the development and responsibility of students. This is especially important for districts like Minneapolis, where low student achievement is magnified by the use of performance testing, and where the diversity of student abilities requires a flexible and dynamic assessment procedure.

Porter and Cleland also underscore the value of portfolio assessment as a means of promoting student reflection. Using portfolios to facilitate student reflection on their own learning and their individual goals can make assessment meaningful for all students, regardless of their level of performance. Additionally, when students can choose the contents of their portfolios, the assessment can be personalized to accommodate the needs and interests of the individual learner.

We can establish, then, a number of criteria for the authentic assessment of writing. Drawing from an extensive literature on performance assessment, we would select the following criteria as most appropriate for the measurement of student performance in writing:

- Assessments should demonstrate skills that students have learned.
- They should give insight into students' overall performance.
- The assessments should measure higher-order cognitive skills.
- They should involve a minimum of artificial constraints on time and resources.
- Assessments should be anchored with actual student work and based on appropriate standards.
- They should be administered fairly, with adequate and uniform instructions.
- Results should provide meaningful, reportable data to the community.

It would seem that portfolio assessment provides a broader range of opportunities than standardized testing for meeting these criteria, especially when one considers the needs of a diverse student population.

PORTFOLIOS AND STUDENT DIVERSITY

The beauty of portfolio assessment is that it allows us to address a variety of issues related to different populations using a single pedagogical device. Despite differences in the cultural backgrounds of students in Minneapolis and the variety of needs that these differences create, we do not need to devise separate assessment tools to address separate needs. In the case of LEP students, for example, portfolios create room for students to make use of their own language to whatever extent they have already been able to develop it. The fact that they can revise or otherwise reconstruct the contents of the portfolio serves two ends. They can perhaps choose to work on topics with which they already have some familiarity and descriptive ability. Portfolios also give students the advantage of confidence by giving them the ability to select areas of study for which they already have some linguistic competency. As they build their portfolios, they will naturally develop language that has relevance to their lives and their interests, and thus they will be more likely to retain and master it.

If Ogbu's (1987) argument holds, portfolio assessment might provide an assessment alternative for those African American students who experience "oppositional culture" and "oppositional identity." By allowing students to control the content of their own portfolios, this assessment alternative may help them past the notion that success in school is about "acting white." For those who are not proficient in the conventions of Standard English, portfolios provide an occasion to master those conventions within contexts chosen by the students themselves.

Portfolios offer something to each of these groups. They foster a developmental focus by accommodating longitudinal assessment, and they focus on the students' language without foregoing students' need to learn Standard English.

PROCEEDING WITH CAUTION

What is likely to happen when we take the best of portfolio practice and make it the basis for assessment? It is difficult to answer this question with certainty, but it is also difficult to imagine students taking risks, exercising creativity, and making authentic choices about the contents of their portfolios when they know that those portfolios are instruments of examination.

Further, the use of portfolios, of itself, is no guarantee that students will be allowed to participate in their own assessment process. It is entirely possible that the portfolio will only give standardized writing assessment a new face. According to Jean Fontana (1995), the forms of portfolio writing assessment can vary significantly from state to state. Fontana uses portfolio assessment programs in Vermont and Kentucky as examples of differing possibilities. In Vermont, the student's portfolio includes "on demand" performance assessments, while in Kentucky on demand assessments are required in addition to a portfolio. In the former case the portfolio is a reflection of student choice, while in the latter it is a reflection of the state's requirements (25).

How do we achieve a balance, then, between classroom practice and accountability within a system or state's assessment scheme? How do we ensure that such assessments provide useful data for teachers as well as authentic measures of student learning? Standardized assessment, whether it involves portfolios or not, can induce teachers to build their teaching programs around political exigencies rather than student needs.

When assessment provides only summative data, it becomes difficult for teachers to interpret the results of tests in ways that allow them to address the needs of their students. It is equally difficult for parents to enter into partnerships with schools and teachers. A whole host of logistical problems arise as well. In inner-city schools, for example, where transiency from school to school is high, it is difficult to keep portfolios and students together.

Thus, we must be careful not to lose the very advantages of portfolios that made them valuable as learning tools in the first place. As Sue Wortham (1995) says,

> It behooves us to ensure that we walk the walk with portfolio assessment. If we cannot implement it effectively for assessment and instructional planning, we can anticipate a revisionist phase of portfolio assessment characterized by articles titled, "Why Portfolio Assessments Don't Work." (32-A)

Wortham's concern in some ways summarizes the problem: If portfolio assessments are not authentic reflections of student work then there is little point to using them for assessment at all. A further danger is that portfolio practice will be distorted in ways that negate the advantages for which we adopted it in the first place.

One other matter worth our attention involves a limitation inherent in portfolio assessment: the variability of the assessment itself. While all assessment of writing is necessarily subjective, the assessment of portfolios adds new criteria to the evaluation process. To what extent is progress judged apart from product? How much does selection

192 John S. Schmit and Deborah A. Appleman

affect the judgments of the evaluators? How might the idiosyncrasies of a portfolio match or oppose the judgments of the reviewer? Are the assessors able to judge portfolios on their own merit, or must they be compared against a set of established expectations?

If the latter is the case, then how does one judge the success or failure of the student's construction of the portfolio? How, in other words, does one norm portfolio practice? John Nidds and James McGerald (1997) summarize the problem:

> Such inconsistency [as was reported in Vermont's statewide assessment program] would seem to suggest that judging portfolios is so subjective as to be practically meaningless for purposes of comparison. One teacher's score of 95 might be another teacher's score of 80, and still another teachers score of 70. Portfolio assessment, in Vermont, is too unreliable to provide the information needed to make intelligent decisions at the local or state level. Portfolio assessment makes more sense when there are no specific educational standards, as at the classroom level. (49)

Again, this argument suggests that if portfolio assessment is to be used for assessment, it should be used in small settings for gathering formative data. If reliability rather than authenticity is important at the levels where policy is made, then portfolios are better left out of the assessment procedures that precede policy decisions.

A final caution concerns the possibility that portfolio practice might be skewed. As Mark Reckase (1995) reports, large-scale use of portfolio assessment creates the opportunity for instructional practice to be distorted (31). The flexibility of portfolios is lost, as is the authenticity of the student's work. One might even argue that the accumulation of student work that is created within such assessment systems is not a portfolio at all but merely a collection of assessment materials.

CONCLUSION

While portfolios serve the purpose of informing teachers about the effectiveness of their practice and the success of their students, as summative assessments they too can become political weapons. A number of troubling answers come forward when we ask questions like, Whose needs do the assessments meet? The governor's? The legislature's? The parents'? The teachers'? Various political entities are likely to fall into conflict about how to best use portfolios as assessment and what those portfolios do and do not indicate about the state of writing instruction in our schools.

On the other hand, as Simmons (1992) reports, when wisely used, portfolios can provide a sensitive and sensible alternative to the blunt and imprecise instruments of other large-scale assessments:

> Portfolio assessment has now developed sufficiently at the individual level to be adapted to large-scale settings. To fail to do so, or to settle in the process of change for only the most superficial or highly constrained forms of portfolios, can only perpetuate the inequalities and inaccuracies of the past. (113)

He also notes that portfolios are able to capture the nuances of literacy and culture in an equitable way. Ultimately, those of us who live in cities like Minneapolis need to find ways to fairly report the current state of student literacy as we continue to develop instruction to better serve the needs of all our students.

REFERENCES

1997 Hennepin County Indicators: Update on Families and Children. 1998. Hennepin Office of Planning and Development and United Way of Minneapolis Area.

Cummins, Jim. 1989. *Empowering Minority Students.* Sacramento: CABE.

"Evaluating Schools: A Step Toward Accountability." 1997. Editorial. *Minneapolis Star Tribune.* January 15, A14.

The Face of the Twin Cities: Another Look. 1995. The United Way of Minneapolis Area.

Fontana, Jean. 1995. "Portfolio Assessment: Its Beginnings in Vermont and Kentucky." *NASSP Bulletin* 79 (October): 25.

Freeman, Yvonne S., and David E. Freeman. 1992. *Whole Language for Second Language Learners.* Portsmouth, NH: Heinemann.

Handbook for Minnesota Basic Standard Test of Written Compostion 1997. Dept. of Children, Families, and Learning. State of Minnesota.

Kutz, Eleanor, and Hephzibah Roskelly. 1991. *An Unquiet Pedagogy: Transforming Practice in the English Classroom.* Portsmouth, NH: Boynton/Cook.

Nidds, John A., and James McGerald. 1997. "How Functional is Portfolio Assessment Anyway?" *The Educational Digest* (January): 47–50.

Ogbu, John U. 1987. "Opportunity Structure, Cultural Boundaries, and Literacy." In *Language, Literacy and Culture: Issues in Society and Schooling.* ed. Judith A. Langer. Norwood, NJ: Ablex.

Olsen, L., and N. Mullen. 1990. *Embracing Diversity: Teachers' Voices from California Classrooms.* San Francisco: California Tomorrow.

Porter, Carol, and Janell Cleland. 1995. *The Portfolio as a Learning Strategy.* Portsmouth, NH: Heinemann.

Reckase, Mark D. 1995. "Practical Experiences Implementing a National Portfolio Model at the High School Level." *NASSP Bulletin* 79 (October): 31.

Rosenberg, Roberta. 1991. "Using the Portfolio to Meet State-Mandated As-sessment: A Case Study." In *Portfolios: Process and Product*. ed. Pat Belanoff and Marcia Dickson. Portsmouth, NH: Heinemann.

Simmons, Jay. 1992. "Portfolios for Large-Scale Assessment." In *Portfolio Portraits*. ed. Donald H. Graves and Bonnie S. Sunstein. Portsmouth, NH: Heinemann.

Title VII Systemwide Improvement Grant. 1995. Minneapolis Public Schools, May.

Wolf, Dennie Palmer. 1989. "Portfolio Assessment: Sampling Student Work." *Educational Leadership* 46(7): 35–39.

Wortham, Sue C. 1995. "Portfolio Assessment: Talking the Talk—Walking the Walk." *ACEI Exchange* (Fall): 32A.

16

SURVIVING PORTFOLIOS
Three Lenses to the Rescue
JUDITH FUEYO

Remember in high school, getting invited (or not) to the dance? There was talk, always talk, of what to wear, who would be there (or not), and so on. By the vagaries of cultural codes, this information was passed on to those who needed it.

Why isn't culture behaving likewise around portfolios? I once believed that inviting students to "represent themselves and their literacy learning" via portfolios was enough. I believed that students would manipulate the form to position themselves as just that: manipulators of the form for their own purposes more or less. I believed students would capitalize on the distinctive features that make portfolios different: their capacity to exploit the medium/message dynamic, and their potential to shift power relations. Some students did and I'll show portions of their portfolios later. But why so few?

It's because I've kept the distinctive features secret, unintentionally, nevertheless, in a very real way. I say "unintentionally" intentionally. I had to find student portfolios that exhibited the medium/message dynamic and the shift in power relations to understand how critical these features are to my image of "successful" portfolios.

That said, I need to rethink ways of responding to the majority of portfolios that seemed less "successful," all the while knowing that I did not yet know how to "teach" portfolios better.

A HALLUCINATORY DREAM

Once upon a time in Portfolioland, semesters then and now, thousands of preservice teachers in their first methods courses were commanded to construct portfolios. Brave uninitiates that they were, they would advance nobly toward Wal-Mart, seizing three-ring binders and plastic sleeves till no more could be found in the kingdom.

Thence, these uninitiates commenced to craft portfolios to which we insiders had to respond. One Among Us, me, had what can only be termed an out-of-body experience. She claimed to see herself hovering above the multitude of portfolios as they sorted themselves into piles of yet-to-be-admitted-to categories whilst strands of Peggy Lee's "Is This All There Is?" wafted in the mauve-hued background.

Off to her left, she watched The Grand Tour representatives assembling themselves into alphabetical order. These portfolios recapped the syllabi verbatim, using assignments and artifacts to prove "Been there. Done that," all with equal emphasis. No matter how hard she looked, One Among Us could see only pale imitations of her better intentions—those syllabi and that portfolio guideline—coopted to carry on school-business-as-usual. She yawned despite her vow to love, honor, and respect. . . .

To her right, hovering still, she gazed on as the I Love Children portfolio pile, accompanied by the Barney theme song, mounted higher even than that of The Grand Tour. So noxious to her was this cliched bunch that she felt justified in ignoring it altogether, despite the seduction of quilted covers and macaroni lettering. "Necessary but not sufficient, this love for children thing," she'd exhorted time and again. And still this? Is there no light in Portfolioland?

She drifted despondently toward that heap labeled The B. S. Circuit. Alas! Here could be heard the language of wider portfolio communication. The B. S. Circuit had appropriated the discourse, even dressed the part (black binders, minimal arts-'n'-crafts touches). Here a shining moment . . . until she remembered how shamelessly the makers of these portfolios came clean in their portfolio exit interviews. In that face-to-face encounter with her, many admitted to learning "the in-words," "decoding the politics of this kingdom." Touché. She couldn't ignore this bunch: Lo, she'd tried on this discourse herself way-back-when. Why, then, did The B. S. Circuit leave her more disillusioned than the others?

It came as some relief, then, when One Among Us spotted the Save the Yearning Masses pile far down to her left. Although this group of portfolios might manifest itself in Engfish, that peculiar brand of illiteracy that poses as academic, it appeared sincere. She hovered close enough to read the inscription on the portfolio atop this pile: "This portfolio is an excellent example of hard-core literacy which is so important and needed by young children which don't read and write." In spite of the self-conscious language, she couldn't fault the uninitiate's intentions. Worse, One Among Us found herself tempted to take a sentimental stance toward this portfolio, out-of-the-closet Romantic that she was.

> The final pile, the I Gotta Be Me representatives. . . . Ach, enough! Seeing these portfolio piles from on high had addled her brain.

Surely it's fun for me to satirize the students' stances—and I intend it as a humorous hook into this piece. Surely, too, I'm not above posturing as the Wizard of Oz, the one behind the curtain, the one who's "getting smart," and who will lead the students to "see" differently. But that approach is a force feeding for many. To better attune myself to my students' intentions, honor them, and still nudge them beyond their present positions I need to find different ways of "seeing."

THREE LENSES TO THE RESCUE

The lighting technician for a theatrical performance uses colored lenses to enhance and interpret the action on stage. Analogically, I will describe how three lenses through which I have come to view preservice teachers' portfolios fit the "action on stage." As a consequence of looking this way, I see things differently. What I once saw as disappointing, I now see in ways more likely to honor the portfolio makers' intentions. What I once saw as successful, idiosyncratic breakthrough portfolios, I now see as serendipitous collisions of my good intentions and student subversions of same which help me to name and demonstrate portfolio potentials I've been imagining for a long time. I am reminded of Annie Dillard's awakening:

> There is another kind of seeing that involves a letting go. When I see this way I sway transfixed and emptied. The difference between the two ways of seeing is the difference between walking with and without a camera. When I walk with a camera I walk from shot to shot, reading the light on a calibrated meter. When I walk without a camera, my own shutter opens, and the moment's light prints on my own silver gut. . . . I cannot cause light; the most I can do is try to put myself in the path of its beam. (Dillard 1974, 30–33)

It's taken me nearly ten years of "doing portfolios" to see and see through these lenses, to be "in the path of (the portfolio's) beam." The three lenses I suggest are not mutually exclusive, but each one values differently qualities that portfolios invite. I call the three lenses the "performance lens," the "aesthetic-repleteness lens," and the "critical genre lens." In this article, I will describe these lenses and their affinity for portfolios as I've experienced them.

At the end of a nine-credit literacy block, preservice teachers must construct a portfolio to "show (your) understandings of theory and practice (as a teacher of) reading, writing, children's literature, and multicultural issues. Frame these understandings around significant issues that best represent you as a literacy educator for our times." Students may choose the audience for the portfolio and are urged to share it with this audience. However, because they must have a thirty-minute portfolio exit interview with a senior faculty member, typically students choose us as audience. This is the first portfolio for most students, and sometimes the first portfolio experience for the graduate teaching assistants.

We keep the evaluative stakes low for the portfolios. Some years we've used Pass/Fail; other years, at the urging of students!, we assigned up to ten points of a possible one hundred for the nine-credit block. We never headed for rubrics, partly out of inertia perhaps, but mostly because of a shared epistemological dream: we hoped to keep open the potential for what portfolios might become.

In the section to follow, I show two portfolios that were more successful in my eyes. But, you need to know that these two students acted upon their portfolios *after* consulting with me. I believe that this interruption significantly changed their portfolios. It is possible that what I'm noticing about these portfolios could have happened in the portfolios I satirized above if I had met with each student during the portfolio process. But, large-block structure—where faculty lecture to 150 preservice teachers three times a week—discourages such one-on-one encounters. Better yet, if I had known what "more successful" portfolios looked like, I could have provided better large-group instruction.

I am hopeful that because of what I've seen of the two portfolios to follow, anomalies both in product and process, I can use them as examples in large-group lectures and interrupt business-as-usual in the future.

THE PERFORMANCE LENS

All portfolios function as performances. But, when I remind myself to note the particular functions of the performance lens for portfolios like those I satirized above, they take on more weight. When I view these portfolios as performances—students trying on new selves as they negotiate their entry into their academic and professional communities—they fare better (see also Bartholomae 1985). In this discussion then, I am borrowing from Tom Newkirk's (1997) *The Performance of Self in Student Writing*, his analysis of undergraduate students' writing. The coherence between kinds of "selves" students compose in his composition classes is similar to the "selves" our students construct in portfolios.

One of the questions I routinely ask a student author when writing a piece is, "What are you trying to do here?" The performance lens functions similarly: It reminds me that the portfolio maker is trying to compose a professional self. To suggest that the performance categories are clichéd attests to their ubiquitousness. Still, to call their performances clichés dishonors students' intentions and distrusts the cash value such performances might have in students' professional becoming. I need to take them at their words, at this time, as they position themselves on stage.

Instead of being disappointed in the satirized categories above, I am going to ask a pragmatic question, taken from Tom Newkirk , William James, and John Dewey: What might be the consequences of positioning oneself within such categories as (choose one): *The Grand Tour, I Love Children, The B. S. Circuit, Save the Yearning Masses,* or *I Gotta Be Me?* Is it possible that, for example, *The Grand Tour* folks really need to summarize the literacy block semester for themselves? that *The B. S. Circuit* is the sincerest form of flattery and these students may one day own this new discourse from the inside? that *The I Gotta Be Me* folks will teach powerfully precisely because they are environmentalists, mountain climbers, Christians, Buddhists, vegetarians, or football players?

Because I suspect each of you could add to the list, I will not provide example portfolios from this category. But I will show portions of two portfolios that break out—each in its own way—from the above categories. The portfolios to follow fare better when viewed through different lenses.

Remember the scene in *The Truman Show* when Truman's sailboat crashes up against the horizon line? That moment when he realizes his life is a made-for-television movie and all his world's a stage? Instead of attempting to portray some essential "me the informed literacy preservice teacher," the students' portfolios below made visible the movie set, its constructions, if you will. Both portfolio makers below understand the possibility for multiple representations of themselves better than most (or at least they bring this understanding to the fore). Both intentionally framed/aimed their portfolios toward an audience other than me, narrowed their focus dramatically, and played with the portfolio form itself. Jen's portfolio stands out especially for its marriage of content and form, thus I use hers to illustrate the fit of the aesthetic-repleteness lens for such portfolios. Later I will show parts of Sara's portfolio because the critical-genre lens best captures her intentions.

Both Jen's and Sara's portfolios, I admit, capitalize on the overlapping features of what's possible aesthetically and critically. *The difference between the two portfolios is in what students emphasize.*

THE AESTHETIC-REPLETENESS LENS

The quality of portfolios that attracted me in the first place was their "repleteness." *Repleteness* is a term borrowed from philosopher of art Nelson Goodman (1968) and means that marriage of form and content such that the artist/meaning maker exploits in a positive sense the unique potential of a particular artistic form. For example, imagine two first graders exploring with lumps of clay. One child flattens the clay and draws a man on it with his pencil tip: The other child shapes the clay into a man. We would say that the second child's product was more replete than the first child's product because the second child exploited clay for what is unique to clay, its three-dimensional mouldability, to suggest meanings.

I imagine that portfolios could be that marriage of form and function, realizing a way to shape teaching/learning/assessment into a seamless thing. Once in a while, this happens.

Jen arrived on schedule for her portfolio exit interview last spring, portfolio completed. Her audience was her hometown school board, because "my school district could definitely benefit from a multicultural curriculum." We talked as we went through it. (Finally, *I* do not turn the pages. It's taken me years to learn that.) As usual, the talk surrounding the portfolio was richer than the portfolio. So I asked, "Jen, how might you capture in the portfolio what you've been saying today?"

I told her how I was trying to write an article using students' portfolios and excerpts from their taped exit interviews. I was interested in showing the richness in the dialectic across their talk and their portfolio entries. I admitted to the inauthenticity of my telling their stories. (The further irony of my telling them here is not lost on me.

Still, I must act, all the while respectful of the partiality of my telling. Lather (1991) warns against using language to give the appearance of objectivity. She suggests instead using data as "the material for telling a story where the challenge becomes to generate a polyvalent data base that is used to *vivify* interpretation as opposed to 'support' or 'prove' (91). Even Jen's story is her story about her story.)

I invited her to find a way to add the interview talk to her portfolio over the summer and handed her some transparencies and markers.

During the second week of the semester this fall, as I was crossing College Avenue, Jen rushed up to me and pulled me to the curb. "I did it! Want to see it?" Then I remembered our conversation from the previous semester and asked her to bring the portfolio in quickly because I was trying to make sense of this article.

Below I reproduce one three-page section, an utterance in the Bakhtinian sense, of Jen's revisioned portfolio: (Figure 16–1) a child's drawing of Jen's farmhouse (artifact); (Figure 16–2) Jen's original reflection on that child's drawing; and (Figure 16–3) the reflection Jen

---

FIGURE 16–1   "This student thought my (farm)house looked like an apartment building."

I included this drawing because it represents my first attempt to read-aloud to a group of multicultural students and my intention to have students perform a response to the book that I read. I read a story about a farm because I live on a farm. I thought that the students would know very little about farms since they live in a "projects" area of Harrisburg. This drawing by a second-grader is a response to the picture book that I read. I gave students the option to write in their journals about what they liked about the story or didn't like and what they expected to see on a farm, or to draw a picture of what they thought my farm looked like. This child thought that my barn resembled an apartment building. I liked the dialogue that they incorporated and their labeling of pictures. I did this read-aloud before I knew how to do a real read-aloud such as the one that we did for workshop. I wanted to share my culture with the students that I was working with because I thought that they would like to learn about something different. In ——————, I was not taught about cities or what I might find there. I think students would find it interesting to learn about an environment that is much different than the one they live in.

FIGURE 16–2   Jen's Original Typed Reflection.

I went to a school that had K–12 in one building. I live 15 miles away from my school in a very tiny farming community. Most of the people in my town are lower-middle class and lower class blue collar working families. Many students do not go to college after graduation or many attend trade and business colleges in surrounding towns.

Going to Penn State was a real culture shock for me. I had never seen so many different races, but instead of being narrow-minded, I encouraged myself to be curious. I love learning about other people's customs and lifestyles. I really feel robbed of a multi-cultural education from my elementary and high school. I think that in some ways, not teaching children about cultures other than their own can create prejudice. But at the same time, it would be better for the students to not be taught about other cultures by a prejudiced teacher.

My area School District could definitely benefit from a multi-cultural curriculum if the staff taught it in a nonprejudicial way.

FIGURE 16–3   Jen's Later Reflection

added on the transparency. (I present the pages in this order to help you understand the impact of the transparency. However, in her portfolio, it was layered between the child's drawing and her typed reflection.)

Figure 16–1 is a third grader's response to a read-aloud about a farm that Jen did in an elementary school surrounded by housing projects in Harrisburg. Because, as Jen said, "In ————, I was not taught about cities or what I might find there, I thought these (inner-city) students would like to learn about my rural community."

Jen exploited the aesthetic quality of repleteness in the portfolio form. She manipulated the form's potential to interrupt a false sense of linearity or monovocality by inserting the transparencies throughout the portfolio. Imagine how Jen's work might look/mean in hypertext which she will learn next semester! I sense a never-ending conversation, just what we want in our preservice folks, and in ourselves, as we wrestle with making sense of our experience.

In addition, Jen exploits the power inherent in the portfolio genre to critique her past educational experiences. Clearly, Jen's portfolio profits from viewing it through both the aesthetic and the critical lenses.

Her final section originally ended with Figure 16–4. But now, she has added a transparency, Figure 16–5, that acts as praxis, that (rare) transformation of theory into practice.

Although the dynamics of the aesthetic-repleteness lens and the critical genre lens are at work in Jen's portfolio, I use her work to vivify the former because her revised portfolio changed its message, became much more powerful because of the change in form—added layers of critique on the transparencies. It appears that Jen's development is at

---

My original publication about Dr. ———— first lecture is included because it shows my passion to learn about the students that I will have in my class room and the extent to which I feel that educators must go in order to provide a comfortable learning environment for all students. Through a writing workshop, I developed a paper that I am really proud of, regarding an issue that I feel very strongly about. I think that ———————— Elementary School would benefit from such a workshop model, and educators should encourage students to write about issues that they feel strongly about. My paper deals with the need for bilingual education, which I feel has a lot to do with multicultural education. By reading this paper, the school board and administrators would see how strongly I feel about multiculturalism and why it should be implemented into the ———————— Area School District.

FIGURE 16–4 Jen's Final Section

I have recently changed my concentration from Science and Math to Spanish. I will be taking my first Spanish class this fall and I will lose 6-9 credits in Science that I paid for but cannot use toward graduation. I recently read an article about the many Spanish speaking children in classrooms, and I know Spanish would benefit me so much more than Meteorology and Geo Sci.

I think that I am fortunate to have been blessed with an open mind. I am learning all of the time about other cultures and I am totally willing to learn about my students' and community's cultures when I become a teacher. I don't know where I will find a job, but I hope that it is somewhere that I am challenged, appreciated, and satisfied.

FIGURE 16–5   I Have Recently Changed My (Academic) Concentration from Science and Math to Spanish

---

least facilitated by, if not born of, the addition of multiple reflective layers over time. Hence, Jen's intentions are best honored using the aesthetic-replete focus. When I see Jen's portfolio through this lens, I appreciate how the portfolio form contributed to what Jen is becoming and how she is coming to see this.

THE CRITICAL-GENRE PORTFOLIO LENS

A critical-genre portfolio lens highlights the power relations embodied in the portfolio as a genre. A social theory of genre in general emphasizes "the shifting relations between language in the spoken and in the written mode, and its relations to shifts in power" (Kress 1993, 36–37). Viewed through a critical-genre lens, the portfolio could provide students a genre for written language as social work wherein relations of power assume overt attention.

Sara: "This Portfolio Assignment Is Stupid."

Thus Sara announced her unexpected arrival in my office late one afternoon three weeks before the end of the semester and the due date for portfolios. So I asked Sara why the assignment was stupid and what would make it worthy. She shrugged, "All my assignments have been handed back with comments and points. What's the use of a portfolio?"

We continued to talk. She told me that she worked in an after-school program nearby. She mentioned how much this new knowledge about literacy was helping her with the children there and their parents. I asked who might benefit most from what she was learning. She decided it would be these parents. So, instead of me as audience, and instead of "making connections across the block" in a vacuum, she agreed to find a way to show these parents what might be useful to know about literacy. As Sara left my office she said, "I'm glad I came in. If I did what you wanted (in the guidelines), I'd just pick five assignments and it would have been just blah-blah-blah" (Sara 12/1/97).

Two weeks later, Sara arrived in my office with a draft of her portfolio. I reproduce two of eight sets of pages that faced each other to show how Sara conceptualized and shaped her portfolio. Like Jen, Sara capitalized on the quality of repleteness and manipulated the portfolio's form to contribute to meaning. But, Sara intentionally manipulated the genre's potential to shift power relations. Instead of aiming the portfolio toward me or even a school board, Sara aimed it at parents who are likely to know less than she about literacy learning, thus positioning herself as expert and inverting the usual teacher-student hierarchy.

The juxtapositioning of Figures 16–6, 16–6A, and Figures 16–7, 16–7A, emphasizes Sara's aha's during the course. The first page shows Sara's initial misconceptions about literacy learning/teaching. The next page shows her new understandings.

Sara, herself, is developing as a literacy educator. But more important, she is conscious of the power relations operating in the portfolio assignment and uses the genre to capitalize on this realization. Sara is aware of her novice position vis-a-vis me as old pro, so she positions herself for herself—as one who knows more than the parents. Her format, facing pages that talk back to one another, exploits the portfolio's dialogic possibility to position her knowledge before and after the course.

I told Sara how successful her portfolio was and asked why. Sara confessed to me "I didn't look at the guidelines, really."

I laughed and said, "Maybe that's what saved you!"

Sara's portfolio, like Jen's, demonstrates repleteness. But, I believe that her intention to shift power relations in the portfolio assignment was uppermost in her mind, hence I use her work to vivify the critical lens. By viewing her portfolio in this way, I give Sara credit for seizing upon the portfolio genre as "social work wherein relations of power assume overt attention." She is the authority, not parents, not her textbooks, not our curriculum, (and, because I am not the audience, not me). Bravo, Sara!

Last summer, before Maggie entered first grade, I did a lot of reading with her. When *she* was doing the reading, I would correct every word that she missed, regardless of the type of error that she made. Later, through my Reading Miscue Inventory with Michael at Elementary School, I realized the many different kinds of miscues that people can make when they read. Not all miscues are bad—they can be seen as windows into the child's reasoning strategies that are in use to decode words. The most important thing for us to monitor is the child's comprehension of what they are reading.

FIGURE 16–6   **"I would correct every word she missed."**

Sometimes children will substitute words that are the same part of speech and have a similar definition (ex. 'said' for 'called'). These types of miscues do not change the meaning of the passage and reveal that the child is using other types of prediction strategies to decode words. As with children's writing, we want to respond to meaning first, so if the child makes a miscue which violates or changes the interpretation of the passage, and he or she doesn't notice, then it is good to call the child's attention to the mistake. Opportunities like this can be used to work on word decoding skills, whether they include repeating the preceding words, phonetically sounding out the unknown word, or skipping the word and trying to predict one that would fit in that slot. Sometimes when children work so hard to phonetically decode words correctly, they lose some comprehension. If they are allowed to fall back on some other strategies that are available to them, comprehension will be maximized, which is the ultimate goal of reading—to understand.

FIGURE 16–6A   **We Want to Respond to Meaning First**

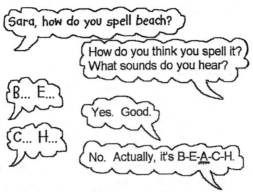

During the summer before first grade, Maggie tried to incorporate written language into many of her crafts and paintings. Whenever she wanted to write a word, she would first ask me how to spell it. I always turned the question back to her and asked her how she thought it should be spelled. She usually got the first letter or two right, but when she moved on to the rest of the word and wrote a wrong letter, I would let her know and tell her the correct one. Basically, Maggie wrote letters until she got one wrong, at which point I stepped in and corrected her. I felt like I wouldn't be helping her at all by allowing her to use invented spellings.

FIGURE 16–7   "Sara, how do you spell beach?"

Now I see that by correcting Maggie's spelling efforts, I was unintentionally doing two things.

First, since she *doesn't* know how to conventionally spell many words, I end up correcting most of the ones that she attempts, pointing out that she is not a 'good speller.' We want children to believe that writing is something that they *can* do, and if mechanical corrections are constantly brought to their attention, confidence in their work and abilities will quickly fade.

Also, by correcting misspellings, I am preventing Maggie from making crucial discoveries about language on her own. Through practice and supportive later editing, she will work closer and closer to adult conventions. I don't want her first worry to be about spelling every time she writes a word, as this will probably only end up inhibiting her creative writing by limiting the vocabulary she feels comfortable using. The use of invented spellings will free up the words that she uses, allowing her to establish a creative writing style, and *then* go back and work on the mechanics.

Under these conditions, writing can become a highly enjoyable activity for children—they understand that the purpose of writing is to convey ideas, and they are allowed to do this without being held back because of unsure spellings.

FIGURE 16–7A "Now I see."

A LITTLE STORY.

Recently, my colleague and I were invited to do a year long inservice for a school district in a down-but-not-out town north of Pittsburgh. They wanted "alternative assessment, especially portfolios." We were able to learn very little about this district before our first day long work with them. Whatever, we reasoned, they could profit from seeing portfolio classroom cultures in action. So, we showed them *Students Find Value in Their Work*, the third in the Hansen and Staley videotape series on portfolios (see Hansen and Staley 1996).

When we discussed this tape, one teacher's words told me most about this district: "We wouldn't dare invite students to critique each other's work. How did those folks establish that community, anyway?" How presumptuous I had been to show the third tape in the series. I told the teachers that there were two other tapes, the first called, *Students Find Value in Themselves*, and the second, *Students Find Value in Each Other*. Overwhelmingly, the they cried, "We need to begin with the first tape!"

My gut reaction to that was, "Of course. And once you develop portfolio cultures, you won't need me or even rubrics," this latter being high on their list of concerns. But, more naiveté on my part. More old-think. I believed for too long that once teachers began working to establish portfolio cultures, by their very nature, these cultures would provoke new ways of doing, being in their classrooms. And many do. But I vastly underestimated how institutionalized doing business-as-usual is. I needed to find ways to demonstrate the qualitatively different power relations portfolios invite into our work. Only when I found a portfolio that did this intentionally, did I recognize how well a "critical lens" suited some portfolios. I needed, too, to find ways to excite students about the meaning potential in this new form, and expect surprises. Once I saw Jen's and Sara's portfolios I realized that these were examples of what I'd been waiting to find (but didn't know how to "teach").

NO MORE PORTFOLIO GUIDELINES.
NO MORE MANDATED PORTFOLIOS.

In what I now see as a misplaced sense of responsibility, I provided "guidelines for portfolios" that no doubt had much to do with the cliched piles in Portfolioland. I need to keep faith with Elliot Eisner (1982) when he reminds us that the very forms we invite either constrain or liberate meaning potential. For portfolios to function as open invitations to new meaning potential, I need to back off, let students play with them, and be open to "seeing" as Dillard suggests.

However, portfolios are not for every student, nor for every course or teacher. I look forward to the day when this assignment is one option among others for a culminating event in our preservice literacy block.

But you bet I'll share Jen's and Sara's portfolios. You bet I'll invite students to use the portfolio genre to interrupt power relations in school—in forms that exploit the reasons for using portfolios in the first place. Especially because these are times where many want to standardize even the way we think, I'm counting on new teachers to marry ways of "seeing" with responsible action on the world. In the best of worlds, portfolios will achieve a marriage of performance, aesthetics, and critical theory. In sum, I'm counting on our new teachers to do much more than survive.

REFERENCES

Bartholomae, David. 1985. "Inventing the University." In *When a Writer Can't Write*, ed. Mike Rose. New York: Guilford.

Dillard, Anne. 1974. *Pilgrim at Tinker Creek*. New York: Harper & Row.

Eisner, Elliot. 1982. *Cognition and Curriculum*. New York: Longman.

Goodman, Nelson. 1968. *Languages of Art*. New York: The Bobbs-Merrill Company.

Hansen, Jane, and Kathy Staley. 1996. *Portfolios: Students as Readers, Writers, and Evaluators*. The Video Series. Portsmouth, NH: Heinemann.

Joos, Martin. 1967. *The Five Clocks*. New York: Harcourt Brace Jovanovich.

Kress, Gunther. 1993. "Genre as Social Process." In *The Powers of Literacy: A Genre Approach to Teaching Writing*, ed. Bill Cope and Mary Kalantzis. Pittsburgh: The University of Pittsburgh Press.

Lather, Patti. 1991. *Getting Smart: Feminist Research and Pedagogy with/in the Postmodern*. New York: Routledge.

Newkirk, Tom. 1997. *The Performance of Self in Student Writing*. Portsmouth, NH: Boynton/Cook, Heinemann.

III
A PORTFOLIO OF PORTFOLIOS

CONTENTS

DAVID WILES' PORTFOLIO, SECOND GRADE
JANUARY 1997–SEPTEMBER 1997

Table of Contents

David Wiles' Portfolio Reflections (Transcriptions from interviews in September, 1997):

Mummy Medicine: "I like this because it's cool and it's funny. I like mummies."

If I Were M.J. (Michael Jordan): Comments in September 1997: "I really like M.J. and I am going to play in the N.B.A. That's why I wrote this."

In January, 1998: "This is not very good. The spelling is bad and it doesn't make sense."

If I Were A Slave: I am Black and I am glad that I didn't live when they had slavery. I am glad I am not a slave."

IF I Was A Rat: "This is good. I liked this book a lot. I wrote this on the computer and it looks good. My teacher liked it."

This thing is well like Funny: "I have a tutor and her and me made this together. I liked it because it was funny and I got to draw funny monsters."

Untitled: When I went to Canada . . . : "This was fun to write for Camelia [David's tutor] so I could tell her about our trip. I loved the gift shops."

The following pages show these pieces in David's portfolio.

January 1997

Dear Camelia

You are Cool becuse You like B Ball and You make me neke and you are OK at B Ball.

Your Friend David

January 20, 1997

Mummy Medicine

Mom when you are sick get
your healing power from a
mummy so you can get
better. If you don't get
find it up! OK you got it!

2-15-97

IF I Was M.J.

I would get my money and get my life supply of Candy but I get it ONCE A Week because I Eat it in a Web. I would get toy + ever that I'm 30 I would get toys. I would not go away from the Bulls. I would get a new home for my mom and dad. I would My Band + a new Corand my friend a new lamborghine. I would get My ___ in dog school. the End

ME

MY Mom

MY Dad

2-27-97   David WILES

What it would be like if I was a sla...

If I was a slave I would
not be with my Mom and dad
I would not have my own house
I would live in a shed. I would
not have every shoe at all. I would
not have good foods because I wo
out in the field. I would be piking
Cotton. I would not have money.
I would try to get away and go to
the north. I would not talk
back to my master because I would
be killed. I would not want to be
a slave because I don't get called
around. by that I mean like
People don't tell me what to do.

Response to
Fourth Grade Rats
by Jerry Spinelli

David Wiles
March 9, 1997

If I Was A Rat

If I was a rat I would get third graders' lunch and put ants in their sandwiches so when they ate their sandwiches the ants would get in their stomaches and they would feel things moving in their stomachs. I would kick their soccer balls so they would have to get the ball. I would race them to the ball and kick the ball again and again and again until recess was over. I would also push them off the monkey bars and make them fall off if I was a rat. After school me and the rest of the rats would get on our scooters and ram into the Angels, the third graders, and make them fall off their scooterboards. I would also trip them. At lunch time I would get my drink and dump it on the third graders' heads. When an Angel was drinking something I would say something like a joke and they would spit out their drink and get in trouble with the teachers. I would get the catsup, mustard, salad dressing, and gravy and dump it on their heads.

I AM A RAT FOR LIFE!

This is what I would do if I was a 4th grade Rat.

this thing
IS WELL LIKE
FUNNY

When I Wihsent to Canada I got so lucky. When I went to old Monmantreeall I must of gone to 15 stores in one day and got stuff in each store. I went with my mom and dad. In this part of Canada they speak frinch there. But most of this part of Canada speick English. There was a place called the O-zone in the O-zone there was a place and your are in a car thing and you go at frirst, but later you go fast very fast! I mean it when you get this note you will fell like you are there. This was in Newport. I kept stoping that it wold stop because it was so scary. You wold try to get out of your seat!

Montreal
speak
french
stores

You can not lift your seat belt

August, 1997

LINDA RIEF, TEACHER, OYSTER RIVER MIDDLE SCHOOL, DURHAM, NH PORTFOLIO GUIDELINES

Building Toward Portfolios:

- immersion in reading, writing, speaking
- time in large blocks
- choices

Teaching Self-Evaluation:

Each quarter, I collect three–four final drafts arranged in portfolio from the most effective to the least effective, with a discussion of the following:

What makes your best piece most effective?
How did you go about writing it?
What problems did you encounter?
How did you solve them?
What makes your most effective piece different from your least effective piece?
What goals did you set for yourself?
How well did you accomplish them?
Based on what you've done, haven't done, know, don't know, what are your goals for the next six weeks?

I ask students to consider similar questions with regard to their reading, too, each quarter.

I introduce the "end-of-year showcase portfolio" as a collection of our best evidence as writers, readers, speakers ("literate human beings"). In it, we consider:

range, depth, growth (effort, improvement, risk-taking . . .)
in school and out of school
across the disciplines
literary, visual, performing

Organization of evidence (artifacts)

"from most effective to least effective"
finished products with all drafts
reflections/evaluations

Or, consider items because you are most proud of them, or because they are most effective, most satisfying, most important. . . .

Each student's portfolio is a collection/story of who he or she is as a literate human being. It should be rich with the evidence of what they know and are able to do, how they know and are able to do that, and why they have included items and organized them in a particular way.

MOLLY FINNEGAN'S
EIGHTH-GRADE PORTFOLIO ('97–'98)
ANNOTATED TABLE OF CONTENTS

Fiction

    A picture book about a quilt, drafts and a Case History/ Evaluation

Textiles

    Introductory prose-poem about quilting

A poem by someone else about quilting

Two different quilt projects, includes Case Histories/Evaluations and photos

Poetry

    Quote by Langston Hughes

    Five different poetry projects w/ case histories/evaluations and drafts (ex: "Patent Leather Agony" final draft, case history, four drafts w/ sketches, ideas from writing journal)

Nonfiction

    Letter about work with historical diaries, two poems, double-entry journal (work done independently of school work)

    Three attempts at personal narrative (ex: unfinished piece about my grandfather, case history/evaluation, photos, a poem he wrote, early drafts, and a journal entry

Letters, Etc.

    A letter and book review from Author Unit (about Barbara Cooney)

Writing Across the Curriculum

    Introductory letter

    Four different writing projects from other subjects (ex: my eighth-grade major experiment, "The Role of Gender in Conversation and Interruption in the Classroom")

Publications

    Artifacts from the four occasions that I have been published

VI. Reading

    Letter on why reading is important to me as a writer

    Quotes on reading

    Excerpts from a few of my favorite books

    Favorite book list and my school year book list

    Reading responses from my journal

VII. Comments & Questions

    A space for audience to ask me or themselves questions, or to comment or compliment

KIM KELLY: KENTUCKY WRITING PORTFOLIO

KENTUCKY WRITING PORTFOLIO
Table of Contents
Grade 12

Student Signature Sheet Included   (Y)   N
(Circle one)

Fill In Number Selected	Category/Descriptor	Study Area At least two pieces must come from a study area other than English/Language Arts	Page
1	*Reflective Writing*		
	Title: Letter to the Reviewer	English	1
1	*Personal Expressive Writing* (Include 1 or 2) Personal Narrative, Memoir, Personal Essay		
	Title: Personal Endeavors: ...	Psychology	3
	Title:		
1	*Literary Writing* (Include 1 or 2) Story, Poem, Script, Play		
	Title: Untitled	English	5
	Title:		
2	*Transactive Writing* (Include 1 or 2) Various real-world forms (see Handbook p. 1.11c)		
	Title: Anthropologists Revisit ...	Science – Genetics	6
	Title: Scientists Explain ...	Science – Microbiology	10
5	**Total (must equal 5)**		

Dear Reviewer:

As I looked back upon those freshman-year pieces that were accompanied by trite illustrations, I saw just how much I have learned about sculpting an idea into a thesis and a thought into a theme.

As I came into high school, my writing displayed untempered emotion, thus many of my pieces were free verse poetry. The third selection listed ("untitled") is an exemplary medium of expression from the first two years of my instruction from high school.

For those years, I wrote for the Oracle, (a student produced literary magazine), and I had a strong aversion to transactive pieces that involved analysis and structure.

However, by the beginning of my junior year, I had taken a strong interest in the sciences, and therefore, it was necessary for me to be able to compile data and information into a concise work. The first few attempts at these were insipidly written, and acknowledged no audience. It was then that I found my way to expressing myself through argument or persuasion essays. This era of potently opinionated works (most regarding religion) led to a piece of personal reflection. The second item listed is an essay concerning how I found myself by constantly questioning the fundamentals of my ideals and morals. In this work, being both structural and expressive, I established myself as not only a creative writer, or persuasive writer, but as an author that could employ systematic elements to enhance creativity.

After evolving to this point, I attempted to master the task of writing research and analysis papers. This development occurred in the latter part of my junior year. Due to the classes I was enrolled in (microbiology, genetics, human anatomy, botany), I found my niche in the biological sciences. This intense interest was reflected in my writing, and I had finally found my way to writing engaging, colorful, informational works. The final two selections included in my portfolio are indicative of how I presently choose to share not only my knowledge, but they also show how one can sew a little piece of who they are into each sentence they craft.

I am hopeful that this collection will not just be another in a stack, and one more closer to you getting home, but that it will enlighten you to the many stages of growth of a young writer.

With respect,
Kim Kelly

DICK HENNESSY
RESEARCH PORTFOLIO, PROJECT ON WASPS
(WOMEN AIRFORCE SERVICE PILOTS)

annotated table of contents:

one-page summary:

Dear Reader,

This portfolio includes all the documents to support my study of WASPs, Women Airforce Service Pilots who served during World War II. Some of the artifacts in this collection are really specific and almost esoteric, such as the copy of one woman's individual flight record, or the diploma from the United States Airforce Academy presented at the end of training, or the outline of the training day given to individual women during training (see pages 3, 6, and 8). I obtained many personal mementos like these during the interviewing process with the remaining WASPs, and they're quite unique.

There is a whole other set of documents that anyone could obtain in a good library: articles about the WASPs and book chapters on women in the history of aviation. Some of the best printed sources turned out to be from military magazines and journals (see pages 4–9 and 15–20).

One of my favorite articles was from *Airman*, a magazine of the American Air Force, called "Put on the Girls," which urges women to join the WASPs by making them seem very glamorous in their flying attire. This article began with a patriotic quote from Eleanor Roosevelt.

The most personal set of artifacts in this portfolio come from my visit to the International Women's Air and Space Museum in Ohio. I have included over 15 pages of photographs from that museum visit, showing uniforms, trophies, replicas of actual planes and many many pictures of women pilots who were WASPs. I found the museums to be among my richest sources of material culture and tried to capture this in my pictures.

In one section of my portfolio, I have included the interview questions, transcripts, and notes I took on the several elderly WASPs I contacted. I also included my phone notes from the messages I left and received about this project. I was able to locate many potential women to interview but none of the actual interviews turned out to be very productive, either because of time constraints or that the women were too elderly to be helpful.

This portfolio is really more valuable than my actual paper which does not begin to reflect the richness of the artifacts I have been able to gather for this project. I am so fascinated by these wonderful and brave women and so outraged at their neglect in history that I plan to continue with this project after the course ends. I hope to write an article about the WASPs which will include some of my photos, material artifacts, and portions of my interviews. I have very much enjoyed the process of putting this together into a portfolio that I can use to continue my research in the future. I hope you enjoy the ride, too.

Sincerely,
Dick

GUIDELINES FOR TEACHERS
AND STUDENTS
BONNIE S. SUNSTEIN

I. **Personal literacy portfolios are the *products* of our *processes*.**
    "Keeping track is a matter of reflective review and summarizing,
    in which there is both discrimination and record of the signif-
    icant features of a developing experience. It is the heart of in-
    tellectual organization and of the disciplined mind."—John
    Dewey, *Experience and Education* (1938)

II. **Portfolios can complement (*not replace*) assessment policies—
    and link subjects together—because they:**

    • Evaluate where we've "been" as literate people (who read,
      write, listen and speak)
    • Assess our literate selves
    • Predict where we want "to go" as literate people
    • Represent our literacy to others

III. **Portfolio keepers who evaluate their own work learn how to:**

    • Collect: gather samples of their literacies
    • Select: decide what will represent themselves as literate people
    • Reflect: write and talk about their decisions
    • Project: set personal literacy goals: reading, writing, and think-
      ing, and then they do it again—and over again.

IV. **Portfolios hold the artifacts of our unique literate histories.
    They illustrate our connections—across subject areas and in
    and out of school:**

    • We need to document, explain, and evaluate how literacies fit
      our institution's expectations (i.e., how does each person meet
      the curriculum? Do we let each person show us?)
    • Reading and writing relate to one another—and to the other
      "subjects" in and out of school
    • Exploring artifacts and researching our own histories—inside
      and outside of school—can lead to topics for writing and re-
      search in integrated content areas.
    • A personal history as it sits in the portfolio leads to important in-
      sights and analysis: for more reading, more writing, research, fur-
      ther goals, and our connection to our institution's expectations.
    • Our choices reflect growth as it sits in the reading/writing
      folder. (example: look at four drafts written over time. How do
      these show change for us as writers? What skills have changed?
      What original goals would we revise?)

- We can ask questions about curriculum and personal growth. What does all this history suggest about our future? What constitutes "best" work? What did we learn from our instructive failures? What artifacts will stay in the portfolio the next time around? Will go? What will improve or enrich writing, reading, thinking?

V. **Reflective analysis leads to self-assessment and goal setting:**
Our research is showing us that the crucial piece of portfolio keeping is the critical analysis that comes with reflection. Portfolios enable us and our students to gather our literacies, identify and organize them, and catalogue our accomplishments and goals—from successes to instructive failures. Talking about the contents of our portfolios—how they got there, what we learned, our hunches about why we made the choices we did at the times we made them—and hearing others talk about theirs will generate new ideas and strategies. And that will generate goals.

Here are a few question/responses students can ask in portfolio-sharing sessions:

1. What do you honestly want to know about what your partner has chosen to put in her portfolio?
2. What theme(s), pattern(s) of literacy do you see in your partner's collection? What subject areas are covered?
3. What do you want to know more about? What seems to be missing?
4. What connections can you see: Between the personal and the professional? Between home and school? Between the past and the present? Across content areas? Between reading, writing, speaking, and listening?
5. How might your partner's portfolio shift the next time? About what does she want to write more? To read more?
6. What might she read that you've read? Recommend one book to her, and tell her briefly why.
7. Where might your partner go next? In reading? In writing? In speaking and listening? In learning with the "literacies" of other subject areas?
8. What kinds of lists or categories does your partner's portfolio suggest? What accomplishments might she document?

> *"Not everything that counts can be counted,*
> *and not everything that can be counted counts."*
> Albert Einstein

JASON CEYNAR, PRESERVICE TEACHER, COLLEGE SENIOR, ENGLISH MAJOR WRITING PORTFOLIO FOR "APPROACHES TO TEACHING WRITING" COURSE

Annotated Table of Contents

I have divided my writing portfolio into two sections: "To Be . . ." and . . . "Or Not to Be." My intention is to express an inner conflict that has plagued me as a writer this semester. The first section, "To Be . . ." includes artifacts which define me as an academic writer who is more concerned with how an audience will react to my words than with my own relationship to the process and product of my writing. The second section, "Or Not to Be," includes pieces written in academic and non-academic settings that are truer expressions of myself because I am thinking more about my relationship to a topic than my reader's reactions to my writing.

Section I: To Be

1. *A thirteen-page research paper entitled "Rembrandt, Milton, and the Protestant Reformation."* In many ways, this piece is the culmination of my career as an English Major. Milton was my final English class and this is the last extensive literary analysis I expect to be assigned as an undergrad. I included this paper because it showcases my ability to synthesize an original, academic (teacher-pleasing?) argument from a variety of sources. It also represents my ability to write in a scholarly tone, a skill that I've picked up after three years of writing literary analyses. I use this voice in order to win over an intelligent audience. My intention was to impress my Milton professor, and I hope that I accomplished this goal. I'll be disappointed if I get anything less than an A on this piece.

2. *A paper entitled "Personal Betrayals" that I wrote for Contemporary British Drama.* Although I told myself at first that I was including this piece because it illustrates my ability to perform a close analysis of a text, I now realize that it is the grade that I was most concerned with. I can't even remember what the paper is about. I didn't want to reread it because I was afraid that I'd discover I was given the A unjustly. This paper represents my tendency to value the grade I get on a paper more than the content of the paper and the learning that I achieve through the process of writing it.

3. *A fifteen-page paper, the result of an extensive ethnographic study of library book shelvers.* Of all the major projects I have completed, I

am the most proud of this one I did in a Folklore class during my junior year. In this piece, I presented the findings of my study and hypothesized about their significance. I am proud of this paper because it represents my obsession with looking for the "deeper meaning" of things. I am constantly analyzing the "data" of my life in hopes of achieving profound insights about who I am, where I'm going, and what life's all about. Essentially, this study is a written expression of my tendency to think about things . . . a lot. It is also a product of a lot of hard work—gobs of time go into data collection, analysis, and synthesis during an ethnographic field study. This paper is therefore representative of my dedication as a student. This is the only piece in this section in which I tried to take on a personal, even conversational tone instead of the academic voice that I used to impress my instructors. It is evident that I was still trying to sound smart, however, in hopes of earning a good grade.

Section II: Or Not to Be

1. *"The Stacks"* is a short essay that I wrote for a nonfiction writing class. This piece is NOT written in the scholarly, academic drone that dominates the pieces in the previous section (with the exception of the ethnographic piece). It is a paper about me and is therefore written in a voice that I consider to be my own. This voice is lively and energetic, full of humor and even a hint of the insight that is a result of my reflective nature. This piece is one of the only things that I've written for school that I've returned to and revised AFTER I submitted it for a grade.

2. A *sonnet*. For my Milton class, we were asked to write a sonnet in a Miltonic fashion. I have included my sonnet in this portfolio because it represents one of the only times that I put a lot of myself into a piece that was intended for academic purposes. I was not concerned with telling my teacher what she wanted to hear when I wrote this. In fact, this poem criticized the "cloistered" nature of college and the inactivity of intellectuals—a criticism that is by no means intended to flatter a Miltonic scholar. My sonnet also expresses some very personal concerns about whether or not I should continue with school or jump into the "real world" after I receive my undergraduate degree. My teacher liked the poem and gave me the coveted A, but I think I would have been proud of this sonnet even if I had received a dreaded B.

3. *"The Big Race, Revised."* It was during the process of writing this paper (for my "Approaches to Teaching Writing" course) that I began to realize that my main goal as a writer is to impress my

audience. I do not write with the intention of learning more about myself or a topic, although I often achieve those results in spite of myself. I write to earn an A, to impress my peers, to win a scholarship. I write to perform. This piece is, in a lot of ways, central to my portfolio because it made me aware of the negative impact that writing exclusively for others has had on my growth as a writer.

4. *My hope for the future.* This is a journal entry that I pulled from the personal journal I started keeping only a few weeks ago. Keeping a journal has been an awkward experience for me because there is no audience to shape my writing. I do not have to use a scholar's voice in order to earn an A or use excessive humor to impress my peers. No one, except for me, will ever see these entries. The lack of an audience is liberating because I can write whatever I want without fearing the consequences. I've written a lot of things that have surprised and excited me, things I never would have written if I knew that my journals would be read by someone else. I'm learning a lot about my "hidden" writer who has been constrained by the demands of an audience. Unfortunately, I still have some problems expressing myself openly in my journal. Every once in a while, my mind nags at me, begging me to consider how a reader would receive what I have to say.

One-page Reflection

When I first assembled samples of my writing for this portfolio, I was concerned because all of my artifacts were pieces that I have written for college courses. I didn't have any writing samples that were written in a non-academic context. I looked at my writing group's collection of personal journal entries and letters with envy. I knew that I had written things outside of school, but most of these pieces were either too personal to share or, in my opinion, insignificant. I pouted about my "lacking portfolio" for a couple of weeks until our professor told us that sometimes a portfolio tells us a lot about who we are as writers by what is MISSING.

I began to realize that I did not exist as a writer outside of an academic setting. I like to write, so I couldn't understand this lack of motivation to write on my own time. My first solution was that I don't have "my own time," but then I thought about the three consecutive summers that I promised myself I would write every day and I didn't.

What did I enjoy about writing the assignments that were in my portfolio? It didn't take me long to make a connection. . . . I was excited about writing things for classes because I was writing for an audience. I admitted to myself that I like to show off when I write. I like to play with a sentence until I'm sure that it will entice either a gasp, a giggle, or a thoughtful chin scratch from my reader. Without an audience, these efforts are wasted. Teachers, the only people I've ever respected as worthy judges of my writing, have given my writings A's and accolades since I was in middle school. You don't get that kind of reinforcement when you write short stories for yourself or letters to your friends who want to hear what's going on, not evaluate carefully constructed prose.

A theme was emerging: assessment. I was obsessed with assessment. This was no surprise. I've always judged my performance as a writer according to the opinions of others. But how did this obsession impact my writing, and what did it have to do with the artifacts that I had chosen? I received an A on everything that appears in my portfolio, but I knew that there had to be a way to further classify my writing. I looked through my artifacts and evaluated my reaction to each one. There were three or four pieces that I was pleased with; I was ashamed by the two remaining assignments even though I had received an A on each one. The pieces that I was attracted to were more personal. I was drawn to the personal essays and poems that expressed myself in relation to the subject matter more than the impersonal "literary analyses" to which I felt no real connection. I decided to refer to the personal pieces as "writing for me" and the more academic selections as "writing for others." Even though all of my pieces were written for the audience of teacher, I went out of my way to impress some instructors with an academic voice while I relied on a personal voice for other assignments (i.e. I use big words in my Milton paper, I don't use big words in my essay about the library stacks). I knew there was something significant about the fact that I was happier with the pieces in which I was writing more *about* myself than *for* the teacher. There was something genuine and sincere about these pieces. When I decided that I would be proud of these artifacts even if the teacher hadn't given me an A, bells and whistles went off in my head. Through the two "academic" pieces, I was define as a writer by the A I received. Through the four "personal" pieces, I was defined as a writer by my writing.

The "To Be or Not to Be" thing just struck me. I'm not sure where it came from. I knew, however, that I wanted to express these contrasting definitions of myself as a writer in my portfolio. Am I "to be" an academic writer, writing to impress others in a voice that may or may not be my own? Or am I "not to be" the writer who is obsessed with his audience, dependent upon exterior approval, and always saying what others want to hear?

I didn't include the personal journal entry until today's version. I knew I had to include this specimen of personal writing because it is a result of what I've learned through the construction processes each time I've reworked this portfolio. My journal is an attempt to embrace a writer who is not obsessed with assessment but can recognize value in his own words.

As a future teacher, I recognize an invaluable lesson that this portfolio has taught me: IT'S NOT ABOUT GRADES. Over the last four years, I have fretted about my academic progress. I wrote with one purpose in mind: to get good grades. I've allowed a lot of personal growth to go unnoticed because I've been focusing my attention on grades. At this point in my learning, I realize the importance of recognizing and fostering personal growth. I am here to improve myself as a writer and thinker—not to impress. If I believe that as a student and a writer, I will believe it as a teacher. I will not encourage my students to impress me, but rather to impress themselves. That's what growth is all about.

INTRODUCTION TO PORTFOLIO, JULY 1999
JONATHAN H. LOVELL

For this portfolio, I decided to gather together some pieces I wrote 12 to 15 years ago, and compare them with some pieces I've written more recently. I didn't have any grandiose plan when I did this. It just so happened that I'd kept some writing I did for some writing workshops I'd organized while teaching at the University of Nevada in Reno from 1983–1987, and so these pieces of writing were ready at hand for me to look over and think about.

What I discovered surprised me, however, and I ended up finding the business of putting together this portfolio both surprising and insightful.

#1: Recalling my initial impressions of Belmont Hill School (written Jan. 25, 1984)

My first surprise: here I was writing about exactly the same experience I wrote about in my introduction to the *To Kill a Mockingbird* workshop I gave 13 years later, in the summer of 1997 (see July 1997 entry). The transition from a co-ed junior high to a snotty all-boys prep school at the beginning of my 10th grade year left a powerful impression on me. I'm struck in rereading this narrative of my impressions of Belmont Hill at how aware I was of the contrast between the warmth of the social environment I'd left as opposed to the coldness of the social environment I was entering. These sharp contrasts become increasingly important to me, and I believe are brought into stronger and more memorable focus as my writing moves towards the present.

#2: Responses to: George Orwell's "Shooting an Elephant" (written Feb. 1985), Emily Dickinson's "A Narrow Fellow in the Grass" (written March 1985), and Ben Jonson's "On My First Son" (written April 1985)

These were pieces of writing I did in the spring of 1985 in some Northern Nevada Writing Project workshops I organized for the purpose of writing in response to works of literature. My own personal quest was to try to figure out a way to make academic writing as compelling as personal writing. I'm not sure I met this goal, in the sense that personal writing still remains for me far more important than academic writing, but I was surprised in reading over these pieces how well written they were, and how much enjoyment I gained by reading them. I was especially moved by the poem to my daughters that I wrote "in the voice of" Ben Jonson. I felt this piece of writing was both a good poem and a deeply felt one. I can "feel" it just as strongly today as when I wrote it 14 years ago.

#3: Letter to my father (written April 1986)

It's with this piece of writing that I begin to hear and feel a deeper sense of connection between the cadences of my words the perceptions they are trying to convey. It was a piece I gave to Dad about four months after I completed it in a Northern Nevada Writing Project writing workshop, and it began a significant and mutually affectionate relationship between us that continues to this day. Once again, what I notice about this piece in rereading it is the way it sets something I value (our sense of togetherness as a family) against something that threatens to undermine this thing of value (our separateness from each other). It's my awareness of the fragility of such cherished moments— here, it's the final day of our family sail on a sloop we'd chartered for a week in Maine—that gives me the incentive, I think, to render these cherished moments in strong and memorable language.

#4: "Reflections on the Writing Project Invitational Summer Institute" (written July 1994)

This is the most self-consciously "public," as opposed to a personal recollection or reflection, in this portfolio. It seemed to come to me out of nowhere when I wrote it, but I now see that the seeds of this piece had been germinating for a long time. The ending of this piece is unusual for me in that I do not generally refer to, or express myself in terms of, conventional Christian religious imagery in my writing. But I'd been listening recently to some of the scholars from the "Jesus Seminar" being interviewed on National Public Radio about their completion of *The Five Gospels*, and being very moved by their very unconventional understanding of the resurrection, I included it at the end of this piece.

#5: "Floating," written July 1995

Somewhat surprisingly, given the fact that maintaining my status as an academic depends in part on my publications, this is the only published piece I'm including in my portfolio. It was not initially written for pub-lication, however, but rather as a small response group piece I wrote during the 1995 Invitational Summer Institute of the San Jose Area Writing Project, in which I served as a full participant rather than co-director. I love this piece, and I love the way it evolved in response to suggestions and queries from the members of my response group. I think of it as partly produced by me and partly drawn out of me by my five other response group members. It appeared in the winter 1996 issue of *California English*, in response to the theme "Waiting to Exhale." Again, a cherished moment—feeling the literal "elevation" of love—is defined against a state of depression and aimlessness, which gives that moment its piquancy.

#6: Introduction to *To Kill a Mockingbird* Workshop, written July 1997

In this introduction to my workshop's focus on "bringing outsider readers into the text," I recall my own experience of reading Shakespeare's *Henry IV, Part I* as a tenth grader at Belmont Hill School. In feeling as if I was inside the words of each of the main characters in the opening scenes of this play, and in being able to answer the teacher's questions about them the following morning, I claim that "literature saved me," giving me a sense of place in the cold and impersonal new environment I'd entered.

In the context of this portfolio, I would now say "reading and writing rescued me" rather than "literature saved me." I would say this because what saved or rescued me here was a feeling of being "inside" the words. This is a feeling I express most powerfully in my "Floating" piece, when I describe my experience of reading the manuscript of *Lessons From a Child* by Lucy Calkins. This is what I feel when I am not only reading but writing words that seem to me to be carrying me along with them. So for me there is almost no difference between being in the presence of powerful words (as in reading *Lessons from a Child*), and being the creator of these powerful words (as in my letter to my father).

#7: "A Medley of Writings," written in June and July, 1998

I'm including this medley of writings that I submitted to the 1988 San Jose Area Writing Project's Summer Institute anthology as the final entry in this portfolio because it ties together so many of strands I've spoken about: the public vs. the personal voice; the trauma of being in a newer, colder social setting and losing the comforting older one; words as steady cadences that one can feel "inside" as one is writing or reading them; my relationship with my father.

But it also suggests, in the final guided imagery piece, that this whole portfolio represents the beginning of a journey, and that in this new journey I will be seeking a harmony of those fierce oppositions that have given such poignance and power to the writings I've done over the past 15 years.

AN AFTERWORD

JONATHAN H. LOVELL AND
BONNIE S. SUNSTEIN

The subtitle of this book uses a term that's become familiar in the "standards" climate of the late twentieth century: a standard ought to articulate "what students should know and be able to do." But we've learned that in order for students to know what they know and do what they're able to do, we must furnish strategies for them to understand the standards. Good teaching charges students to show us—one at a time—to demonstrate how their internal learning meets our external standards. But to do this a student cannot simply succeed at a game with a number two pencil, bubbling in the answers to multiple-choice questions. Setting a portfolio standard requires careful thinking—about what one knows, what one is able to do at a particular time—and how that fits inside a much bigger bubble of what one's world expects. To set a portfolio standard requires critical analysis and careful study, for every student, of what it is to "know and be able to do." Thus, each portfolio sets a unique standard while it satisfies common ones. Each portfolio becomes a single voice in a noisy conversation about learning and accomplishment. Each portfolio, because it displays breadth and depth of multiple knowledge, ought to be "measured" in multiple ways.

And, we believe, that's exactly what we've shared with you in our book. Our collection of chapters offers a large geographical range, proving to us that the practice of portfolio keeping in one form or another has in the past ten years spread to virtually every region of the country. And, we suspect, you've seen the dazzlingly creative and richly experimental ways our colleagues are using portfolios, and discovering new modes of "knowing" and "doing" in the process. So it seems a particularly appropriate time to take stock of where we are, what we've learned, and where we might go from here. We'd like to conclude with a few broad observations drawn from our authors' collective wisdom:

1. Portfolio keeping, however we do it, helps us and our students learn and teach together.

The articles in this book show how consistently the activity of portfolio keeping engenders an ongoing and reciprocal process of learning between students and teachers. Mentor teacher Don Hohl and university faculty Ron Strahl and Joe Potts express this discovery, "it is the professional contacts and conversations that preserve teachers have with mentor educators and university professors and, ironically, professors with professors, that make the portfolio a valuable process." If this were the only value in maintaining and encouraging the practice of portfolio keeping, it would be a strong enough argument for doing so. Portfolio keeping simply improves our own practices as teachers by helping us become more aware of who our students are and how our students learn.

2. Portfolio keeping is difficult and counterintuitive because it's "higher-order thinking" about the self.

Self-indulgent? Hardly, but a superficial portfolio can look that way. Counterintuitive? Maybe, because we're supposed to be learning about subject content and a world of others' ideas. It is a difficult and arduous task to maintain an ongoing reflective portfolio, to maintain a look at oneself in the process of filtering others' knowledge into one's own. Look at Section III again, and read what second grader David, eighth grader Molly, twelfth grader Kim, college student Dick, preservice teacher/college student Jason, and professor Jonathan learned about their learning. The deep and fundamental value of continual self-reflection, self-assessment, and self-presentation is the most important contribution portfolio keeping has made to our teaching practices in the eight years since the publication of *Portfolio Portraits*. We've learned that teachers must actively guide students in this process, as Judy Fueyo discovers with her preservice teachers in Pennsylvania, and we've learned that teachers must practice this form of reflective portfolio keeping themselves. The chapters and guidelines in Section III offer helpful models for cultivating and sustaining such reflective portfolios in our classrooms.

3. Portfolios can't be mere accumulations of artifacts intended to meet prespecified criteria.

It is better to understand the mandated portfolios that we see in statewide, districtwide, or school-wide portfolio assessment programs as "collections of assessment materials," John Schmit and Deborah Appleman persuade us in their chapter. But that's not the only way to use them; in fact, a simple "display case" can discourage the practice of using portfolios to monitor complex growth. We agree with Danling Fu's contention that "portfolio assessment and standardized assessment represent two different philosophies and value systems. They may co-exist, but there is no middle ground." Well-meaning policy makers have spent too much time and energy over the last decade in the exhausting and frustrating task of preparing students for large-scale, mandated portfolio assessment programs.

4. But, on the other hand, even mandated portfolios have gotten us writing, selecting, and reflecting.

But, to argue with ourselves, the introduction of such large-scale portfolio assessment programs like the Kentucky project Liz Spalding writes about has, at the very least, started teachers in all subject areas talking about the types of writing in which their students should become proficient, and has helped them develop common standards for assessing the pieces of written work, even though the writing is "mandated." And so what we're left with is two kinds of portfolios and a distinction we must make: First, as an artist might present her work to a buying public, portfolios can be exhibits of achieved proficiency, containers for the display of finished products. But more important, we believe, portfolios can be demonstrations of the unfolding process of learning. In these more consequential exhibitions of their learning, students include both finished and unfinished pieces in order to lay out their evolving sense of what they know, what they are able to do, and their hunches about what goals they want their work to address in the future. These two different kinds of portfolios cannot and should not look the same. But it doesn't hurt to keep two. In fact, learning to keep one kind can enhance learning to keep the other.

5. Ongoing self-evaluation is a habit both valued and necessary in contemporary society.

The larger world our students enter after they finish their schooling will be one in which it is extremely likely that they will be "taking stock," continuously, changing jobs from five to seven times in the course of their careers. In such a complex contemporary climate, it's critical to develop a capacity for ongoing self-reflection and self-assessment. This is a skill—a habit, in fact—that we do not foster with simple test mastery. It is far more critical, more self-reflective. It requires the difficult and challenging habit of watching the self in relationship to one's changing environment, watching "what one knows" in relationship to what others "know," watching "what one is able to do" in a world where others are "doing" in new ways all the time. It is the habit that acknowledges lifelong learning. Meagan, the undergraduate college student that Marilyn Barry and Yaso Thiru write about in their chapter, expresses this insight, "This [portfolio] project has given me the chance to plan more effectively for my immediate future so that I can graduate with a clear vision of what I want to do, where I want to go, and how I'm going to do it."

6. New communication technologies will enlarge our students' capacities for portfolio keeping.

Look at any Website and you'll see a portfolio. This is the realm of portfolio making we expect will grow most in the decade to come. Our own collection of chapters focuses primarily on print-based portfolios because these are the easiest types of portfolios to represent in book form. But, at our 1998 conference, participants were treated to a wide range of electronic portfolio keeping strategies and practices, from sound effects design to cartooning to CD-ROM and network possibilities. Peter Reynolds, the artist who brings us the drawings on our cover and section header pages, entranced conference participants with his ways of connecting computer generated visual graphics to smart and practical teaching. Peter's portfolio itself brings educational ideas to life on a screen as well as a drawing board. It is this kind of work that will make the greatest difference in the look and shape of portfolios in the future. These technologies are powerful new ways our students can truly take the lead—as they continue to surprise us with what they know and are able to do.

ABOUT THE AUTHORS

Deborah Appleman is Professor of Educational Studies at Carleton College in Minnesota, where she teaches English education and directs the Summer Writing Program for high school students. She has published numerous articles and book chapters on adolescent response to literature. A co-editor of the multicultural anthology *Braided Lives*, she has recently completed a book on teaching literary theory to secondary students.

Marilyn Barry directs the writing program at Alaska Pacific University and was chair of the committee that developed the General University Portfolio Guidelines. She has taught, written about, and presented workshops on writing, linguistics, literature, and writing theory for over twenty-five years in state and private universities in California, Washington, and Alaska.

Julie Cheville is Assistant Professor of English at Elizabethtown College in Pennsylvania, where she teaches nonfiction writing and English education. She co-edited, with Bonnie Sunstein, *Assessing Portfolios: A Portfolio* (1997). Her forthcoming book from Heinemann/Boynton/Cook is entitled *Splintered Learning, Splintered Lives: Athletes on the Court and in the Classroom*.

Elizabeth Chiseri-Strater is Associate Professor of English at the University of North Carolina, Greensboro, where she directs the freshman writing program. She teaches courses in literacy, ethnography and nonfiction writing. Her work includes a co-authored book with Bonnie Sunstein, *Fieldworking: Reading and Writing Research* (1997) and an ethnography of writing across the curriculum, *Academic Literacies* (1991) published by Heinemann.

Molly Finnegan is a junior at Oyster River High School in Durham, New Hampshire. She is interested in writing, drawing, and painting and other fine arts. She attended the Bread Loaf Workshop for Young Writers in 1999 and has worked as a performer and assistant director of a community youth theatre. She is currently helping her mother transcribe and research a local nineteenth-century schoolteacher's diaries.

Danling Fu is Associate Professor at the University of Florida; and formerly professor of English at Nanjing University in the People's Republic of China. She teaches courses and seminars in literacy, studies writing development, and works closely with classroom teachers.

Danling has consulted for diversity programs in public schools in Florida, California, and New York City, and is author of My *Trouble Is My English* (Heinemann, 1995) among many other publications in both English and Chinese.

Judith Fueyo is Associate Professor of Education at Pennsylvania State University where she teaches courses in reading/writing development, emergent literacy, assessment, and teacher research. She has published articles in *Language Arts, Teacher Research,* the *Journal of Natural Inquiry,* and many other professional journals, as well as chapters in several books for teachers.

Cinthia Gannett is Associate Professor of English at the University of New Hampshire where she directs the Writing Across the Curriculum Program. Her scholarship has focused on diary and journal traditions, resulting in a book, *Gender and the Journal* (1992), and various articles. She is also interested in the uses of portfolios across the curriculum.

Don Hohl teaches English at Marina High School in Huntington Beach, California. With twenty-five years in his writer's portfolio, Mr. Hohl is a charter member of the California Writing Project and emeritus Director of the South Basin Writing Project. He teaches composition and English education courses at California State University, Long Beach.

Jonathan Lovell is Professor of English at San Jose State University, where he teaches courses in methods of teaching English and young adult literature as well as supervising student teachers in English. He serves as the university-based director of the San Jose Area Writing Project as well as having hosted, with his co-director Charleen Delfino and co-editor Bonnie Sunstein, NCTE's "Inside Portfolios" conference in January 1998. His chapters and articles have appeared in professional publications including *Language Arts, California English,* and *The Quarterly* of the National Writing Project.

Mary E. McGann has taught at the university level for twenty-four years. As a founding member of the Rhode Island Writing project, she spent many hours working with elementary and secondary students in their classrooms. She has directed Writing Centers and Basic Writing Programs, and currently directs the Prior Learning assessment/Portfolio Program in the School for Adult Learning at the University of Indianapolis.

Sandra Murphy is Professor in the Division of Education at the University of California, Davis. She teaches graduate courses on the teaching of reading and writing and has taught high school English and freshman composition at the college level. She coauthored *Designing*

Writing Tasks for the Assessment of Writing (with Leo Ruth) and *Writing Portfolios: A Bridge from Teaching to Assessment* (with Mary Ann Smith) and has written several articles on the acquisition of literacy and the assessment of writing.

Miriam Dempsey Page is Associate Professor at the University of Puerto Rico in Mayaguez, and has taught at several universities and colleges in the United States. She has published several articles in rhetoric and composition and is currently working on two books relating anthropology and ethnography to the composition classroom.

Joe Potts is Assistant Professor of English at California State University, Long Beach, where he teaches literacy education courses. A former high school language arts teacher, he believes deeply in the power of the portfolio to promote conversation, collaboration, and reflection. His current projects include two books on strategies for mentor teachers.

Barbara Wells Price is Director of Standards and Assessment for an educational services agency in western Wisconsin. She has taught writing and literature courses at Central Missouri State University and the University of Iowa. Her experience in assessment includes working as scoring center manager and scoring director for NCS, and as writing assessment specialist for ACT and consultant to their work in Brazil.

Linda Rief is a language arts teacher at Oyster River Middle School in Durham, New Hampshire. She is the author of *Seeking Diversity: Language Arts with Adolescents* (1992) and *Vision and Voice: Extending the Literacy Spectrum* (1999). She has been an instructor in the University of New Hampshire's Summer Reading and Writing Program for the last ten years, and co-editor with Maureen Barbieri of *Voices from the Middle*, an NCTE journal, for the last five years. In the spring of 1999 she designed and hosted a series of eight television programs called "Tales Out of School: Reading and Writing Beyond the Classroom" for the Massachusetts Corporation of Educational Telecommunication.

John Schmit is Associate Professor of English at Augsburg College in Minneapolis, where he teaches composition, linguistics, and American literature. He is also president-elect of the Minnesota Council of Teachers of English. His recent research has focused on assessment and the standards movement and on cultural influences on contemporary students.

Elizabeth Spalding teaches general secondary education and English education at the University of Kentucky. Previously, she was Project Manager for Standards at the National Council of Teachers of English, where she worked in the NCTE/IRA project to develop K–12 content standards and in the New Standards Project to develop performance assessment tasks and a portfolio assessment system. She has taught in public schools in West Virginia and for the Department of Defense Dependents' Schools in Korea and the Philippines.

Thomas Stewart is a department chair and runs the tutoring program at Kutztown University in Pennsylvania. He has taught writing, literature, and education courses at colleges in Pennsylvania, New York, and Hong Kong. His research has focused on portfolios and on understanding the experiences of developmental students.

Ron Strahl is Professor of English at California State University, Long Beach, and Director of the South Basin Writing Project. He teaches courses in literacy studies, rhetoric and composition, and English education. He is co-author of *Literacy: Language and Power* and has placed articles in *College Composition and Communications, Journal of Advanced Composition, Clearinghouse,* and other journals in the field.

Susan Stires has taught for thirty years in rural and urban elementary schools, most recently as a primary teacher at the Center for Teaching and Learning in Maine, and now works as a consultant in literacy acquisition and development. Her publications are about teaching reading and writing to elementary and special education students and include *With Promise* (1991), a collection she edited. She is currently working on a book about teacher research in reading and writing with the support of a Spencer Grant.

Bonnie S. Sunstein is Associate Professor of English and Education at the University of Iowa where she teaches nonfiction writing, ethnographic research, and English education. She has taught in public schools and universities throughout New England. Among her published books, poems, and articles, she is co-editor, with Donald Graves, of *Portfolio Portraits* (1992), author of *Composing a Culture* (1994) and, with Elizabeth Chiseri-Strater, *FieldWorking: Reading and Writing Research* (1997). With Jonathan Lovell and Charleen Delfino, she co-chaired NCTE's "Inside Portfolios" conference in January 1998.

Yaso Thiru teaches accounting, management, and portfolio development, and coordinates the credit-for-prior-learning portfolio program at Alaska Pacific University. She has also worked in industry both in Alaska and overseas.

Terry Underwood is Assistant Professor of Language and Literacy at California State University, Sacramento, where he teaches courses in literacy assessment and instruction. He is the author of a forthcoming book to be published by NCTE entitled *The Portfolio Project: Assessment, Instruction, and Middle School Reform* and has published several articles in scholarly journals.

Jeffrey D. Wilhelm is a long-time English and reading teacher, and currently Assistant Professor at the University of Maine. His work revolves around helping at-risk learners through the use of drama, art, and electronic technologies that can assist learning performances and make these performances concrete and visible. Such performances can then be critiqued, manipulated, revised, and even put into electronic portfolios!

James D. Williams is director of faculty development at Cal Poly Pomona in California, where he teaches courses in rhetoric and English education. His teaching experience ranges from high school to research universities, and he has been involved in teacher preparation since 1981. His most recent publications include *Preparing to Teach Writing* (1998) and *The Teacher's Grammar Book* (1999).

ABOUT THE ILLUSTRATOR

Peter H. Reynolds is an author, illustrator, animator, and award-winning creator of media for children and families. He is also a passionate educator, traveling across the world helping countless teachers explore how technology, media, and storytelling can be used effectively in the classroom. As author/illustrator, Peter has published a book titled *The North Star* (*www.fablevision.com/northstar*) along with a companion classroom *Teachers Resource Guide* as tools to help people of all ages follow their dreams and navigate their true potential.

INDEX